VIRGIL'S ELEMENTS
PHYSICS AND POETRY IN THE
Georgics

DAVID O. ROSS, JR.

VIRGIL'S ELEMENTS

PHYSICS

AND POETRY IN THE

Georgics

PRINCETON, NEW JERSEY

PRINCETON UNIVERSITY PRESS

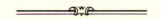

MCM·LXXXVII

COPYRIGHT © 1987 BY PRINCETON UNIVERSITY PRESS
PUBLISHED BY PRINCETON UNIVERSITY PRESS
41 WILLIAM STREET, PRINCETON, NEW JERSEY 08540
IN THE UNITED KINGDOM
PRINCETON UNIVERSITY PRESS
GUILDFORD, SURREY

LIBRARY OF CONGRESS CATALOGING IN
PUBLICATION DATA WILL BE FOUND ON
THE LAST PRINTED PAGE OF THIS BOOK
PUBLICATION OF THIS BOOK HAS BEEN
AIDED BY THE WHITNEY DARROW FUND
OF PRINCETON UNIVERSITY PRESS

ISBN 0–691–06699–X

THIS BOOK HAS BEEN
COMPOSED IN LINOTRON BEMBO
CLOTHBOUND EDITIONS OF PRINCETON
UNIVERSITY PRESS BOOKS ARE PRINTED
ON ACID-FREE PAPER, AND BINDING
MATERIALS ARE CHOSEN FOR
STRENGTH AND
DURABILITY

★

PRINTED IN THE UNITED STATES OF
AMERICA BY PRINCETON UNIVERSITY PRESS
PRINCETON, NEW JERSEY

For Pamela,
Ian, Eric, and Peter

CONTENTS

CONTENTS

PREFACE

My interest in the *Georgics* became a major preoccupation well over a dozen years ago, when I noticed a recurring pattern of the elemental oppositions of fire and water, hot and cold, and the like throughout the poem, but was unable to find in commentaries and other studies any discussion—or for that matter any awareness—of what seemed a purposeful and insistent emphasis on the ancient elements. I was soon led into areas where I had never been before, *terrae incognitae* where a reader of Virgil perhaps had no reason at all to venture, for the more I seemed to be directed by the poem towards Greek science (physics, medicine, ethnography, astronomy, botany, and so on), the more I realized that Virgil (and it is one of the tokens of his stature) had very few scientific "sources." Others, I am sure, must have pursued some of these trails before, only to find that Virgil seldom "uses" or "refers to" any specific author or work; but I then began to see that he had made all his own whole traditions of scientific thought and, as seemed likely, must have been relying as well on popular conceptions that we can know very little of (our literary sources being so seldom "popular"). Real science is the beginning of the poem, and the elements are the basis of the physical sciences: that all this had not been taken account of previously may be due simply to the compulsion felt by traditional scholarship to find specific, demonstrable sources and models, without which connections are not to be made.

I thus spent a great deal of time following trails into byways and on into blind alleys (that is, those at the end of which there was no welcoming fragment of Empedocles or a pre-Socratic, no specific Hippocratic passage as Virgil's model, no page of Theophrastus that suddenly illuminated or made immediate sense of a Virgilian complex of ideas), but I came to realize that what I was able to learn and understand about these areas (in which I am still the dilettante) did gradually make a great deal of the poem clearer for me. The more I understood the physical elements, the more I thought I could see the elements of Virgil's poetic structures.

This book, then, attempts to view the whole poem after careful consideration of certain details in certain passages, with specific purposes in mind. My view of the whole is not complete, and the reader will find all sorts of omissions (I have nothing to say, for instance, of such important poetic predecessors as Callimachus or Lucretius, nor do I discuss the Golden Age as such, nor do I say anything about Augustus or Maecenas). This is not an introductory survey of the poem. Likewise, though most of the poem is covered, there are several major panels barely touched on (such as the opening 48 lines of Book II—which we have recently learned to read so differently in the light of the Lille papyrus of Callimachus), and some passages that are actually rather important for my view of the whole are somewhat sketchily covered, for various reasons. In an attempt to keep the book brief and readable, I have tried to reduce repetition to a necessary minimum, for such is Virgil's weave, with one detail connected to so many others in his patterns, that interpretative repetition is the greatest danger. Thus, for example, my discussion of the first half of Book I presents Virgil's opposition of fire and water, and leads to a survey of oppositions and balances in (especially) early Hippocratic writings: when Virgil, throughout the rest of the poem, returns to these oppositions, the various passages in which he does so are seldom given detailed analysis (though I have called the reader's attention to them), except insofar as previous ideas are developed or themes varied; and though there occur many passages later in the poem in which the ideas of the Hippocratic writings are directly relevant, these works are seldom mentioned again. My Introduction contains further warnings and pleas for the reader's indulgence, but in general I hope that it will always be kept in mind that it was never my intention to deal exhaustively with the poem, but rather to examine certain details in exemplary passages, often leaving Virgil's further development of the same or similar details for the reader to pursue. To have done otherwise would have produced a far longer and more tedious book, and one not necessarily more helpful or satisfactory.

I have tried to write both for the scholar and serious student of Latin poetry, and for the reader with a more general or casual interest in the *Georgics*, an admirer of Virgil who may not be entirely comfortable reading the poem in Latin. Neither of these two individuals, who have been reading over my shoulders, can be entirely satisfied, but the scholarly reader will most frequently find reason for annoyance. An apology is thus necessary for the absence of footnotes throughout, bibliographical and otherwise. Any footnote considered necessary has been embedded in the text, often obviously and awkwardly; unnecessary footnotes are simply not offered, which may distress those who delight in this minor genre of scholarly writing. More distressing will be the infrequency of my acknowledgment of the work of others and their contributions to which I am indebted. Scholars who have worked on the poem will easily supply for themselves the bibliography relevant to any particular discussion, and for those less well acquainted with the basic work and criticism I have supplied the Bibliographical Notes, which I hope will suffice as an introduction and guide, and to which the reader may easily refer when the work of a modern scholar is mentioned in the text. My main objective, again, has been to be as readable as possible and to present my line of argument unencumbered by asides of any sort, but those who point to places where further details, helpful parallels, fuller illustrations, or specific useful bibliography might have been given, will point to sources of my own anxiety as well.

I have offered my own translations, which I intend only to be helpful and literal. I have not generally translated words and phrases occurring in the text, because I imagine that such words will be intelligible to all readers; and when sometimes I have not translated longer citations (of, say, Servius), the reason is that the gist of such citations is clear from the discussion and the Latin is of interest only to the specialist in a position to read it.

The first draft of this book was completed during the academic year 1981–82 during a sabbatical leave granted by the University of Michigan. I am grateful to the American Council of Learned Societies (and to the National Endowment for the Humanities) for a Fellowship which made the year's work possible.

An anonymous reader for the Press supplied a lengthy list of corrections of various sorts. Special thanks are due to Joanna Hitchcock for her long interest in the project and for her exemplary expertise and thoughtfulness in receiving and overseeing the final manuscript; and to Elizabeth Powers for her careful editing.

A succession of Michigan students, in various seminars and classes, have contributed with enthusiasm and interest to the growth of this study, as have my departmental colleagues with their encouragement and help, especially my friend and former chairman, J. H. D'Arms, with his proddings. I owe a special debt to James E. G. Zetzel, who read an early draft and produced both specific criticisms and general directions for revisions, and corrected a final draft as well. Richard F. Thomas has been in on all of this almost from the beginning and has offered specific help right through the end; much of what is here has been shaped by discussions with him, as will be apparent to those who know his work: to him my sincere thanks.

My greatest debt is owed to those to whom this book is dedicated.

JANUARY 1986
Ann Arbor, Michigan

VIRGIL'S ELEMENTS
PHYSICS AND POETRY IN THE
Georgics

CHAPTER ONE

INTRODUCTION

Virgil is by no means an easy poet. The *Odyssey* is read by school children, and the *Iliad* can be understood by the average college student more easily and (I think) more accurately than any other work of classical literature likely to be encountered in survey courses. The *Aeneid*, however, often seems tedious and mechanical to these same students and more often than not frustrates the lecturer who tries to convey to a general audience some idea of the depth and beauty of Virgil's verse and the poem's profound power over mind and emotions. Yet the *Aeneid* is far better understood, and more readable, than the *Georgics*, and the *Georgics* than the *Eclogues*. Why is Virgil so difficult, but less so from work to work? One answer can be had by setting the periods of his creative life against the history of his time.

The experience of Virgil's youth was of bloody civil war and political chaos, but his maturity coincided with unexpected, and almost unhoped for, stability in the Roman state. Virgil, born in 70 B.C., was twenty-one when Caesar crossed the Rubicon: he had thus grown up knowing only political uncertainty, and though rural Mantua must have been far more peaceful than the streets of the capital city (which, in the middle fifties, were the scene of increasing violence, terrorized by armed gangs of political thugs), the years of the First Triumvirate made it clear throughout Italy that balanced power must soon become unbalanced and that armies, controlled by individuals, had supplanted reasonable authority, whether the Senate's or the People's. When Virgil was thirty, he had (we can presume) been working on his *Eclogues* for two years: Caesar had, over five years, emerged victorious in protracted battles over Pompey and the state, and had been murdered; the Second Triumvirate had proclaimed its purposes and principles most clearly by its notorious proscriptions (300 senators and 2,000 knights were murdered, according to one ancient estimate; in December of 43 B.C. Cicero's head and hands decorated the Rostra, from which recently he had spoken out against Antony to the people in the forum). When the *Eclogues* were finished (in 35 B.C., as now appears probable), a Roman army was again preparing, inevitably, to face a Roman army: again political chaos was to find resolution only through armed conflict. Civil war had come to seem a curse inherited from the fratricidal foundation of the city. In the *Eclogues* there is little certainty, and what little there is exists only in an idealized world that has barely the substance of a dream. *Tityre, tu patulae recubans sub tegmine fagi . . .* : Tityrus has his farm and peace, but where is he?

In September of 31 B.C., when the battle of Actium left the world with a single leader, Virgil had been writing the *Georgics* for four years, and, though he had enjoyed the patronage of Maecenas during these years, we should not imagine that Octavian's victory filled him at the time with either hope or joy unbounded. The reality of a single man, with a single army, must have been unsettling at best, and in reality, too, this was the man of the proscriptions of 43. Octavian remained away from Rome until the summer of 29, when he returned to celebrate the triple triumph and when no one, still, could have felt much certainty about the future—other than to acknowledge that opposition was no longer possible. If this was peace, it must have seemed only the result of desolation, already a particularly Roman accomplishment. These were the years of the *Georgics*, a poem concerned above all with irrational destruction, with uneasy balances between opposing elements, and with the unreality of hopeful visions.

The *Aeneid*, still without Virgil's finishing touches at his death in 19 B.C., is the product of the years of slow realization that peace was a fact, that the Pax Augusta had brought the blessed calm of a spring day even to Rome itself. Virgil, though, and Horace, were never able to trust this peace—their own experience had been so different, and they knew too well what it had cost and how it had been achieved: in the *Aeneid* we hear of peace and order, but always in the future; Aeneas' experience is otherwise, from beginning to end.

This brief reminder of Virgil's times may serve two purposes. First, we must always be aware, when reading the "Augustan" poets, that the experience of the older poets (Virgil and Horace) was totally different from that of Propertius or Tibullus, and again from that of Ovid, who was born in 43 B.C. and thus knew only Augustan peace and stability. Much of what is still written about Virgil (and especially about the *Aeneid*) neglects entirely the experience of his first forty years, as if he had lived in Victorian England or grown up during the Eisenhower administration. I admit to reading Virgil as a poet of deep pessimism: I cannot see that it could be otherwise.

Second, if we try to understand what Virgil had known and experienced while writing the *Eclogues*, then the *Georgics*, and then the *Aeneid*, we can see how his poetry becomes, outwardly at least, more understandable. His world began in chaos, with uncertainty and random violence; understanding was possible only by imposing abstract patterns upon disorder, the result of which was far removed from observable reality. In the *Georgics*, however, the real world appears prominently and has a certain stability, though not to be trusted, and perhaps not at all as real as it seems; consequently the poetic conception and its expression are more clear, less dreamlike, though there remain (as we will see) visions of peace and order that prove too fragile in this real world to be ultimately satisfying or viable. The *Aeneid*, finally, is Virgil's Rome: as chaos and inexplicable violence had yielded at last to order and indeed to the rituals and formal ceremonies of the civil and religious past of the city, it was natural that Virgil and Horace would shape this experience through these public and therefore comprehensible expressions. Virgil could never forget blind violence, the irrational madness that is never alien to human nature and is a constant in the universe, but at least the world itself came finally to have patterns and designs of a tangible reality (intellectual and spiritual, historical and religious) against which *furor* could be comprehended.

We can see, then, that Virgil's own experience (the history of his time) made it inevitable that his first expression of this experience would be private, the construction of his own mind, for outwardly there was nothing but disorder and confusion. From 29 to 19 B.C., however, an order emerged in the external world which just a few years before had seemed beyond hope, a stability that must have been welcomed with intense relief even by those who had suffered losses they could never forget: Virgil's private constructions remained (they were never replaced) but began to appear in altered forms, clothed or masked on occasion so as to seem to be the public expressions of the Augustan peace. Virgil became more comprehensible—on the surface.

If we are to understand the middle years and the *Georgics*, we must understand especially the first private reflections of the poet. It was only intellectually and imaginatively that Virgil at first could give form and meaning to disorder and violence: thus, what is most Virgilian (and this is true still for the *Aeneid*) is what is private, reflective, and allusive. Understanding of his poetry can come only from reconstructing the private world he created. His material at first was primarily poetic: the *Eclogues* are made of poetry almost entirely. The *Georgics* (as the real world begins to offer comprehensible shapes and patterns), while no less a poetic structure and built of poetic material, is a poem of science and uses the intellectual structures of scientific literature; both these creations will be altered, finally, in the historical vision of the *Aeneid*, which thus remains, essentially, a poem (and a very private one at that), not a work of historical rationalizing.

My study of the *Georgics* is largely an attempt to reconstruct Virgil's private creations (or at least some of them to some extent) by finding and examining some (at least) of the pieces he used. These pieces are such things as ash trees, infatuation, violent storms, the shepherd's song, glory, or peace. The most obvious difficulty is that although these pieces exist in the world we share, our conception of even the most mundane of these can be (and probably is) vastly different from the Roman conception (that is, the common ground within the idea of "ash tree" or of "peace" shared by every Roman), which in turn will differ from that particular aspect of the conception that Virgil will want to suggest, perhaps paradoxically, in a particular instance: we must first see an ash tree as a Roman would have seen it, and then as Virgil conceived it for a particular purpose, where it might acquire its own special significance from an earlier poetic context, perhaps, or as part of an established literary topic, or as a recurring element in a private pattern being constructed by the poet himself.

We are of course foreigners in the Roman world, in language, culture, and thought, as every classicist is aware. We do not feel anything sinister or magical in an ash tree. Infatuation, for us, is the proper concern of psychiatrists. We know what causes violent storms, our hurricanes and tornadoes, and in the case of the former, at least, we know beforehand exactly when and where they will strike; and we have agencies, public and private, to pick up the pieces afterwards and pay insurance claims. Glory is a concept we know only by hearsay, a somewhat archaic notion that has been replaced by notoriety or celebrity. Peace, on the other hand, which Virgil regarded only as a deceptive possibility, we see as a reality, something that is our right. We must try to find out what Virgil's readers knew instinctively (though it is possible to do so only in a limited way), since it is with such pieces that Virgil creates, bending and transforming the shared and the general to his own purposes.

Virgil was a reflective poet, which explains both why he worked so slowly and why his three poems present such a coherent whole. His reflections are both private and literary, from the beginning: allusion made his inner world real and tangible. He reflected by setting pieces of reality side by side, by making a simple pattern of objects and ideas, then putting this pattern up against another; later, a different object may be substituted in the pattern, or others added, with an entirely new result, or several new ideas may upset a balance previously contrived. Virgil, like Horace, gives us his reflections by manipulating a succession of concrete images, which may be as tangible as an ash tree or may be an idea or concept such as peace or the Golden Age. Allusion helps here, especially when an image is literary, as when adaptation of a few lines from the *Iliad* can suggest Achilles and fire and war, or when a Theocritean tag may summon up sleep in a summer's noon. Allusion, too, can suggest, often by one word, a whole previously established pattern. We must be aware, though, that Virgil's process of reflecting does not allow any pattern to remain for long and that no pattern will be definitive.

All of this is to say simply what it is to be a poet, and what makes poetry different from geometry, psychology, history, or philosophy. "Language is by no means our only articulate product," Suzanne Langer wrote. Music is expressive, but it can make no statements, and the visual arts, while they can present images, cannot argue a case. Virgilian poetry (I am tempted to say "real poetry") is more like music and the visual arts than it is like history or philosophy, but since it uses words (not just sounds, shapes, and colors), it is often thought to be discursive or analytical, or to carry a logical argument forward to a conclusion, which then is assumed to be Virgil's meaning. But Virgil's meaning is not of this sort, any more than (to take a useful but trivial example) is Hogarth's. *The Rake's Progress* says a great deal to us with a range of expression (humor, sadness, pathos, disgust), but what it says cannot be reduced to any such statement as, "The degenerate life is bad." As Virgil reflects, he gives us patterns of images which, as they continually change, affect us in part emotionally, as does music, but ultimately alter our intellectual awareness and understanding of the world. There are, however, no answers, no messages that we can repeat at the end of our reading. Langer again: "An idea that contains too many minute yet closely related parts, too many relations within relations, cannot be 'projected' into discursive form; it is too subtle for speech."

We might remember, too, that it is the business of science to

classify and define: order and meaning are established from
chaos by separating one thing (or group of things) from another, by excluding. Definition establishes the set of characteristics shared by one group only. Ash trees are different from maples in certain ways; a word is defined to mean what no other
word means; the concept of Justice, or the Good, is established
by rejecting false concepts and excluding misleading similarities. Art, on the other hand, finds connections between apparent
dissimilarities, by suddenly revealing patterns of associations in
the chaos of appearance. Discursive thinking must attain clarity,
whereas art can confuse what had seemed to be clear and can
disturb our passive acceptance. Thus the poet never intends to
tell us about Hamlet what the philosopher or psychologist (or
most critics) want to know, and as well he can leave us with
doubt and uncertainties that we ought not to attempt to resolve.
Virgil gives us connections, not definitions, and reserves the
right to find patterns whose clarity unsettles our preconceptions.

It seems necessary to begin with this simplified view of Virgil
and his poetry as a non-discursive art because so many studies
want to find the wrong sort of answer in his puzzle, to reduce
what he has created to a bald generalization (and often to a bland
inanity of the sort found in the popular moralizing of a Sunday
magazine): "Civil war is bad; madness is destructive, as is anything that goes too far; the peace of rural self-sufficiency is the
proper ideal for men." Virgil's meaning can hardly be in such
messages. We should try to get the right pieces in the right
places: the pictures that result will be the meaning the poet intended.

My goals in studying the *Georgics* are essentially two: first, to
see as clearly as possible what things meant for Virgil and his
contemporaries, and second, to see what things meant for Virgil
in the evolving context of the poem, his own vision. Since these
goals are frequently suggested to be impossible (with the consequent assumption that we shouldn't even try to read as a Roman read, or attempt to understand Virgil's mind and intentions), it is worth answering that we can do a great deal better

than we have done previously. If we do not see any point or possibility in trying as best we can to comprehend a Roman's reaction to "ash tree" or "death," then why read a Latin poem in Latin—why not be content with a paraphrase, or even an outline?

These are, in one sense, the Virgilian elements I will be concerned with—the pieces used to make the poetic patterns, the elements of poetic thoughts.

★

My preoccupation with the *Georgics* has come more and more to focus on the question, "Why did Virgil write on farming?" We tend to take for granted that farming was a suitable, even natural, subject for a poem, for a variety of reasons: because it is after all a fact and one of the first facts we learn about Latin literature, and the familiar is always what we question the least (Nicander's poem on snakes, by contrast, is one of the last things we learn of Greek literature, and therefore the subject seems immediately odd); because Hesiod had written on farming; because we call it a didactic poem, and feel comfortable with that generic designation; because we find that even though plowing or grafting may not be of great interest, the poem is really a grand metaphor for life. Such reasons, however, dull our appreciation of just how unusual, or even strange, it was for Virgil to have decided on the subject, and turn us from asking exactly what it was that farming not simply allowed Virgil to say, but offered positively, as no other conceivable subject did.

Hesiod's precedent is not at all like Homer's for the *Aeneid*. The style and manner of the *Aeneid* is thoroughly epic, and therefore ultimately Homeric to the extent that what is so strikingly Virgilian and original is not immediately apparent. The *Georgics*, however, is Hesiodic only in a few places where Virgil has actually translated a few lines from the *Works and Days*, or adapted a passage such as "how to make a plow" or the impenetrable lines on good and bad days; only the first book is patterned on works and days, but even here the Hesiodic model is vague. Hesiod provided an important (Callimachean) precedent involving poetics or literary genealogy (which does not require further discussion here), but Virgil's subject—farming—can hardly be explained as a Hesiodic debt. Of Nicander's poem on farming we know little, and that little does not correspond to anything in Virgil's poem, which may be significant: had Virgil owed more to it, the tradition of ancient commentary (including Gellius and Macrobius) ought to have recorded samples of the debt. The fact is that there is no good literary precedent for Virgil's choice of subject. (Why, we may wonder, did he not write a Hesiodic *Theogony*, if he wanted to be *Hesiodus Romanus*? or why did he not choose to write, in the tradition of Hesiod and such eminently acceptable Alexandrians as Aratus and Eratosthenes—with so many others available to draw on in part—on astronomy, its universal forces and its mythology?)

No compelling precedent existed for a poem on farming: Hesiod, and perhaps Nicander's *Georgics*, allow such a poem but do not explain it (even if there were a few other versifiers unknown to us, such as the Menecrates of Ephesus, who wrote on agriculture, mentioned by Varro). There was, though, a large number of prose works on the subject, works of philosophy and natural history as well as technical handbooks: Varro (*RR* 1.1.7–10) mentions "more than fifty" authorities available, both Greek and Latin. Here is a suggestion, at least, that Virgil may have been more interested in the practical realities of agriculture than we tend to believe: he may have been drawn to write about farming not because of poetic precedent, but simply because of the appeal of the subject itself.

Is the poem, then, didactic? Should we simply accept its subject as something which interested Virgil sufficiently to allow him to exercise his talents as instructor, or as a rival to Lucretius (or, again, even to Hesiod as a "didactic poet")? In other words, should we see didacticism as the primary urge and the subject matter as only secondary (and therefore acceptable or excusable without further questioning)? This aspect of the question will take care of itself, I hope, but the very nature of the poem's didacticism ought to be faced. The day has passed when it could be assumed that Virgil was trying to get Romans back on the

farms and was giving them enough practical instruction to en-
able them to make a go at it. It ought to be quite clear that no
one could possibly learn enough from the poem about any one
thing to be able to go out and do it, whether it be when to plow
or plant, or how to construct a threshing floor: Virgil, clearly
enough, had no interest in teaching agriculture. There is, however, an important consideration that ought to be remembered
at the same time: Virgil *is* interested in the practical details of agriculture, far beyond the extent indicated by most modern
scholars and critics of the poem. He knew the subject thoroughly, and records details of the why and how of practical and
theoretical agriculture far beyond what would seem necessary.
He does not give all the information necessary, but what he
gives is precise, exact, and scientific: he *is* concerned, therefore,
with the real content of the poem.

Viewing the poem as didactic has a further consequence,
which once exercised scholars and still has a lingering influence
on our reading. If the poem's intention is to instruct, then we are
likely to find ourselves reading not one but two poems, as we
do when we read Lucretius: one that is instructive and practical
and tells how to make a plow or a bee hive, and one that is hon-
eyed, digressive, and impractical, intended to get the reader
from one how-to-do-it part to the next. (Seneca's remarks, *Ep.
Mor.* 86.15, are often referred to—that Virgil wrote not *veris-
sime*, but *decentissime*, not to instruct farmers, but to delight
readers—*nec agricolas docere voluit sed legentes delectare*.) No one, I
think, is still prepared to proclaim that the passages of instruction are merely excuses for the digressions (such as that on the
great storm or on civil war in Book I, or the three major digressions in Book II), but it is clear enough that the digressions do in
fact receive far more attention from critics, who frequently do
little more than paraphrase the instructional sections.

The most recent general view of the poem still does not face
the basic question, "Why farming?": this view, current for several generations of scholars, finds that Virgil's subject matter is
a metaphor for life itself. With very few notable exceptions, the
basic assumption, often tacit, of readers today is that when Vir-

gil writes about methods of plowing, or the care of pregnant mares, or setting out young vines, he is actually writing about something else: it is still assumed that Virgil is not really interested in agriculture or husbandry, that the details he presents are not in themselves relevant and therefore may be passed over quickly or even ignored. The best recent interpreter of the poem, M.C.J. Putnam, has presented this view (along with much else) with succinct eloquence (1979, p. 15): "The *Georgics* is a unique flowering, an imagined fiction with a pretense to be practical, a didactic treatise in a recognized generic tradition, manifestly teaching us how to deal with nature but in fact forming a handbook bent on showing us ourselves. What purports to offer a methodology to cope with the external world is actually one grand trope for life itself." It is clear that two assumptions are implicit here: that the conception (a poem on farming) is Virgil's own ("a unique flowering"), devised in his imagination ("an imaginative fiction"); and that its subject matter is only a pretense ("manifestly," "what purports . . .") allowing and enabling the expression of other, different, and vastly more important ideas ("one grand trope for life itself"). Generally (I think it is fair to say) these assumptions are implicit in every interpretation of the poem in our time; our reading of the poem, then, while seeming to accept the poem's agricultural content, reduces that content to the point where it is of and in itself of little significance, merely carrying a higher level of meaning that was Virgil's real interest. This view still fails to explain Virgil's choice of subject (one may still ask why farming rather than, say, astronomy) and still in practice tends to elevate the digressions at the expense of the didactic sections.

The *Georgics* is a poem about life more thoroughly and intensely than any other I know, and is so precisely because it is not simply a metaphor or a trope for life. Any given technical passage does suggest other ideas and does relate to other passages (as we began to outline, a few pages above), but its content is real, carries its own meaning, and is important in itself—it is not simply a metaphor or symbol of what it manages to call to mind. In what follows I hope to be able to explain enough of the poem's hard content to make this assertion acceptable and help-ful. There is much, of course, that I cannot explain, and much that my ignorance of technical areas will have gotten wrong, but I have consistently had the same experience in trying to under-stand the poem: the more I have understood of the technical content of a passage, the more that passage contributes to the larger patterns of Virgil's thought—not metaphorically, but with extraordinary directness.

Likewise, all of this is Virgil's devising, of course: but neither the pieces nor the metaphors are his. Agriculture is not his imagined fiction, and is not unique: to see it as his unique devis-ing is to miss its extraordinary background and history as an an-cient science, related intimately to all other ancient sciences (physics, astronomy, medicine, ethnography, and so on, as we will see). It was not Virgil's idea that agriculture could stand for, or be about, the forces of life, because for many centuries agri-culture was the study of nature: Virgil was dealing directly with nature (with creation, birth, growth, and death—with life) in every passage of the poem, and doing so not from his own imaginative constructions, but by using terms and ideas reach-ing back to the beginning of Greek understanding.

What follows is an attempt to uncover Virgil's patterns of thought by examining the whole poem, the technical didactic passages as much as the larger ideas (e.g., civil war, the rural ideal) of the digressions. (My impression is that much in our current views of the poem is the result of reading for the mes-sage of the digressions, then finding that message metaphori-cally presented by the didactic content.) What I mean by my as-sertions that the subject matter is not a metaphor, and is not of Virgil's own devising, will thus become clearer only much later (it is not, I hope, a quibble), but there are several points about agriculture and life that contribute to answering the question, "Why agriculture?", and that may best be made in a general in-troductory way here.

I would suggest, first, that there is a special, Italian reason for the *Georgics*: the Romans were a people who remained close to their pastoral and agricultural origins in many important ways, a few of which may be mentioned here. Roman society, at all levels, was basically rural in values and outlook. In their social attitudes, in important aspects of their political and economic systems, in religious instincts, in language, in intellectual habits and reflexes—in many ways the Romans had never left the country, and the country was the farm. There are important differences here between Rome and Athens (and between these Romans and later western societies that may seem to have similar roots in, or yearnings for, an agricultural past). I cannot explore this question in any detail: the brief outline that follows will suggest what I have in mind when I make the claim for rural values and outlook, but at any point in this outline, as in any outline that attempts a description of "the Roman Mind" or "the Greek Way," I am well aware that the reader will easily recall individual writers or specific passages that contradict the generality. I am concerned here only with the norm, with intellectual territory shared by all—not with the observations or contributions of original minds, which, by definition, will differ and depart from the commonplace.

To begin with, consider what is suggested by *urbanus* in Cicero's Rome and ἀστεῖος in Aristophanes' Athens. Contrasted with their opposites *rusticus* and ἄγροικος, both epithets suggest elegance and wit, and while both may be extended to include the notion of the "dandy," ἀστεῖος is generally a term of praise, connoting someone clever or astute. *Urbanus*, however, has a whole range of meaning not shared by ἀστεῖος: departing from "dandy," the epithet moves on down the scale to include "effeminate" and "degenerate," and so reverses the values of city and country, with the result that the country becomes morally upright, the city morally bankrupt. For Catullus and his set, *urbanitas* was everything: clearly, however, their values were revolutionary and were intentionally presented as a social challenge (the *urbani*, the *delicati*, the *facetii* and *venustiores* had arrived). The challenge was accepted, for example, by Cicero, who finds the new *urbanitas* a convenient way to attack Clodia and her degenerate friends: at one point in the *Pro Caelio* Cicero summons up that man of *gravitas*, one of the *severissimi*, Appius Claudius himself, to harangue these urban effeminates, but then declines such an easy triumph: *Sin autem urbanius me agere mavis, sic agam tecum. Removebo illum senem durum ac paene agrestem; ex his igitur sumam aliquem . . . qui est . . . urbanissimus* ("But if you'd prefer me to give you a taste of your own urbanity, so I will: off then with that uprighteous old pillar-of-the-community, practically a hick: and on with one of your own sort . . . who is . . . one of the city's brightest lights," *Pro Caelio* 15.36). The opposition of City and Country can stand for much, and for many different ideas, and at Athens as well as at Rome virtue can be said to reside in the country, certainly: but only at Rome, I think, can *urbanitas* be condemned on occasion as the equivalent of degenerate modernity, of bankrupt morality, not just by Cicero, but by almost every moralist. Why? Catullus and Cicero both make it clear that social values are at issue here, values that would appear to be far more highly charged, to carry far more emotional potential, at Rome than at Athens. Further exploration of *urbanus* and ἀστεῖος would, I think, soon reveal that for the Romans the country had an importance it did not have for the Athenians, and that it went far deeper: hence, at Rome, the conflict of highly charged social values could find expression in these terms.

In politics and economics, too, a case could be argued for a difference between Rome and Athens that would again reveal how deeply imbued is the Roman mentality with instincts primarily agricultural. Again, it is a shared emotional content (if this is the right phrase) that we must consider, not real topography and not necessarily the occasional observations of certain individuals. Athens must have had the feeling of a large country town, after all, and a stroll of a few minutes would have taken one from the agora to the open fields beyond the walls, where the plane tree by Ilissus' stream provided shade for Phaedrus and Socrates. By the fifth century, however, Athens had become proudly urban, its rural origins largely forgotten or conveniently ignored, a city where the political and economic realities had awarded the present and promised the future to manufacturers and merchants. In Cicero's Rome the senatorial aristocracy was forbidden to engage in trade and banking. There were ways to get around such limitations, or course, through agents and various fronts, but it is remarkable that the facade was preserved without a public crack—never did the aristocracy question this code out loud. If banking and trade were anathema, what then? They had their politics and their estates, and from these estates came not only a steady income but their values as well, by repeated reference to which they could keep the rest of the state in line. This aristocracy set the tone and wrote the social rules, and they did so, in a very real sense, from their farms, as their grandfathers had before them—who would argue with the precedent established by Cincinnatus (among so many others)? Cato, of course, is the *locus classicus*. His strictures against the moneylender ("worse than a thief") and merchant ("a dangerous and disastrous career" are coupled with his praise of the good man (*et virum bonum quom laudabant, ita laudabant, bonum agricolam, bonum colonum*), in a passage often noted (the preface to the *De Agricultura*): can anyone imagine such terms used for public praise in Periclean Athens? Roman values, both public and private, remained essentially rural: the Sabine farmer stood for an ideal for both Cato and Horace.

The Latin language clearly shows its rural origins. Marouzeau wrote a study examining the rural element in the basic vocabulary, evident in spite of the attempts of purists to *eradicate* (as even they would have said) *rusticitas* from urbane speech. Such words as *laetus, felix, fecundus, locuples, frugi, egregius, sincerus, imbecillus, caducus*, and *rivalis* are only a beginning, most of which are dead agricultural metaphors (a rival, for instance, is someone who shares irrigation rights to the same stream). Formulae, metaphors, and proverbs of country origin abound (such as *purus putus, sceleris semen, caballus in clivo*—note the alliterative pairs in each example). Marouzeau then discusses and illustrates a country mentality evident in the form and quality of the language as well, a traditional and conservative character in the formulae and clichés of Roman speech. The point to be taken is that Latin never left its rural origin very far behind.

If Roman values and the Latin language retain a close connection with the Italian countryside, we ought not to be surprised at, or to ignore, the terms in which intellectually sophisticated Romans think about the forces of life—conception, birth, life, and death. Myth, religion, and philosophy are foreign: when a Roman thinks as a Roman, he turns naturally to the countryside for the terms in which he casts his thoughts. The *De Senectute* provides a fine illustration. Agriculture is to be one of the delights of old age. This in itself ought to be of interest, but it might be thought to be simply "in character" (the elder Cato, author of the handbook on farming as well as a notoriously rigid countryman, is of course Cicero's mouthpiece in the treatise). Then Cicero writes one of his most remarkable sentences:

Quamquam me quidem non fructus modo, sed etiam ipsius terrae vis ac natura delectat. Quae cum gremio mollito ac subacto sparsum semen excepit, primum id occaecatum cohibet, ex quo occatio quae hoc efficit nominata est, deinde tepefactum vapore et compressu suo diffundit et elicit herbescentem ex eo viriditatem, quae nexa fibris stirpium sensim adulescit culmoque erecta geniculato vaginis iam quasi pubescens includitur, ex quibus cum emersit, fundit frugem spici ordine structam et contra avium minorum morsus munitur vallo aristarum.   (*De Sen.* 15.51)

(For myself, though, I am delighted not simply with the produce of the earth, but with its productive power. When the earth has taken into its lap (made receptive by our plowing) the scattered seed, first it keeps the seed hidden (it is from this process of "hiding" that the term "harrowing" derives), then it opens the seed with the warmth of its moist embrace and brings forth the blade's green freshness, which matures gradually, sustained by its fibrous root system, and in its adolescence, as it were, now erect on its jointed stalk, is enclosed in a sheath, from which, when finally released, it shows forth the grains of the ear, arranged in rows, and is fortified against the bites of smaller birds by its spiked rampart.)

In a single movement, Cicero sees the entire cycle, from seed to ripened ear—conception, birth, growth, maturity. This is not simply an exercise in stylistic cleverness, but is the work of a man who has spent time, repeatedly, observing the process he describes; it is not just the observation of an objective naturalist, but the thoughtful reflection of a natural farmer.

If it were asked just how the Romans thought of the forces and processes of life, what would very frequently come to mind would be the forces and processes known to them from their farms. *Natura* means "birth," and comes to represent the process of life, just as Cicero's remarkable sentence is introduced as the example of *ipsius terrae vis ac natura*, "the force and productivity of the earth itself." Virgil will play with the etymology of *natura* more than once, as we will note. (Φύσις is similar in root meaning, but has in fact a very different history and range of meanings. It occurs in Homer only once (of the "nature" of the plant "moly" which Hermes gave to Odysseus, *Od.* 10.303), and Hesiod never used the word; it became, however, an immediate favorite of the philosophers, which contributed to the development of the Latin word.) *Natura* is an active concept, not a static abstraction: the phrase *de rerum natura* suggests more of the processes of life than of the quality of the world. Lucretius' poem begins with Venus, spring, and procreation for a good reason:

> quae quoniam rerum naturam sola gubernas
> nec sine te quicquam dias in luminis oras
> exoritur neque fit laetum neque amabile quicquam,
> te sociam studeo scribendis versibus esse.   (1.21–24)

(Since you alone [*sci.* Venus] govern natural productiveness, nor without you does anything arise into the bright shores of light or become fruitful or filled with love's power, I am eager that you be my ally in writing this poem.)

I have translated *rerum naturam* as "natural productiveness" here, rather than the more usual "the physical world," in order to bring out what Lucretius must have in mind quite specifically: the poet, at the beginning of this long work, calls upon Venus to aid him in the production of the poem, just as she represents the *na-tura rerum*.

The forces of nature (our "nature," for now) were represented for the early Greeks by their gods: Aphrodite is love and sex,

Ares is the destructiveness of anger, as Poseidon "the earth shaker" is the destructiveness in the physical world, Apollo is beauty and order, and so on. The Olympians do, of course, have other functions and other characters and purposes varying with time and the individual, but it is a valid generalization to say that storms, hostility, sexual passion, or the beauty of dawn were conceivable to the early Greeks most readily in terms of their gods, who became in the process less the objects of religious feelings and more the figures of symbolic abstraction. Philosophers carried the process further, removing the gods, retaining the abstractions, categorizing and defining the physical world, until Socrates took the process beyond the physical. By contrast (and it is only for the contrast that I offer these generalities) the Romans had no gods and no mythology, but knew only those obscure, numinous forces of their fields, forces like Mavors, who lurked grimly just outside the boundaries of the field, or like Robigo, a fact, not an abstraction; and the Romans never settled easily into philosophical abstraction.

There are two observations to be made here, while we are briefly considering Roman religion. First, the most important annual rite of the fields and farm was the Ambarvalia, at which the *suovetaurilia* (pig, sheep, and ox) was driven three times around the boundary line before sacrifice. Now, the *lustratio* was not so much a purification of what was within this religiously established boundary, but rather served to keep out, as if by a wall, spirits of evil that existed outside. (The establishment of the *pomerium*, and the ceremony of the *amburbium*, is a related and similar lustration.) The farm itself became an island of security in a hostile environment, as we can see from Cato's prayer to Mars (*De Agr.* 141): *agrum terram fundumque meum suovetaurilia circumagi iussi, uti tu morbos visos invisosque, viduertatem vastitudinemque, calamitates intemperiasque prohibessis defendas averruncesque*; followed by the prayer that field, vineyard, flock, home and family, be granted health, *bonam salutem valetudinemque*. Outside the farm's *termini* existed not only the visible wolves and wild growth, but forces unseen and nameless. Tibullus' composite lustration shows clearly what was intended:

di patrii, purgamus agros, purgamus agrestes:
  vos mala de nostris pellite limitibus,
neu seges eludat messem fallacibus herbis,
  neu timeat celeres tardior agna lupos.   (2.1.17–20)

(Gods of our fathers, we make pure both fields and country folk: do
you drive evil from our boundaries, that the crops do not deceive the
harvester with weeds, that the slower ewe does not fear the quick
wolves.)

The consequence of this deeply rooted view of the natural world
is very important, and can be stated simply: wilderness held no
attractions for the Italian spirit, but was a source of malignity
and fear. "Nature" was the farm, not the wild and terrifying
world just beyond.

A second and related observation. Cyril Bailey made a point
that has not, to my knowledge, been sufficiently appreciated:
"Italian animism was in no sense a worship of the powers of nature . . . In two cases alone [*sci.* Jupiter as sky-god and Tellus]
could it be held that there was a 'nature-worship' at Rome."
Whatever truth or significance this statement has for Roman religion, I cannot say, but in any case it is of great importance for
understanding what the Romans felt about "nature," in present-
ing a paradox: that is, Roman religion begins with, and even
after Etruscan and Greek importations of all sorts remains close
to, nature, but at the same time is "in no sense a worship of the
powers of nature." The explanation is simple, and depends on
recognizing the reality of what "nature" meant for the Romans:
"nature" was not the world of flora and fauna and other natural
forces that it is for us, or for the American Indians or the Eski-
mos, but the world of cultivated growth within the farm's sacred *termini*.

This glance at Roman religion has taken us immediately and
inevitably back to the cultivated fields and pastures, just as when
we considered social and political values, or language, or if we
were to consider the Twelve Tables and law, or the actual history and growth of Rome itself, the city and its heroes. When
we say that Romans of Virgil's time were close to the soil, we

do not mean simply that they had grown up in the country or returned to farms or country estates whenever the pressure of business allowed. What we mean is that their intellectual and emotional inheritance is rural, in a way that the Greek "mind" was not, and in a way that perhaps no Western society has been since. It is not a question simply of living close to the fields: the mentality of Homer and Hesiod, for instance, is not rural in any similar sense. It is rather that the terms of thought which seem so frequently and so naturally to occur to Roman writers are those belonging to the agricultural countryside. An example: when Horace writes most simply and deeply about human life and mortality, it is not the terms of Greek literary thought that he gives us, but rather the passing seasons and aspects of the Italian landscape, its storms and intervals of quiet, its rites, its trees and animals, all that he knew and loved. In this, Horace is not unique among Roman writers.

I have been suggesting, and returning to, three main points, which may be restated here before we continue. First, when the Romans thought of the forces of nature, they frequently and instinctively did so in terms of their own countryside: the agricultural metaphor was a deeply and widely rooted cultural inheritance (social, religious, linguistic, etc.) and had not been replaced or superseded by any other as powerful.

Second, the terms of this metaphor were specifically agricultural: "nature," for the Romans, was the countryside of their farms and cultivated fields. This is a point worth more consideration than it will receive here, for it affects our understanding in several important ways. Wilderness, for the Romans, was full of terror, inhabited only by wolves and, worse, vague spirits. One particularly striking example: before the Capitoline Hill became Jupiter's and golden, it was possessed by some unknown and terrifying *numen*, as Evander pointed out to Aeneas—*iam tum religio pavidos terrebat agrestis / dira loci, iam tum silvam saxumque tremebant* (*Aen.* 8.349–50). Our "nature" (that of Audubon and the 19th-century naturalist explorers, including the Mountain Men of the West) is precisely what was abhorred by the Romans. For us, man is an intruder or observer; for them, the farmer is central, is in fact in possession, and is in fact the creator of "nature." We must thus be extremely careful with the concept of "nature" (as with all such concepts), where we enter totally foreign territory. "Nature" is agricultural, is inconceivable without man, and is his creation: but herein lies, and lay, an obvious paradox, which is indeed a central paradox for the *Georgics*: *natura* ("begetting") is the direct result of man's knowledge and effort, but there exist as well external forces (diseases, storms) which can interrupt and even destroy the *natural* cycles of growth. *We* consider such forces (locusts, hail storms) to be Nature: *our* devastated crops are *not* Nature, but are our intrusion upon Nature and are therefore vulnerable. For the Romans, I think, the storm that destroys and the pests that attack are un-natural, are forces dire and hostile like Mavors, wolves, and the terrifying *numina* of forest and thicket, whereas the grain and vine are the embodiment of the natural cycles of life. It comes down to this: if man is the creator, or at least the fostering attendant (the *agri-cola*, the *colonus*), then he is in league with nature—and not just co-operating, but controlling and guiding with experience and knowledge; the *Georgics*, however, reveals the paradox, because it shows us the larger world, where pests are the natural inhabitants, where the oak and pine (not man's grain and vine) are in fact nature's own, where storms are part of some universal order; and it shows a world in which man intrudes rather than belongs, where his intervention and manipulation, rather than fostering, perverts and even destroys. I believe, then, that our greatest difficulty in understanding the *Georgics* is that it is basically a strangely modern poem. Virgil's paradox is rather close to our own instinctive view, which we assume as our starting point, but with this assumption we get it all backwards. We must begin with a view of "nature" totally different from our own: for the Roman, the farmer did not intrude upon the natural world, but rather fostered or even was responsible for nature (*natura* as productive growth). We must then see Virgil subjecting this instinctive conception to revisions and inversions: for example, that the world outside the boundaries of the farm has its own order and "natural" laws, that the farmer can actually destroy rather than create. We must thus make a conscious effort to see a paradox in what seems (for us) an obvious given.

Third, seeing the forces of life and death in agricultural terms has important consequences for our comprehension of the sort of metaphor involved. Horace's nature poetry is vastly different from Wordsworth's in this respect: Wordsworth had to create his Neoplatonic nature, which had no reality before him and does not exist without him. The idea preceded, needed expression, and was happy to meet with the leech-gatherer, who became truly a metaphor for the pre-existing abstraction. Horace's farm, however, did not occur to him either at a sudden stroke of inspiration or gradually over a long time, as the suitable expression for various ideas and abstractions: his farm was the reality co-existent with, if not in fact preceding, the ideas expressed thereby. We think in words and images, which flow through our minds happily satisfying our nebulous thoughts until precise expression becomes necessary, at which time begins that search for the *mot juste*, the precise sequence of phrases which will convey as nearly as possible what we mean. Horace's nature, I would say, corresponds to that flow of words and images that enables us to think at all—it supplied, in fact, a good part of the fleeting mental patterns through which his thoughts of life and death, or man and the world, presented themselves to his consciousness. For Wordsworth, I would say again, Nature came on only to supply the *mot juste*, or, like a gradually and painfully evolving written sentence, served as a conception unifying similar pre-existing ideas, giving structure and expression to formulations that had already come into his mind in other terms and images. Such, I think, is the difference not just between Horace and Wordsworth, but between the Roman metaphor of agricultural nature and that which can be found readily at other times: it is a matter of directness, which I am hard put to define precisely, though one further example may help. In the *Iliad* we have the world of men; "nature" is met with only in the similes, in which a fighter's controlled fury is visualized through the likeness of a hungry lion. When these similes first took shape (and the artifacts would suggest that their origin was Mycenean) the lion must have been the direct expression of "fury," with no intervening abstraction, and so would have a directness similar to what I claim was the directness of the agricultural metaphor in the thought of Horace and his contemporaries. In our *Iliad*, however (and whenever), the similes would have lost this immediacy: the fighter would suggest fury, the concept of μένος, which then found expression in a lion, or a fire on a mountainside *observed by a shepherd*. When Homer composed the *Iliad*, nature already had been superseded as the vehicle of the direct expression of abstractions.

Agriculture, then, is not a grand trope for life, but *is* life in a very real sense, and while we can still speak of the agricultural metaphor, we should understand clearly that the poem's explicit subject is metaphorical in a far more direct and immediate way than it is for us. We should also understand that the metaphor was in no way Virgil's unique conception.

★

In these pages we have been trying to see why Virgil wrote the *Georgics*, why agriculture is the subject matter of this poem of unequalled depth and intensity. The third general point, just above, suggests an aspect of the poem which we can focus upon here, by way of introduction. There is a characteristic of the *Georgics* which we will have opportunity to comment upon frequently enough in this poem to suggest that Virgil must have been aware of it as he composed. In the *Georgics*, abstractions of all sorts have become realities. A well-known example from the *Aeneid* will serve to illustrate: the stock imagery of love, the fire and the wound, appearing and re-appearing throughout the fourth book, becomes a reality at the end, as Dido, on the pyre, falls upon the sword Aeneas has left behind. (So too in the second book the serpent and the flame are both image and reality.) In the *Georgics*, however, we see this happening in a variety of ways: a Homeric simile, for instance, will be clearly suggested, but the subject of Homer's simile will be the real matter of Virgil's lines; or a literary *adynaton* will suddenly have become not only possible, but observable fact; or a pastoral conceit will exist in the real world of the poem. Again, a few examples will make this clear. We will return more than once to the Homeric fire that represents the μένος of the hero: Virgil has taken this destructive force but removed it from its setting in simile and image; it appears as a real fire burning off the stubble in real fields, or as a conflagration in an olive grove, or as the actual fever burning in the veins of animals. So much of poetic simile and image had been drawn from the natural world, for the obvious reason that poets who write of men and their deeds, from Homer on, compare human activity to natural processes and phenomena. Virgil must have seen from the start that his subject was the stuff of poetry, that what had been the image was now to be his reality. Since our reading of the poem will explore this in repeated details, we need do no more than state the principle here, but it must have been this possibility as much as anything that attracted Virgil to the strange idea of writing a poem on farming: the very subject allows metaphor to become reality.

Virgil's agricultural world is continually changing: nothing stays for long as it first appeared. (This is one obvious reason for the interpretative difficulties the poem presents—values shift constantly.) Transformations are effected in two general ways, which may, also by way of introduction, be stated here. One way is by extension: Virgil will isolate the important characteristics, the essential nature, of a piece of our world, and then magnify this nature until it is taken to its extreme. This is the principle governing the development of the third book, for example: the essential characteristic of the pastoral world is its warmth; Virgil plays with this in a variety of ways, until at the end of the first half of the book this warmth has become, by extension, the destructive fire of love, and in the second half the fire of disease. The other way is by inversion, by which values become their opposites. There was a principle of physics (as we will see) that opposites are, at their extremes, the same—the extreme of heat, for instance, is cold. Again the third book provides a convenient example (discussed in detail later): Scythia there appears as an inverted pastoral world, in which the char-

acteristic pastoral warmth has become the Scythian cold, allowing Virgil yet another means of testing and exploring the very
essences of his subject, the pastoral idea. Again, it must have
seemed to Virgil that the possibility of reflecting reality, appearance, and illusion in such ways was inherent in the very subject
matter of the poem.

A few other points relating to method can be introduced here.
First, the *Georgics* (as we noted earlier) is a progression of patterns: motifs, themes, and ideas recur, blend with one another,
form contrasts, change their appearances, carry different suggestions from context to context in a continual flow, from
which meaning results, such meaning as we would get from a
similar flow of suggestive images on a screen, not from a discursive logical argument. We said before that there is no way to
state what Virgil means, as one could state, without undue distortion, what Lucretius or Tacitus mean; but it is also impossible even to follow the course and development of his patterns,
because simply to describe any one pattern means that others
must also, at the same time, be described. Fire, for instance, is
everywhere throughout the poem, but has a wide range of suggestions and values, ranging from the fire that provides the
warmth necessary for the generation of life to that which is the
element of absolute destruction: in any one passage fire may
have one prominent connotation, but others may be obviously
suggested at the same time, and still others may be implied: to
spell them all out, at each occurrence, is clearly both impossible
and undesirable. My intention, then, in what follows is to clar-
ify certain suggestions and associations which I think are now
unclear, and to trace some of these through the poem; I do not
intend to say what the poem means, though I hope that our understanding of its meaning will profit from my observations.

Much of Virgil's web of suggestion is managed through "recall" and "allusion." When does Virgil actually allude to another
poet or recall an earlier line or passage of his own? I have tried in
this matter to act with extreme caution, because I think the general trend now is to find recalls everywhere. I propose no rules
or guidelines here, and will offer only a few cautionary obser-

vations. No single word ought to be regarded as a recall or allusion. Latin poetic vocabulary is very limited, and thus even noun-epithet combinations can recur where we should not assume intentional association (even if the combination occurs in identical metrical positions). Furthermore, words simply represent ideas: it may be that two lines are similar in ideas and thus have a word or words in common. *Dixerat* may begin two hexameter lines: an interpreter might say that the word in one serves as a recall of the other (with further interpretative implications), but what the two lines actually share is simply the idea of the conclusion of a speech—which idea is hardly enough to associate the two lines. For a word or phrase to act as a recall, it ought to be in some way special, significant in itself. The question of verbal echo is too complex to enter into here, but is worth mentioning because so much of recent interpretation relies so heavily on finding such "parallels." I have tried to follow Virgil's ideas, not his words, and have tried to justify the recalls and echoes which I do consider valid and significant.

If one line does, clearly, suggest another, then we must ask, in every instance, why? It cannot be assumed that recall of context must be the poet's intention. Every instance should be considered on a scale, at one end of which would be the totally unconscious use of the precedent line, and at the other end the intention of recalling the entire context in which the precedent line had occurred: in the middle is an area in which the poet (e.g., Virgil) did consciously rework a line of another (e.g., Lucretius), but only to convey some required tone (e.g., of philosophical cosmogony), not to contrast contexts or recall the idea. While I have always kept such a scale in my own mind, I have not argued each instance: I have tried again to act with caution, and have tried not to base the associations I find solely on the assumption of a certain sort of recall or allusion.

The longer I have been with Virgil, the more I have become convinced that he used no proper name or adjective gratuitously. Every geographical designation, for instance, has, I feel sure, some real purpose. Many, of course, will remain inexplicable, but I have so often found unexpected precision in these designations that I feel confident in Virgil's total integrity in this matter, as will be seen.

Another principle I have kept in mind has to do with the technical passages. I mentioned above that although Virgil does not (quite obviously) intend to instruct—the opposite is often the case—he does know precisely whereof he speaks. He has selected what he presents from a great deal of possible detail, and, being Virgil, can be trusted to have done so for good reason. Thus, in any one didactic passage, there will be a common thread running through the diversity of information and instructional detail, which, if it can be found, will show clearly the purpose of that passage, the general idea it presents. I mention this, which would seem to be self-evident, only because the technical passages have received relatively little attention, and because often the connections between the details are in themselves somewhat technical and therefore have not been properly understood in some cases.

One last point of introduction: Servius' commentary will be quoted frequently in what follows. I have come to find Servius of far greater value than anything written on Virgil since. Servius' commentary is a compilation, a variorum, part of which must go back four centuries to comments of various sorts made soon after the first publication of Virgil's poems. (For this reason I have not found it worthwhile here to attempt to distinguish consistently between Servius and Servius Auctus—the Donatus commentary.) These notes are often valuable in two ways. First, they illuminate because so frequently they provide us with a set of ideas entirely different from our own, an entirely neglected view of a word, or phrase, or passage that proves reasonably to have been Virgil's intention, long forgotten or overlooked simply because his own terms had been forgotten; understanding the *Georgics* is so often a matter of seeing the exact terms used in any passage. Second, even when a comment seems to us trivial, unnecessary, or silly, it often indicates that in antiquity some problem existed, that a line that seems clear enough to us seemed then to call for explanation, either because we simply don't see what bothered an ancient reader, or (as I

suspect may frequently be the case) a comment, good and informed in itself, elicited another (but trivial) comment later,
after which the informed comment dropped from the tradition,
leaving only the dross to mark the place. I cite Servius, then,
whenever I feel that what is there recorded provides a possible
indication of the truth, known once and since forgotten.

*

I discussed above why Virgil was drawn to farming as the subject for a grand poem, how the material itself had roots deep in
Italian soil and supplied, for the Romans, a natural metaphor for
the cycles and forces of life and the universe. This is only a part
of the answer. The *Georgics* is an artful poem of science. Virgil's
science, as I would define it, is the attempt to understand ration-
ally the workings of the universe and man's place within it: as
Virgil himself says (*Geo.* 2.477–82), science comprehends the
motions of the stars and planets, eclipses of sun and moon,
earthquakes and tides, the procession of the seasons. To know
the world is to be able to control it—to know what makes crops
productive, when to plow and when to prune, how to care for
flocks and herds. The farmer requires all knowledge, for his
farm and the diversity of life it supports is a miniature universe,
subject to all its forces and laws. All the sciences (not so rigidly
distinguished in antiquity, of course) contribute to agricultural
knowledge—astronomy, physics, biology of plants and animals, geography and ethnography, medicine: indeed, at the beginning of Greek science, knowledge presented a similar unified
appearance. Agriculture thus provided Virgil with a subject
comprehending, as no other subject would, all of human
knowledge.

   The physical world, as we will soon see, was reducible to the
four elements (earth, air, fire, and water), with which were associated four qualities (hot, cold, wet, and dry). Aristotle's authority had canonized these elements and qualities: previously
their associations and correspondences had not always been so
neat or exclusive, and in later times the more creative thinkers
tended to ignore the rigidity imposed on the world by this sys-

tematization, though the existence of these four prime elements was never denied outright. In popular thinking, though, the appeal of these tetralogies was universal, and with good reason—everything can be explained in simple terms, if the explanation is not pressed too hard. For Virgil the pre-eminence of the elements and qualities was a given, not just because their existence and universality was assumed as easily and as completely in his day as the existence and the nature of the atom is assumed in ours, but because, again like the atom, all matter can be understood thereby. But for Virgil the four elements and qualities offered more than the atom offers in our time: fire was not only a constituent of the physical world, but had of course been a powerful element in symbolic thought, poetic and otherwise. Strife and its resolution, creation and destruction, all of life was understandable in terms of elemental oppositions. As all things, physical existence and intangible forces, are reducible to four elements and qualities, so too do these serve to connect everything, to form the smallest pieces in the ever-changing patterns of things.

Knowledge, understanding, control, and power: science then is remarkably similar in its goals to science now. The more we understand Virgil's intellectual world and Virgil's own mind, the more we are permitted, and often required, to see a strange relevance in his poem. Intellectual understanding is necessarily a process involving conflict, just as the resulting control and power are synonymous with domination. The farmer's knowledge is control and power over nature (this is especially true of the Roman farmer): but there are forces (often, literally, supernatural) that exist in the universe as well that seem to belittle and destroy his power, and so at every level conflict and destruction continue.

I said above that the Virgilian elements I will be concerned with here are in one sense "the pieces used to make the poetic patterns, the elements of poetic thoughts." In another sense they are the four elements of ancient science, which, as we will now see, dominate the poem's opening movement.

CHAPTER TWO

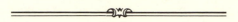

BOOK I

The PINGUIS ARISTA

The *Georgics* begins with a simplicity of vocabulary and word order that would be natural enough to prose, a four-and-a-half line statement of the subjects of each book in order:

> Quid faciat laetas segetes, quo sidere terram
> vertere, Maecenas, ulmisque adiungere vitis
> conveniat, quae cura boum, qui cultus habendo
> sit pecori, apibus quanta experientia parcis
> hinc canere incipiam. (1.1–5)

> (What makes fields fertile, under what constellation to plow the earth, Maecenas, and to tie vines to the elms, what care there is for cattle, what practice for the maintenance of flocks, how much knowledge for keeping thrifty bees—this is the beginning of my poem.)

Virgil's professed subject is agricultural knowledge: what makes field crops productive, when to plow, the methods of animal husbandry, the lore of the bee-keeper. *Cura, cultus,* and *experientia* are practical words, useful for someone who knows, from trial and error and the experience of others, what to do at the right time to get results.

A long and elaborate invocation follows, as if Virgil had suddenly remembered what a poet was supposed to be doing, but even here, in language grand and highly stylized, there is a break with tradition. He begins with a clear reminder of Varro, who at the beginning of his *Res Rusticae,* invoked the twelve Dei

Consentes of agriculture—not, of course, the Muses of Homer and Ennius, and not the twelve urban Dei Consentes (*invocabo eos, nec, ut Homerus et Ennius, Musas, sed duodecim deos Consentis; neque tamen eos urbanos . . . sed illos XII deos qui maxime agricolarum duces sunt*, 1.1.4): Jupiter and Earth, Sun and Moon, Ceres and Liber, and so on in pairs. Virgil begins with the sun and moon (*vos, o clarissima mundi / lumina, labentem caelo quae ducitis annum*, 5–6) and Liber and Ceres, omitting Varro's Jupiter and Earth, and omitting to point out (because Varro had) that he thus begins *not* in the manner of Homer and Ennius, *not* with an invocation to the Muses, a notable departure in an ostensibly Hesiodic poem. Just as in the opening statement of subject, Virgil seems to indicate that he is consorting not so much with poets as with practical men.

Though the Muses are snubbed and the great poets neglected, Virgil's language, suddenly elevated, reveals the hand of the poet at work:

> Liber et alma Ceres, vestro si munere tellus
> Chaoniam pingui glandem mutavit arista,
> poculaque inventis Acheloia miscuit uvis.　　　　　(7–9)

> (Liber and fostering Ceres, if by your gift the earth exchanged the Chaonian acorn for the rich ear of grain, and mixed Acheloian cups [of water] with the newly discovered grape.)

These three lines are pure Virgil, thoroughly characteristic of the *Georgics* in the hard clarity of their surface, like black ice on a pond, revealing figures and patterns frozen in the surface itself but allowing other shapes and forms to be seen dimly moving beneath. The two deities invoked by name in the first of these lines, Bacchus and Ceres, are of the greatest importance in the poem; their contributions to civilization, wine and grain, each receive a line (8–9), each of which is a highly stylized poetic construction containing two nouns, two attributes, and one verb, and each with an obviously learned geographical epithet demanding attention. We mentioned above, in a profession of methodological faith in Virgil's poetic sincerity, that no geographical designation is used gratuitously, or simply ornamentally; we noted too that what is preserved in Servius' commentary will often point the way; and we are obviously presented here with two of the most prominent "pieces" that recur again and again in the patterns of the poem. These lines call for leisurely consideration.

Ceres was traditionally derived from *gerere (fruges)* or from *creare*, as Varro (*quae quod gerit fruges, Ceres. antiquis enim C quod nunc G, LL* 5.64) and Cicero (*a gerendis frugibus Ceres tamquam Geres, ND* 2.67) both reported. Virgil's epithet *alma* is thus an elementary gloss, as Servius implied: " 'alma' ab alendo, 'Ceres' a creando dicta." Elementary though this is, it serves to alert the reader for what follows. The two proper adjectives likewise function as aetiological glosses. On *Acheloia pocula*, Servius noted (along with much else), "nam, sicut Orpheus docet, generaliter aquam veteres Acheloum vocabant" ("before the discovery of wine, as Orpheus teaches, the ancients generally called water 'Achelous' "); and on *Chaoniam glandem*, "Epiroticam, a loco, in quo abundant glandes, quibus antea homines vescebantur" ("Chaonian is equivalent to Epirotic, where acorns are plentiful, which men ate previously"). In the *Aeneid* (3.334–35) Virgil will give a fuller aetiology: Helenus called Epirus "Chaonia," after the Trojan hero Chaon. The purpose of "Chaonian" here is clear enough: our attention is thereby called to the actual location, to Epirus with its famous oaks, the oracle of Jupiter. Virgil will soon, of course, develop this connection in detail: Jupiter and Ceres are to be as dominant in the poem as Juno and Venus are in the *Aeneid*; the acorn and the grain will be recurrent motifs, and so will Bacchus and the vine. The learned use of the etymological and aetiological glosses serves to underline these important concepts right from the start.

This much, though, is well marked and therefore fairly obvious, but there is another etymological gloss in these lines that has not been noticed since Servius, and which is as important as those which illuminate and connect Ceres, Liber, and Jupiter, and more important in some ways, because through it Virgil identifies another complex of ideas which will also dominate much of the poem—the language and the terms of physical science. By Ceres' gift man exchanged the acorn for the "rich ear," *pingui arista*, the most prominent token of agricultural civilization and therefore central to the poem. Let us start with Servius: "aristam modo pro frumento posuit. et adfectate ait pinguem aristam, cum proprie arista ab ariditate sit dicta." That is, the word *arista* (the ear of grain) is derived from "dryness" (*ab ariditate*), and Virgil studiedly indicates this etymology by glossing the term with an adjective meaning the opposite, *pingui* ("fat, oily, plump, succulent"). We must ask first of all whether Virgil was aware of this etymology; and, if he did use the epithet *pingui* "studiedly" (*adfectate*), we must then ask just what he had in mind. The first question can be answered easily and with certainty; the second will take us much farther into the poem before any reasonable certainty can be gained.

Varro gives the etymology of *arista*, among other words pertaining to grain, in the *Res Rusticae* (1.48.2): "*arista dicta, quod arescit prima.*" This by itself almost guarantees that Servius' comment was valid for Virgil, but we can do better. Varro's derivation is probably traditional, not his own, since it must lie behind a rather prominent play on the word by Catullus. In poem 48, Catullus claims he would not have enough of Juventius' kisses even if "the field of our kissing should be denser than dry grain" (*non si densior aridis aristis / sit nostrae seges osculationis*, 5–6): commentators, not recognizing the etymological gloss in *aridis*, have wondered needlessly about the propriety of the word ("dry") in the context of kissing; here again in Catullus' polymetrics the learned mingles with the playfully posh. A different field occurs in the epyllion, where Achilles will mow down the Trojans like the ears of grain dried under a burning sun: *namque velut densas praecerpens messor aristas / sole sub ardenti flaventia demetit arva*, 64.353–54). Virgil quite obviously has both Catullan lines in mind, where the etymology is again prominent, in the *Aeneid*: *vel cum sole novo densae torrentur aristae* (7.720: the Catalogue is rich in etymological aetiologies—this section begins with the descent of the Claudian *tribus* and *gens* from Clausus and includes the recognized glosses *Rosea rura* and *Tetricae horrentis*, 712–13). Servius comments on this simile (a comment, of course, that is earlier than the comment on *pingui arista* in the *Georgics*, since he wrote the *Aeneid* commentary first), "sed tunc [*sci*. prima aestatis parte] non sunt aristae, quas ab ariditate dictas esse constat." Play on the etymology of *arista* continued after Virgil; Ovid's Oenone, in her letter to Paris (*Her*. 5.111–12), looks to both Virgil and Catullus: *et minus est in te quam summa pondus arista, / quae levis adsiduis solibus usta riget* ("you are lighter than a spike of grain, which, weightless, burned dry by constant sun, is brittle").

There can be little doubt that a traditional etymology of *arista* (*ab ariditate*) existed before Catullus, which Virgil certainly knew from Catullus' poetic use of it and from Varro's report. *Pingui* serves as an etymological gloss, giving the opposite, a variation on the *lucus a non lucendo* type of etymology. Some seventy lines later Virgil contrasts *aridus* and *pinguis* specifically, and in a related context (*arida tantum / ne saturare fimo pingui pudeat sola*, 79–80, where Servius explains *pingui fimo* with "vel umido vel fertili"). *Pinguis* is an important word in the *Georgics* and will concern us again more than once. Just as there is point in the proper adjectives in these lines (*Chaoniam, Acheloia*) and in the simple and immediately recognizable gloss *alma* (*Ceres*), so too we can assume that there is more than a demonstration of poetic learning in *pinguis arista*.

There are two details still to be observed in these opening lines which will suggest intriguing possibilities and will certainly reinforce the assumption that *pinguis arista* is more than etymological playfulness. The first seems to me clear enough. In lines 14–15 an unnamed benefactor is introduced: *et cultor nemorum, cui pinguia Ceae / ter centum nivei tondent dumeta iuvenci*. Why this anonymity? When a learned poet omits a proper name, the rules of the game dictate that a clue be given by some reference. Prominent in the hymnic relative clause that identifies this *cultor nemorum* is the geographical reference *pinguia Ceae / . . . dumeta*. The epithet *pinguia*, six lines after *pinguis arista*, provides the clue to the hero's name, Aristaeus. The second detail, connected with this, is far from certain, but well worth our notice because it is in itself intriguing and may be significant. The Bern scholia, which often shows independence from the Servian commentary, gives a story about Aristaeus that is unique: it relates that certain Greek cities, at a time of pestilence, were told by Apollo to vow white (*candidissima*) bullocks to his son Aristaeus, which they did, leaving them (for no apparent reason) on the island of Cea. Obviously all this is intended to explain what the rest of the tradition leaves unexplained—why the bullocks are *nivei* and why they are in Cea—and is therefore very likely to be the worthless fabrication of some later scholiast. Not only did this unique nonsense displace the usual explanations of Aristaeus, but it occurs where it has no business to be: it is not to be found explaining *cultor nemorum* in line 14, but after the lemma ARISTA in line 8. A simple misplacement? Perhaps, but it is also possible that, rather than misplaced, it actually displaced a mention of Aristaeus made at line 8 which connected the *pinguis arista* with Aristaeus, discoverer of the agricultural arts. However this may be, the connection was certainly made by Virgil, according to the conventions of learned poetry. Whereas other learned poets often play by the rules simply for the sake of the game itself, Virgil always does so for a good reason, making particularly significant that which he draws attention to.

Aristaeus was significant for Virgil in a number of ways—as the son of Apollo and Cyrene, as an agricultural benefactor, as a figure sufficiently malleable to be set against Orpheus at the end of the poem. We will see there that Aristaeus significantly acquires knowledge in sharply contrasting settings—first by a descent beneath the cool blue waves to a watery realm where he is received and consoled by his sea-nymph mother, and then in a struggle in the blazing heat of midday in midsummer as the sun's fire scorches the earth. For Virgil the name itself was significant: Aristaeus is connected here at the very beginning with the *pinguis arista*, itself a contradiction, the result of man's craft and art taught to him by Aristaeus (among others); but this is only the beginning.

The *pinguis arista* is the product of the agricultural process, a process which concerns practical men who must live by their knowledge and experience, but which as well extends back in time to a defined beginning, when Jupiter's acorn was replaced by Ceres' gift of grain. It is therefore an important token in the *Georgics*, being a paradox, a contradiction in terms—in terms which are in fact the most important physical opposition in the poem, dry and wet, fire and water. Man's knowledge produces this meeting of elemental oppositions, this "moist dryness." We will explore some of the history of this elemental opposition later in this chaper, and in subsequent chapters we will never be far from the real world of physics, the world of the four elements and the four qualities. The *Georgics* is a poem of science, which is to say of knowledge, by which man controls his world, altering its nature for his purposes, manipulating, achieving balance and harmony where otherwise there would exist only opposition and strife. The ripe ear of corn shows what he has learned to do, the result of a balance created between the wet and the dry, between water and fire.

★

To understand the relevance of the word play in *pingui arista* and its thematic importance in the introduction, we need only look at certain details in the poem's first didactic panel, lines 43–175. In the *Georgics*, however, a proper awareness of the details in any passage comes only from a recognition of the place that passage has in the overall structure of a larger unit or of the book. This first book is generally recognized to fall into two Hesiodic halves, a "Works" half and a "Days" half (so in the poem's first line, *laetas segetes* and *quo sidere*): the division clearly comes after line 203.

The "Works" half, however, is not Hesiodic in its structure, but rather Varronian (though this does not appear to have been recognized). Varro's division of the subject of agriculture is assumed by Virgil, but this division is itself of little importance: what is important is that once Varro's division is recognized, we can then see Virgil's purpose in adopting it.

Varro divided agriculture into four parts (*RR* 1.5.3):

1. knowledge of the farm's situation and soil;
2. necessary equipment;
3. what must be done and
4. when it must be done.

Each of these four parts (Varro goes on to say, 1.5.4) has two sections; and it is according to this outline (with further subsections) that the first half of Varro's book is composed (1.6–1.37.3). (The second half follows a different disposition of material, given at 1.37.4, of six stages—preparation, planting, cultivation, harvesting, storing, and marketing.) Virgil was not interested in reproducing Varro's arrangement (had he wished, he could have followed it explicitly), but he saw that these divisions comprehended his entire subject and were therefore useful without being restricting. As we will observe, there is only one omission in Varro's outline, and that is the farmer himself, a figure Virgil's perspective includes: Virgil will, in fact, focus on the farmer as part of the farm's equipment. Thus it is with Varro's arrangement generally in mind, and with the assumption that it would be generally in the minds of his readers, that Virgil has disposed the material of the first half of his first book:

43–70: Introduction, which (see below) itself assumes Varro's four-part disposition.

71–99: what must be done and

100–17: when it must be done;

118–59: the nature of the farmer's world;

160–75: necessary equipment.

176–203: summation, conclusion, transition.

It will be immediately apparent that Virgil has changed Varro's order (3 and 4, then 1 and 2): Varro's order has more instructional logic, but Virgil's is far more dramatic, at least as he has developed it. It will be apparent, too, how vastly different Virgil's scope is, when seen against Varro's: for instance, Varro's first part, the farm's situation and soil, has become an extraordinary exposition of the nature of the farmer's world and historical (and theological) causality, evil, and necessity.

We now consider each of these sections in order and in (what may be tedious) detail. It is important to see as clearly as we can what Virgil is concentrating upon—what are the elements—in these first didactic passages of the poem.

The introductory section (43–70) establishes the terms and indicates the scope of what follows. Varro does what all ancient technical writers did—he gives an outline (1.5.3–4) with clear headings and subheadings of the material to follow. Virgil is here doing the same, but with a difference: his lines are a perfect ring structure, with a series of *exempla* at the center.

    A   (43–44): when (*vere novo . . . cum . . . Zephyro . . .*)

    B   (45–46): what ("let the bulls begin to plow")

    C   (47–49): the farmer (*avari agricolae*)

    D   (50–53): knowledge of the farm's situation

    Exempla (54–59): 3 × 3

    D'   (60–61): the farmer's world as universe

    C'   (61–63): the farmer as Man (*durum genus*)

    B' ⎫   ⎧ what ("let the bulls plow") and

       ⎬ (64–70): ⎨

    A' ⎭   ⎩ when (*primis a mensibus anni . . . sub ipsum Arcturum*)

This outline, while too schematic and rigid, is helpful in revealing the movement from the agricultural to the universal. *D* clearly corresponds with Varro's first division, the *cognitio fundi*, which has to do with the farm itself (its soils and fields) and its larger situation and environment, whereas *D'* (*continuo has leges aeternaque foedera certis / imposuit natura locis*, 60–61) looks to nature's eternal laws about the fixed characters of places: when Virgil, in lines 118–59, comes to speak of the nature of the farmer's world, the scope will be even wider. Likewise *C'* is concerned with Man rather than with the farmer (the *avari agricolae* of *C*), specifically with the *durum genus* descended from Deuca-

lion's stones. Here (*CC'*) Virgil must depart from Varro's topics, but we may be permitted to put the farmer under the category of equipment, for the moment: lines 160–75 are clearly
devoted to Varro's equipment, the *duris agrestibus arma* (160),
where the farmer and his tools are much the same. *A* and *B* distinguish the "when" and the "what," but lines 64–70 avoid schematic rigidity by combining these topics into a single B'A'
movement.

With this much clearly in mind, let us look at the six-line cen-
terpiece:

> hic segetes, illic veniunt felicius uvae,
> arborei fetus alibi atque iniussa virescunt
> gramina. nonne vides, croceos ut Tmolus odores,
> India mittit ebur, molles sua tura Sabaei,
> at Chalybes nudi ferrum virosaque Pontus
> castorea, Eliadum palmas Epiros equarum? (54–59)

(Here grain crops, there grapes come more productively, elsewhere
fruit trees grow strong and, unbidden, pasturage. For you see, of
course, how the Tmolus sends the scent of saffron, India its ivory,
the soft Sabaeans their incense; but the naked Calybes produce iron,
and Pontus the beaver's musk oil, strong-smelling, and Epirus the
victory-palms of Olympian horses.)

These *exempla* follow naturally from the admonition (*D*) to observe the *patrios cultus habitusque locorum*, and fall into three sets
of three. The first set is specific and, like all that has preceded, is
limited in scope to the farmer and his farm: one area is suitable
for grain, another for the vine and another for fruit trees, and
another for pasture—these are the subjects of the first three
books of Virgil's poem. The next two sets of *exempla* effect a
sudden change in scope, from the limited context of the particular farmer and his land to the whole inhabited world, a wid-
ening of scope that continues as the constraints of the farm's situation (*D*) become the eternal laws imposed globally by nature
(*D'*, *has leges aeternaque foedera certis / imposuit natura locis*), and
the individual farmer (*C*, *avari agricolae*) becomes the human
race (*C'*, *unde homines nati, durum genus*, of Deucalion). These

two sets of *exempla* oppose the East (Tmolus, India, the Sabaei) to the North/West (the Calybes, Pontus, Epirus); perfume, ivory, and incense are opposed to iron, beaver oil, and the horse. The opposition of East and North/West may perhaps seem unjustified cartographically (this traditional perspective is Greek, however, and thus Pontus and Epirus are opposed to sites obviously oriental and exotic), but iconographically and ethnographically there is no doubt. Servius recognized the precise point of Virgil's opposition in his comment (on line 57), " 'molles' . . . quod sub aere clementiore sunt." This is a commonplace of long-standing, as old as the beginnings of ethnographical thinking, and one to which we will return again and again: the climate of the eastern (and of course southern) lands, being warm, requires little of its inhabitants, and hence produces men soft and unwarlike (*molles*) and natural products of similar character (perfumes, ivory, incense, for instance), useless, effeminate, luxurious. The north, with its demanding cold, produces men of rigorous and martial disposition, manly rather than effeminate, and as well iron, castor oil, and the horse. The significance of iron is obvious, and it will be obvious, too, that the horse's sphere in the *Georgics* is entirely that of war or war-games. But castor oil? This is Virgil's contribution, as far as we can discover, a poetic concoction, in the learned manner, though probably without poetic precedent. We know enough about beavers to be able to see what Virgil did with the popular conceptions (see the *Thesaurus linguae latinae*, s.v. *castor* and *castoreum*)—curious but relevant.

Beavers were trapped not for their fur but for the glandular secretion, used medicinally, which was popularly thought to be secreted by their testicles, and hence the exemplary story common in antiquity that beavers castrated themselves to avoid capture—so Servius here, "castores autem a castrando dicti sunt." Virgil's point, then, is conveyed (again) by the gloss *virosa* (*castorea*), not simply "strong (smelling)," but "manly," which lends then further significance to the topic of the manly West. But Servius records as well the comment, " 'virosa' autem venenata . . . et 'virosa' dicta ab eo, quod est virus," saying that abortions are caused by the smell, a silly explanation probably invented simply to explain an original gloss "venenata" or "quod est virus." Poison, as will be seen, is a frequent motif in the poem, and thus is set forth in this characteristic, and poetically vivid, "learned" manner. *Vīrosa*, then, includes easily and inevitably the meanings of *vīrus* ("animal sperm," "poison") and *vĭr* ("man"—ancient etymologies are not concerned with vowel quantities, of course), with inevitably as well an echo of *vīres* ("strength")—all of which popular beaver lore invites the reader to contemplate.

To sum up. The standard agricultural precept (D) that each sort of land has its own character (a single farm may be composed of several different sorts of land), is illustrated with *exempla* that are the subjects of the first three books of the poem. The next two sets of *exempla* suddenly extend the scope—not the farm, but the inhabited world becomes Virgil's focus: the traditional geographical opposition, moreover, brings with it the inevitable contrast of rigorous martial disposition with luxurious effeminacy. Then Man's universe and nature's eternal laws (D'). We are thus presented with one of the poem's most important thematic complexes, and one that shows us clearly what the scope of Virgil's poem (on crops, trees and vines, and pasture) is to be. As we discussed earlier, a Roman would see, in the farm, just how *natura* (as "the power of growth") is responsible for diversity, for products of vastly different character; ancient ethnography saw the differences between people and places in very similar ways—as the result of the differences in situation; and Virgil, in moving from the specific farm to the inhabited world, is establishing his connection between agricultural instruction and the scientific study of Man, between the farm and the world, with the result that his *natura* will be not just that force that the farmer must use to be successful within the *termini* of his own preserve, but that force and power that somehow extends to the chaos beyond the farm's sacred boundaries. So much, at this point, is only stated, not explained, by Virgil, and we should (and must) leave it just as it is, for the present.

These *exempla*, then, present us with images of basic oppositions that we will do well to remember. There is still another related and equally important aspect to this introductory section
that hasn't as yet been touched upon and that will take us back
to our point of departure. The ring structure of this section is
reinforced, in addition to the four Varronian subjects enclosing
the *exempla*, by the *umor* of the first and last lines (43 and 70) and
by the repetition of *glaeba/glaebas* (44, 65). These are not verbal
echoes, strictly speaking (both words are too common to allow
any sort of recall); the repetition is not of words, but of ideas.
This is an important distinction, because what opens and closes
this section is in fact a further opposition, of wet and cold (the
umor of 43 is *gelidus*, the spring run-off from mountains still
white (*canis*) with snow) versus the hot and dry; at the end of the
passage, spring is mentioned again (*primis . . . a mensibus anni*)
as the proper time for plowing rich soil (*pingue solum*—note the
epithet), which will be cooked by dusty summer (*pulverulenta
aestas*); but scanty moisture in sterile sand should be preserved
by a fall plowing, *sub ipsum Arcturum* (at its heliacal rising of mid
to late September). The purpose of plowing (the bulls of 45 and
65) is to achieve a balance of these opposed elements—that is
what the farmer must do, and why he must do it at the right
times. Here, again, we are simply presented with these details;
as yet they have no context, no explanation, and hence the present explication may seem exaggerated or distorted, an unwar-
ranted singling out from certain casual details the elemental
qualities of wet and cold, hot and dry. One more observation,
though, remains to be made.

When Virgil advises recognition of the land's character and
situation, he is doing more than including a Varronian topic, or
one that is of obvious importance to any writer on agriculture
(so Cato, at the beginning of the *De Agricultura*, 1.2–3: *uti bonum
caelum habeat, ne calamitosum siet, solo bono, sua virtute valeat. Si
poteris, sub radice montis siet, in meridiem spectet, loco salubri . . . ,*
etc.). Virgil's advice to the new farmer (*ventos et varium caeli
praediscere morem / cura sit et patrios cultusque habitusque locorum,*
51–52) is the same as that given by Hippocrates to the physician

who has just come to a strange city: "first it is necessary to learn by observation the seasons of the year . . . then the winds, both the hot and the cold . . . then the powers of the water . . . and to consider the city's situation . . . and the land . . . and the way of life (regimen) of its inhabitants" (πρῶτον μὲν [χρὴ] ἐνθυμεῖσθαι τὰς ὥρας τοῦ ἔτεος . . . ἔπειτα δὲ τὰ πνεύματα τὰ θερμά τε καὶ τὰ ψυχρά . . . δεῖ δὲ καὶ τῶν ὑδάτων ἐνθυμεῖσθαι τὰς δυνάμιας . . . διαφροντίσαι χρὴ τὴν θέσιν αὐτῆς . . . καὶ τὴν γῆν . . . καὶ τὴν δίαιταν τῶν ἀνθρώπων, *Airs, Waters, Places* 1; I have excerpted phrases from the opening paragraph, which has much else of interest and relevance). The point and purpose of this clear suggestion of the Hippocratic treatise will be considered in detail later. For now, I simply make the claim that this Hippocratic voice serves to anticipate the ethnographic turn that the introduction suddenly takes with the second and third sets of *exempla*, and as well to give prominence to the elemental qualities with which the section opens and closes. Since all of this will occupy us in much of the following investigation, we must again leave it as it stands, calling attention to it, as does Virgil.

After this introductory section comes Virgil's first real lesson in basic agriculture. We must remember that (1) on the one hand Virgil is not writing an instruction manual or text book, and thus has been selective as to what he has included in these didactic passages, and (2) on the other hand what has been included is real agricultural fact, based on knowledge and ancient theory. We may be confident, then, that (1) every detail is there for a good reason and that the purpose of any passage ought to be apparent if (2) we can only see the pattern of the details purposely chosen and understand the reality of each detail.

Lines 71–99 are concerned with Varro's third division of the subject, *what must be done*. Various topics come in quick succession—allowing fields to lie fallow, crop rotation, fertilizing with manure and ash, burning the stubble, proper harrowing and plowing: obviously this is a miscellaneous collection and obviously it is too brief a treatment of each topic to be of any help to any farmer. Still, there is a clear theme running through the passage that connects the topics: the farmer's work, as Virgil had it at the beginning and end of the preceding introductory section, is to effect a balance, to alter the natural character of his land and soil so as to bring about a productive equality of elemental oppositions. Each of the operations touched on here has this as its aim. The section falls clearly into three parts. First (71–83), crops burn the land (*urit . . . urit . . . urunt*, 77–78), but balance can be restored by rest or rotation. Second (84–93), the farmer himself ought to do the burning sometimes, for a variety of possible reasons. Third (94–99), the farmer must command his fields in other ways as well. The first two parts focus on burning, which is counteracted by the farmer in the first but employed by him in the second. The fields exhausted by crops have been burned dry (*arida*, 79) and must be restored by rich manure (*fimo pingui*, 80), the very opposition that initiated our inquiry. Rest (both from rotation and lying fallow) is as well an important part of this restoration (*segnem situ durescere*, 72, and in the concluding lines of this part, *requiescunt . . . inaratae gratia terrae*, 82–83). When the farmer employs fire, however, its aim is somehow to produce rich food for the soil (*pabula pinguia*, 86–87), or to cook away an excess of moisture (*inutilis umor*, actually equated with a *vitium*, 88), or allow moisture (*sucus*, 90) to penetrate or remain (91–93). The philosophical origins or implications of these alternatives need not detain us (it was not Virgil's purpose to list the schools of thought that these eclectic possibilities may be related to): what is important is to see that here it is the farmer who restores the balance between the dry and the wet, the hot and the cold. We may pause to observe Servius' note on the final word of this part, *adurat* (*aut Boreae penetrabile frigus adurat*, 93): "et ad solem et ad frigus pertinet: nam uno sermone duo diversa conclusit, quae tamen unum effectum habent. nam et frigoris finis est caloris initium, et summus calor frigoris est principium . . . *hoc est quod Graeci dicunt* ἀκρότητες ἰσότητες" ("The verb *burns* pertains both to the sun and the cold, for in this one word [Virgil] includes two opposites, which nevertheless have one end, because the end of cold is the beginning of heat, and extreme heat is the beginning of cold . . . *This is what*

the Greeks mean by 'extremes are equalities' "). The third movement of this section continues with the farmer as the agent, but
(and this is a logical extension of his burning the fields, as we
will see shortly) as a soldier, or commander, training and com-
manding his fields (*exercetque frequens tellurem atque imperat arvis*,
99), and with the introduction of the military metaphor comes
a definite suggestion of violence (*frangit . . . trahit, . . . proscisso
aequore . . . perrumpit*, 94–98). It will be evident that the section
concludes directly opposite its starting point, with violent training and exertion rather than rest and ease.

The next section (100–117) concerns (ostensibly) the proper
times for work, Varro's "when." It begins with summer and
winter (*Umida solstitia atque hiemes orate serenas, / agricolae*, 100–
101), lines that have caused some difficulty, but it ought to be
clear enough that the "wet solstices" are simply the poetic opposite of *hiemes serenas*, "dry winters" (so *hiberno pulvere* in the
next line), and that one of Servius' explanations is not only
right, but apt: "dicit autem, optanda haec quae per naturam non
sunt, quo possit utriusque temporis asperitas mitigari, et aestatis
calor pluviis et frigus hiemis serenitatis tepore" ("He says,
though, that one must hope for what does not occur naturally,
that the harshness of each season can be tempered—the heat of
summer by rain and the cold of winter by the warmth of clear
skies"). Winter is naturally cold and wet, summer hot and dry:
the farmer prays for a balance (yet again) between these oppositions. The section closes with reference to spring and fall, the
incertis mensibus (115), as Servius notes again (and as we will see
again in greater detail in passages where the traditional uncertainty of these months is of greater importance: "incerti autem
menses sunt veris vel autumni: nam et hiemis certum est frigus,
et aestatis certus est calor" ("the months of spring and autumn,
however, are variable: for both the cold of winter and the heat
of summer are fixed"). This section, then, is marked at its beginning and end with reference to the four seasons and thus indicates its place in the Varronian division of the material—we
clearly have Varro's "when." But we do not get the expected list
of times to plow, plant, and harvest. The seasons are here for a

different purpose, and as we read, we see that Virgil is in fact using the seasons only to continue with the themes of the preceding section—the opposition of the elements, particularly of fire and water.

The farmer's task is to achieve a balance between the opposed elements, by irrigating (104–10) or draining (113–17), or by reducing luxuriance of growth (111–13). Virgil's emphasis on the basic oppositions of water and heat is apparent on a first reading of these lines (for example, in line 107, *et, cum exustus ager morientibus aestuat herbis*) and is marked by verbal play as well (as in line 110, *scatebrisque arentia temperat arva*, where noun and epithet anticipate the important etymology of the last word in the following line, *aristis*). The farmer brings about a balance: *temperat* (110) is a key word; *temperies* (or εὐκρασία) will concern us later.

In this section, though, the farmer appears as he was at the end of the previous section (another continuity that again should alert us to Virgil's special intentions). *Quid dicam, iacto qui semine comminus arva / insequitur* (104–5): the metaphor is that of a legionary, who, having thrown his javelin (*iacto semine*), then rushes to close with the enemy in hand-to-hand combat (*comminus*). The military metaphor goes far beyond this, however, and is combined in an extraordinary (and thoroughly Virgilian) way with the central theme of the opposition of the elements. To start with a detail: *nullo tantum se Mysia cultu / iactat et ipsa suas mirantur Gargara messis* (102–3). Why Mysia and Gargara? (In reading Virgil, again, we should start with the assumption that no geographical reference will be either gratuitous or merely decorative.) Mysia was a general designation of the area of Asia Minor containing the Troad and Phrygia (Servius, though reading *Moesia*, discusses the same area, not the province in central Thrace), and Gargara was a town at the foot of a mountain of the same name, or called Ida, also in Phrygia. Neither was synonymous with rich harvests of grain (though the area was productive), and Macrobius (5.20) in a long discussion of these lines goes to great lengths to find an explanation for Gargara's appearance here. What must come to mind (and it is the general and unspecified character of the place names that al-

THE *pinguis arista* 49

lows it to come) is Troy and the Trojan War, a fleeting suggestion inevitably arising from the mention of this area.

It is the total context, though, that suggests Troy, not simply
these place names: why Virgil makes this apparently pointless
suggestion is vividly revealed just a few lines later. The farmer,
"who casts the seed and attacks the fields in hand-to-hand combat," then opens the irrigation ditches:

quid dicam, iacto qui semine comminus arva
insequitur cumulosque ruit male pinguis harenae,
deinde satis fluvium inducit rivosque sequentis,
et, cum exustus ager morientibus aestuat herbis,
ecce supercilio clivosi tramitis undam
elicit? illa cadens raucum per levia murmur
saxa ciet, scatebrisque arentia temperat arva.   (104–10)

(Why should I mention him who, when he has cast his seed, closes
with the fields hand-to-hand and routs the mounds of poor sand,
then conducts a small stream, obedient channels, to his young plants;
or who, when the scorched field seethes with heat, its grasses dying,
brings forth a wave of water from a ridge down a sloping channel?
That water in its fall produces a loud growling in the smooth pebbles, and tempers the fields' dryness with its bubblings.)

We noted above the emphatic language of these lines, "the
burned field seething with heat with its dying grass," the word
play at the end, *arentia arva*, with *aristis* ending the next line.
Modern commentators have sometimes noted the precedent for
these lines, but critics and exegetes have seen little of significance in Virgil's use of the precedent, even when they are aware
of it. The lines are based clearly enough on a simile in the *Iliad*,
near the climax of Achilles' battle with the Scamander, just as
the river begins to drive the hero back:

φεῦγ', ὁ δ' ὄπισθε ῥέων ἕπετο μεγάλῳ ὀρυμαγδῷ.
ὡς δ' ὅτ' ἀνὴρ ὀχετηγὸς ἀπὸ κρήνης μελανύδρου
ἂμ φυτὰ καὶ κήπους ὕδατι ῥόον ἡγεμονεύῃ
χερσὶ μάκελλαν ἔχων, ἀμάρης ἐξ ἔχματα βάλλων·
τοῦ μέν τε προρέοντος ὑπὸ ψηφῖδες ἅπασαι
ὀχλεῦνται· τὸ δέ τ' ὦκα κατειβόμενον κελαρύζει

χώρῳ ἔνι προαλεῖ, φθάνει δέ τε καὶ τὸν ἄγοντα·
ὡς αἰεὶ Ἀχιλῆα κιχήσατο κῦμα ῥόοιο
καὶ λαυψηρὸν ἐόντα· θεοὶ δέ τε φέρτεροι ἀνδρῶν   (21.256–64)

(Achilles fled, but the stream followed after with a great rumbling. Just as when a farmer irrigating leads a stream of water from a dark spring through his plants and fruit trees, holding a mattock in his hands to break through the little dams in his channel; as it runs ahead, all the pebbles beneath are swept on, and flowing swiftly down a steep place it growls and outstrips the one leading it: just so the wave of the stream always overtook Achilles, swift as he was, for gods are more powerful than men.)

Why has Virgil suggested so clearly (and especially audibly) this simile here? We may assume again that no allusion of this sort is simply gratuitous.

Cedric Whitman, in *Homer and the Heroic Tradition* (Cambridge, 1958), has a superb chapter on "Fire and Other Elements," in which he shows that fire as an image is restricted to the *Iliad* (that is, it is not used as an image in the *Odyssey*), that it is restricted in its applications (not used, for instance, of love), and that its associations, "death, sacrifice, the fall of Troy,—coexist in each occurrence of it" (p. 145). Paramount is the fire of Achilles, which transforms itself from an image to what we can only term a symbolic reality in Achilles' *aristeia*, when Hephaestus, fire itself, intervenes against the Scamander, as Whitman so vividly recounts:

> But when Achilles reaches the river, his *aristeia* is no longer merely that. It becomes a battle of the elements, in which the protective river of Troy rises up against the hero and attempts to drown him . . . Homer is seldom as directly symbolic with his divine figures as this, but he has a special reason. Xanthus threatens to quench the fire of Achilles, and fire itself must answer the challenge. Hephaestus "aims the divine fire" like a spear, burning first the plain with the bodies on it, and begins to restrain the water. Trees and shrubs are consumed. The fish are tormented, and at last the water itself burns, or boils, and cries out in surrender. Achilles himself, in the middle of it, is untouched. All naturalism is left far behind, and the basic imagery of the *aristeia* of Achilles has completely run away with the action.
>
> (pp. 139–40)

The simile occurs just at the moment when the river begins to drive Achilles back, and the simile itself is a stage in the gradual domination of the action by the imagery: Achilles is like a farmer opening his irrigation channels, but the river is like the stream chasing after the farmer, a strange simile in which the comparison is identical with the compared. I suspect Virgil knew and appreciated the process Whitman has described (fire, after all, is one of the major images in the *Aeneid*, which frequently, especially in the last six books, functions in Homeric patterns) and was well aware that in the *aristeia* Achilles' destructive fire becomes a dramatic reality. It is Virgil's practice in the *Georgics*, as we frequently observe, to turn literary topics, abstractions, similes, metaphors, and the like into realities, and in some ways the poem itself can be seen as a metaphor made real. Here, to return to the passage at hand, the simile from Homer has become real. The burned field seething with its dying grass (compare the trees, clover, and other flora burned by Hephaestus as fire, *Iliad* 21.350–52) is a reality for Virgil, as is the irrigation channel with its bubbling stream.

There is something of a paradox here, or at least a conflict posed and unresolved. It is the farmer's function to effect a balance between opposing elements, here and in the previous section, as Virgil makes clear by selecting details all of which involve the qualities hot and cold, wet and dry. Yet at the end of the preceding section the farmer had become a military commander, and in this section geographical references to the Troad anticipate the direct suggestion of Achilles and his *aristeia*, his fire and destructive fury. Throughout the poem the farmer will often act with similar violence and will cause further destruction in a world that often opposes him as definitely as the Scamander opposes Achilles. For now, though, the conflict of both aspects of the farmer's activity, balance and destruction, is left unresolved.

The next two sections can be passed over rather quickly at this time, for they present other themes that will be of more importance later in the poem. No passage, however, has received more attention than the next, dealing with the imposition of Jupiter's order and containing, along with much else, the well-known *labor omnia vicit*. For now, though, only two observations—on its subject and on its structure.

Lines 118–59 are, in the Varronian outline, concerned with "knowledge of the farm's situation and its proper soil": we expect this, at least, from the introductory section, in which lines 50–53, paraphrasing Hippocrates, clearly state this essential precept (Cato's, in fact, as much as Varro's—a commonplace, for that matter, with a long history before Cato), and we are ready for Virgil's transformation of the precept from lines 60–61 of the introduction (*continuo has leges aeternaque foedera certis / imposuit natura locis*, from Deucalion's time). Varro's farm has become Virgil's world, its character the result of natural laws imposed now by Jupiter. It will be helpful, I think, to keep in mind that his passage is essentially an expansion, and transformation, of Varro's first division of his subject (*cognitio fundi, solum partesque eius quales sint*, 1.5.3). Anyone who takes the trouble to review what Varro actually says about the farm and its environment (chaps. 6–16), however, will see why Virgil has been able to leave Varro so far behind: Varro divides this division into a total of eight subsections and still allows himself a remarkable freedom (chapter 8, for instance, part of his discussion of types of soil, is actually concerned with various methods of supporting vines).

The structure of this section is again a ring, but unbalanced. It begins and ends (as Servius notes on 155) with clearly marked correspondences—weeds (*amaris intiba fibris*, 120 = *herbam*, 155), birds (*anser, grues*, 119–20 = *avis*, 156), and shade (*umbra*, 121 = *umbras*, 157): these are plagues attendant upon the farmer's efforts (*labores*, 118). The passage continues: Jupiter's responsibility—before him the earth bore freely (121–28); Jupiter's specific acts and their results (129–35); man's specific discoveries, the *artes* (136–45); and the attendant plagues (145–59). Here are the *patrios cultus habitusque locorum*, the *leges aeternaque foedera* imposed by nature, or Jupiter: continual opposition between man and his world, his *artes* and *labor* against its pests and plagues. The specifics will concern us later.

So, too, the details of Virgil's version (160–75) of Varro's

"Means: Men and Equipment" will find more appropriate context for discussion later: here the correspondence of Virgil to Varro is clear enough. We noted earlier how Deucalion's stones, *unde homines nati, durum genus* (61–63), are assumed here in the opening words, *Dicendum et quae sint duris agrestibus arma* (160). Again, the language associated with this hard race is full of violence, force, and domination, and *arma*, "equipment," inevitably suggests the weapons of the soldier.

We may summarize before considering a more general question. First of all, the didactic content of these opening lines is real, necessary, and scientific in the best sense: in the first section, for instance, Virgil discusses how to preserve or restore fertility—one must practice succession planting with fallow periods, crop rotation (with an awareness of the nitrogen-fixing capacity of legumes), manuring, burning, good plowing methods, and irrigation and drainage. Still, no one could learn to farm from Virgil's instructions: within this wide range of subjects (all presented in just thirty lines), it is obvious just how much Virgil has selected and omitted, and obvious as well what common ground there is to the details (all sharp and precise) he has chosen for mention. Virgil's real subject is fire and water—the opposition of these two prime elements. The farmer thus appears as the "realization" of the ἀνὴρ ὀχετηγός (the "irrigator") of Homer's simile, just when Achilles' symbolic fire is about to become Hephaestus' real fire, opposing Scamander's water. The farmer, now, emerges as a duality. Like Achilles, he is a military commander, or a soldier engaged in hand-to-hand combat, associated (through a vivid and sustained metaphor) with violence, domination, and even destruction—the embodiment of Achilles' fire. But at the same time, in contradiction, the farmer's efforts are directed towards resolving the elemental conflict, towards achieving a balance between hot and cold, wet and dry. The token of his efforts is Ceres' gift, the ear of grain which replaced the acorn, the *pinguis arista* which is itself a paradox. In the lines that are based on the Achilles simile from the *Iliad* (104–10, quoted above), we noted the word play *arentia temperat arva* (110) anticipating the last word of the next line, *aristis*, but we did not note that just a few lines before the "thin sand" (the furrows that the farmer levels and irrigates) is termed *male pinguis harenae* (105). The *pinguis arista* is a paradox and a contradiction, the co-existence of opposites. The farmer, in Jupiter's reign, has learned to bring about such balances through the skillful tempering of opposites, through which the natural world becomes productive and useful. But—and we are forced back now around the circle that Virgil leaves us with in these lines—the farmer, to achieve a balance, must use one element against another and in so doing becomes either the agent of the elemental conflict or an opponent in the struggle, like Achilles.

Historically, the conflict is attributable to Jupiter's new order, necessitating the arts and assuring as well a world of continuing conflict due to the plagues and pests (weeds, birds, and shade, among others) that are an inevitable part of the new order. One word will sum up all that we have had in this first movement of the poem (and which covers all that Varro defined as *agri culturae . . . initium et finis, RR* 1.5.1): opposition. We have been shown opposition and conflict in various related spheres that touch and intersect, conflict now resolved and then again resumed, but always returning to the prime opposition of fire and water. The *pinguis arista* will be Virgil's subject for the rest of the poem, a primary element of his poetic reflections, and symbolic of the primary elements of the physical world.

The Background of the Elements

We must now survey the general background of some of these ideas we have seen Virgil working with. Any sketch I can present will be unsatisfactory, for several reasons, making a note of caution and a plea for indulgence necessary here at the start. An intellectual history of the elements and their qualities in antiquity is, first of all, well beyond me, and, second, would be irrelevant to Virgil's poetry. I will thus limit my survey to a selective notice of a few areas, in none of which, however, can I claim more than an amateur's interest: specialists will be able to supply a great deal of detail, but I hope will not find that I have misrepresented the substance of the picture. On the other hand, it can be argued that the details I do present, while superficial, are at the same time largely irrelevant to the *Georgics*, since seldom can Virgil be shown to be "using"—much less referring to—any particular source.

I can answer only that the importance, or even the existence, of the background to be sketched in what follows is unknown to those who write on the *Georgics*, particularly in those books which give a general interpretation of the poem: it seems necessary, therefore, to go out on a limb over very thin ice. My excuse for the limb is that specific relevance to the *Georgics* is not really essential, for two reasons. Virgil very seldom "borrows" any single doctrine from any one philosopher or school—more often than not a particular passage will turn out to be a mixture of diverse ideas (Pythagorean, Democritean, and Stoic elements, for instance, can rub elbows happily within a few lines). Not only is Virgil generally eclectic, but as well he is using ideas that were often commonplaces in his time, though for us they can appear rigidly labelled. A modern novelist, for instance, can use Freudian ideas, or even terms, without being "Freudian" and without even suggesting the psychologist Freud to his readers: so Virgil can draw on a general awareness of the opposition of fire and water without suggesting any particular philosopher or school, or even a particular branch of science, to his readers. My excuse for the thin ice over which my limb sways is that the history of the elements in ancient thought is a large subject indeed, well beyond my capacity, and that even in any single area of thought I must rely on reading which is only a survey and on modern scholars whom I may misunderstand only too easily: but I hope that what I can do will be of some help to readers of the poem.

We observed above that Virgil does make one specific reference to the beginnings of Greek science, to the introduction to the Hippocratean *Airs, Waters, Places*: the new farmer must observe the nature of his land (1.50–53) just as Hippocrates' physician is to observe the situation of a strange city. This reference establishes a great deal: the scientific context clearly pointed out will be repeatedly suggested, assumed, and expanded upon not only in the following lines, but throughout the poem, without Virgil having to make further specific references to individual scientists, schools, or definite theories (though occasionally he will make such allusions). The Roman reader would be receptive to certain terms and ideas that were part of his general intellectual world but which have been lost, for modern readers, along with their general contexts. Putting the *Georgics* aside for the moment, we can try to sketch out some background, beginning as Virgil does from Hippocrates, that may remind us of some of the context, and its terms, that Virgil assumed for his contemporary readers.

The *Airs, Waters, Places* is among the earliest of the writings in the Hippocratic collection and is of particular general interest, being perhaps the most "philosophical" treatise, and being composed in a style of archaic and austere elegance. Only two points need concern us: that its basic philosophical assumption is man's intimate relation to his environment, and that it assumes, as the explanation of this relation, a humoral theory.

We summarized above the opening chapter. Ἰητρικὴν ὅστις βούλεται ὀρθῶς ζητεῖν, τάδε χρὴ ποιεῖν: whoever wishes to investigate medical science properly—we may note here the definite appeal to the amateur rather than the professional physician, which may explain the philosophical outlook of the treatise—must observe the seasons, the winds (that is, the prevailing character of the air), the water, the situation of the land, and the life style (δίαιταν) of the inhabitants of any city. To this author, the stars, the seasons, air, water, diseases and one's bowels are connected, and therefore, as he concludes his introduction (chap. 2), astronomy makes a major contribution to medicine (εἰ δὲ δοκέοι τις ταῦτα μετεωρολόγα εἶναι, εἰ μετασταίη τῆς γνώμης, μάθοι ἄν, ὅτι οὐκ ἐλάχιστον μέρος συμβάλλεται ἀστρονομίη ἐς ἰητρικήν, ἀλλὰ πάνυ πλεῖστον). The author then considers the effects of different prevailing winds (3–6—the city's situation and direction of exposure is crucial here), of waters (7–9—standing waters, spring waters with the direction of its exposure, rain and snow waters), and of seasonal changes and characteristics (10–11). How, precisely, do such environmental considerations affect the body? The author shows his awareness of scientific medical theory in the assumptions he sporadically offers. For instance, in a city exposed to hot southerly winds (chap. 3) men will have heads that are moist and full of phlegm; the opposite exposure (chap. 4) will produce hard cold waters and men who are bilious (χολώδεάς τε μᾶλλον ἢ φλεγματίας): behind this lies a connection between winter, the cold and the wet, and phlegm, and likewise between summer, the hot and the dry, and bile, though the author (who may be somewhat confused—how do south winds produce moist phlegmatic heads, and the converse?) is not inclined to press these correspondences systematically, due to other interests which predominate. Easterly exposure is best (he continues in chap. 5) because such a situation is most like spring in its balance of the hot and the cold (ἔοικέ τε μάλιστα ἡ οὕτω κειμένη πόλις ἦρι κατὰ τὴν μετριότητα τοῦ θερμοῦ καὶ τοῦ ψυχροῦ), and westerly exposure is worst. In the following discussions of waters and seasons the author reveals similar assumptions and outlook: though he recognizes bile and phlegm, he does not pursue humoral theory systematically or exclusively, even though these two humors are already connected with what primarily interests him—the qualities of hot and cold, wet and dry, and their influence upon the body and relation to the seasonal and physical environment.

In the second half of the work the author's philosophical tendency predominates: he compares the climates of Asia and Europe, and shows how each affects the characters of different inhabitants, particularly the Libyans (a section most unfortunately lost) and Scythians. Climate and season influence character (this is the basic premise). Violent changes in seasons (especially between hot and cold) produce vigor and passion, and sameness leads to passivity: so (in chap. 16) Asians are without spirit and valor, because in Asia the changes between winter's cold and summer's heat are more moderate, less violent, than in Europe. (περὶ δὲ τῆς ἀθυμίης τῶν ἀνθρώπων καὶ τῆς ἀνανδρείης, ὅτι ἀπολεμώτεροί εἰσι τῶν Εὐρωπαίων οἱ Ἀσιηνοὶ καὶ ἡμερώτεροι τὰ ἤθεα αἱ ὧραι αἴτιαι μάλιστα, οὐ μεγάλας τὰς μεταβολὰς ποιεύμεναι οὔτε ἐπὶ τὸ θερμὸν οὔτε ἐπὶ τὸ ψυχρόν, ἀλλὰ παραπλησίως). We have seen Virgil making use of this idea, which had become a commonplace: the eastern Tmolus, India, and the *molles Sabaei* (Servius: "molles . . . quod sub aere clementiore sunt") are contrasted, in their products, with the north and west (1.56–59), just following Virgil's paraphrase of the *Airs, Waters, Places*: the effeminate East versus the warlike West.

A temperate climate produces men of mild and gentle disposition, a rough climate the opposite. These ideas were very much in the air at the time, are the basis for ethnographical thinking already well established in Herodotus, and continue prominently in later geographical writings: for these reasons they are well known to classicists, though their importance for Virgil in the *Georgics* has only recently been noted and discussed. For the present we will just take a quick look at the terms used to express these ideas in the *Airs, Waters, Places*, especially those most relevant to the *Georgics*.

The ethnographical half begins (chap. 12) with the statement that Asia differs from Europe in the nature of their plants and their men (ἐς τὰς φύσιας τῶν συμπάντων τῶν τε ἐκ τῆς γῆς φυομένων καὶ τῶν ἀνθρώπων—a connection to be noted). In Asia everything grows larger and more beautiful, the country less wild and the men gentler and of a better disposition: the reason is the temperateness of the seasons (ἡ κρῆσις τῶν ὡρέων), since Asia lies farther toward the equator to the east and farther from the cold than Europe. *Crasis* is the key word here, being the standard term in geography (as we will see) to designate a balance (literally "mixture") of elemental opposites, the Latin equivalent being *temperies*; this term is frequent in medical writing, normally used to refer to a healthy balance in the body of opposing elements or humors. The author of *Airs, Water, Places* continues with an explanation of Asia's capacity for growth and mildness, "[since] nothing prevails by force but equality rules" (ὁκόταν μηδὲν ᾖ ἐπικρατέον βιαίως, ἀλλὰ παντὸς ἰσομοιρίη δυναστεύῃ): the metaphor here is from politics, ἰσομοιρίη being equivalent to ἰσονομία, a political term that we know was used by the early physician Alcmaeon, the first to see health as an equilibrium (ἰσονομία) of opposites (especially of the four qualities), and disease as the rule of one (μοναρχία), a domination elsewhere called ἐπικράτεια (cf. ἐπικρατέον here). For our purpose, though, it is enough to note this intimate connection between early medicine, geographical theory, botany and ethnography (the plants and men of a region are similar, due to similar causes), political theory (there is more of this later in the *Airs, Waters, Places*), and even cosmology (the idea of ἐπικράτεια seems to have been important in the cosmological speculations of Anaximander).

To continue now with chapter 12: the "rule of balance" (ἰσομοιρίη δυναστεύη) holds throughout Asia, but especially in that part which lies "in the middle of hot and cold," for "it is not excessively burned by heat, nor parched by drought and lack of water, nor oppressed by cold, nor wet and drenched by much rain and snow." We note how easily the opposition of hot and cold comes to mind, and in fact leads to all four qualities in the author's archaic paratactic explicitness. This introductory section then concludes with two statements, an expansion of an earlier remark, one about the flora, the other about the men of the region. It is interesting to note an idea that was of basic importance in Greek botany (as its inert appearance here demonstrates) and will be equally important for Virgil, that plants are divided into those which grow from seeds (ὁκόσα τε ἀπὸ σπερμάτων) and those which come spontaneously from the earth (καὶ ὁκόσα αὐτὴ ἡ γῆ ἀναδιδοῖ φυτά): this division will become more precise and practical in Theophrastus, and far more suggestive and significant in Virgil, who will expand upon the wild and cultivated that this author also touches upon in the very next clause (ὧν τοῖς καρποῖσι χρέονται ἄνθρωποι, ἡμεροῦντες ἐξ ἀγρίων καὶ ἐς ἐπιτήδειον μεταφυτεύοντες). Beasts and men, likewise, are fine and large, the author concludes, due to the temperateness of the seasons, which is in fact like spring (though, as we shall see, this view of spring, as a time of balance, in spite of its apparent logic, is unusual in ancient climatology), but instead of the manly and martial virtues, pleasure

rules (ἀλλὰ τὴν ἡδονὴν ἀνάγκη κρατεῖν—at which point occurs
the large lacuna that contained the description of the Asian character, illustrated by the Egyptians and Libyans). The details
(such as the equation of temperate climate and pleasure) are of
great interest and relevance, but again it will be enough to note
the main idea, that men resemble lands: indeed, this is the basic
premise of ethnography.

The discussion of Europe begins and ends with restatements
of these same premises, that climate affects landscape, and both
affect men and plants, so that (in chap. 13) some men (φύσιες)
actually are said to be like wooded and watered mountains,
others like smooth (bare?) and dry mountains, others like
swampy or dry plains. Land and water (the author concludes,
chap. 24), these are the determinants of men's characters and of
plants (καὶ τἄλλα τὰ ἐν τῇ γῇ φυόμενα πάντα ἀκόλουθα ἐόντα τῇ
γῇ). Where the land is rich, soft, and well watered (πίειρα καὶ
μαλθακὴ καὶ ἔννδρος), there the inhabitants will be wet, lacking
in endurance, weak in character; as far as concerns arts and crafts
(ἐς τὰς τέχνας), they will be "fat, neither fine nor sharp" (παχέ-
ες καὶ οὐ λεπτοὶ οὐδ᾽ ὀξέες—the first two adjectives are worth
notice!). Conversely, the products of the rough and rugged will
have vigilance (τὸ ἄγρυπνον) among their qualities, and will be
better at the arts and at warfare. The treatise so concludes, and
so may we. Echoes of these ideas in the first part of the first book
of the *Georgics* will come to mind: the idea of the *luxuries segetum*
that must be controled (1.112); similar ideas which occur
throughout the passage in Book II, *nunc locus arvorum ingeniis*
. . . (2.177–225), as we will see; the idea of war and the arts in-
stituted by Jupiter at the end of the period of ease and sloth. To
be more specific in tracing such correspondences would suggest
that Virgil in fact made direct use of *Airs, Waters, Places*, which
I think would be misleading: of course he knew it, as he knew
and had studied other treatises, but what he actually uses is a
generality that was not his alone but was the common property
of his time, and which we can best grasp by continuing our survey with a few other works.

Another of the early Hippocratic treatises that deserves a review here is the *Nature of Man* (Περὶ φύσιος ἀνθρώπου), since it provides the most systematic exposition of humoral theory. It is generally dated to 440–400 B.C., and to turn to it after a reading of *Air, Waters, Places* is to catch a vivid impression of the excitement of the intellectual life of the period. *Airs*, as we have seen, is thoroughly philosophical, based on speculative though wide-reaching assumptions concerning the intimate relationship of geographical environment, vegetation, and man: its medicine, though, is unsystematic, practical, and perhaps amateurish. *Nature*, however, is the work of a real physician, though one who responded, almost in spite of himself, to the current enthusiasm for rational synthesis. The opening chapter speaks of the debates of philosophers, who argue repeatedly in public but never win three times in a row—a sure sign that persuasiveness, not logic or truth, controls the debates. Such philosophers assert that man is either air, or fire, or water, or earth, saying that an essence is "the one thing and everything" (τὸ ἕν τε καὶ τὸ πᾶν). Then (in chap. 2) the author turns to physicians, who fare no better because they follow similar principles of reason, giving man a single humor (blood, or bile, or phlegm) instead of a single element, explaining that this single humor is changed by hot or cold into sweet, bitter, white, black, and all such. The author, though, claims that there are many (he will shortly settle for four) constituents in the body, which produce disease when altered in nature *by the agency of one of the four qualities* (πολλὰ γάρ ἐστιν ἐν τῷ σώματι ἐνεόντα, ἅ, ὅταν ὑπ᾽ ἀλλήλων παρὰ φύσιν θερμαίνηταί τε καὶ ψύχηται, καὶ ξηραίνηται καὶ ὑγραίνηται, νούσους τίκτει). It is interesting to see the compelling force of the four elements and the four qualities even on this man who dismisses with contempt the philosophers' claims for the supremacy of any single one: in the next chapter (3) he argues that the four qualities must be balanced equally for generation, and that at death each returns to itself, wet to wet, dry to dry, etc. (τό τε ὑγρὸν πρὸς τὸ ὑγρὸν καὶ τὸ ξηρὸν πρὸς τὸ ξηρὸν . . . καὶ τὸ θερμὸν . . . καὶ τὸ ψυχρὸν . . .), for such is the nature of all animals and everything else (and we may note how philosophical enthusiasm again drives this man of medical science to a generality about the physical nature of all being).

In chapter 4 the cat is out of the doctor's bag: the body has four humors (namely blood, phlegm, yellow bile, and black bile), these are the nature of man's being (ταῦτ᾽ ἐστὶν αὐτῷ ἡ φύσις τοῦ σώματος), and through these come health and sickness, as these are balanced and well mixed or separated and out of balance. These humors, as such, have no part to play in the *Georgics* (although ancient medical thinking consistently assumed some form of the theory), but they are relevant nonetheless, due to the urge to systematize that we have been observing even here. These humors differ (5), not only in color but in feel: they are not similarly hot, or cold, or dry, or wet (οὔτε γὰρ θερμὰ ὁμοίως ἐστίν, οὔτε ψυχρά). The four qualities, and the compulsion to relate and systematize natural phenomena, again force themselves upon the proto-scientist, to the point that his grand achievement (chap. 7) is an exercise in pure rationalization, synthetic in every sense, and can in fact be represented schematically. Each season, characterized by the conjunction of two qualities, produces in the body an excess of the corresponding humor, and so the medical year proceeds from season to season (see facing diagram).

The author of the *Nature of Man*, beginning with a rejection of the assumptions of philosophers, nevertheless came to base his own work on similar assumptions, in which in fact the elemental qualities play much the same role as they do in the natural speculations he dismissed. Our purpose is not to write a history of scientific thought, but simply to review how ineradicable were certain patterns of thought, even during the intensity of the discovery of intellect during the last third of the 5th century. *Ancient Medicine* went much further than *Nature* in its attempt to establish a scientific methodology for medicine, and failed completely. Here again, especially in its introduction, we have a revealing glimpse of the current discussion and debate of fundamental philosophical issues. (The author gives a vivid indication of just how real this debate was, when he says, in chap. 13, οἶμαι γὰρ ἔγωγε πολλὴν ἀπορίην τῷ ἐρωτηθέντι παρασχεῖν, "I think

WINTER
(cold and wet)

PHLEGM
(cold and wet)

(little bile)

SPRING
(warmer and wet)

AUTUMN
(dry and colder)

BLOOD
(hot and wet)

BILE (black)

(least blood)

(phlegm still strong)

SUMMER
(hot and dry)

BILE (yellow)

(blood still strong)

(phlegm weakest)

I've really stumped my interlocutor now.") The author rejects the speculations of all who assume a hypothesis for their work, either hot or cold or wet or dry (ὑπόθεσιν αὐτοὶ αὐτοῖς ὑποθέ-μενοι τῷ λόγῳ θερμὸν ἢ ψυχρὸν ἢ ὑγρὸν ἢ ξηρὸν ἢ ἄλλο τι ὃ ἂν θέλωσιν), just as had the author of *Nature*; but his reasoning and practice are remarkably consistent—never do the qualities return to play even a small part in his own theory (which has to do with diet and regimen), and never does he omit an opportunity to argue against the qualities as causes of disease. It is worth noting, too, that he views humors as compounds of the sweet, bitter, sour, and the like, unrelated to such essences as bile and phlegm, which were becoming, or had already become, associated with hot and cold, and were emerging into the complete system of four humors we have just seen in *Nature*.

In chapter 13 he returns to what he calls "the current fashion" (τὸν καινὸν τρόπον), that is, reasoning ἐξ ὑποθέσιος, to the point where the physician will treat cold with hot, wet with dry, etc: a losing battle, since treatment *ex contrariis* remained the fundamental procedure of medicine until modern times. There is much in his argument in the next pages that is of interest, but we will note only two points. First, in chapter 16 he argues that in fact hot and cold are the weakest of the powers ruling in the body (ψυχρότητα δ᾽ ἐγὼ καὶ θερμότητα πασέων ἥκιστα τῶν δυναμίων νομίζω δυναστεύειν ἐν τῷ σώματι), an argument interesting for its spirit of combativeness—he has taken on the two most powerful of the elemental qualities—and for the political metaphor we noted earlier, one, as we saw, with a long history. The reason he then gives for this (outrageous) claim is again one we are familiar with: hot and cold have no real power in ruling *simply because* they exist in a state of mixture and balance (κρῆσις καὶ μετριότης): he argues against the prevailing theory by using, remarkably, the precise terms of that theory. Our other observation is on chapter 20, where again we can see clearly the relevance medical debating must often have had: "Certain doctors and philosophers (σοφισταί) say that no one can know medicine who does not know what man is (ὅ τί ἐστιν ἄνθρωπος)." The very nature of man (not just his aches and pains) was the issue, but precisely because of this arose the difficulty we have observed again and again: was the subject of study to be philosophy or scientific medicine? "In their case [i.e., those who would know first what is man] the subject reaches philosophy (τείνει . . . ἐς φιλοσοφίην), just as Empedocles or others who wrote on the physical world (περὶ φύσιος) and concerning man's basic nature." Philosophy has nothing to contribute to medicine (τῇ ἰητρικῇ τέχνῃ), he argues, but, just the reverse, it is medical science that can make a real contribution to philosophical speculation.

Our survey of these three Hippocratic treatises was intended to present three main points which are relevant for the *Georgics*. First, the world and everything in it are related intimately: plants, animals, and men are equally the products of, and are affected by, landscape and climate, which in turn are affected by

seasons and larger geographical or even cosmological considerations. There exists, in fact, a chain of being, but without rank
or theology. As a result of this postulated unity in nature, one
can search for an essence, or several essences, and similarly for
essential forces: the intellectual life of the time will therefore be
characterized by (and no doubt owes a great deal of its excitement to) the feeling that the final unity, the ultimate secret, of
the universe is about to be, or in fact just has been, discovered.
(This excitement seems to have returned recently to modern
particle physics, with the possibility of the discovery of a grand
unifying theory.) Second, although each of these three authors
takes a very different position (the last two polemically) on the
relation of philosophy and science, as we have noted, even the
most determined scientist (the author of *Ancient Medicine*) shares
the urge to find the unity assumed for nature and to answer, ultimately, the question "What is Man?", which is basically philosophical. "Science," then, is at this time (and remained for Virgil), something different than our own understanding of the
word, and after all, what we have been calling "science," as it
occurs in *Nature* and *Ancient Medicine*, is simply "the doctor's
craft" (ἡ ἰητρικὴ τέχνη). However, what concerns us is only
that philosophy and science were for most thinkers one and the
same, and that just as there existed really but one word (philosophy), so all knowledge, understanding, inquiry, and observation had a unity of subject and purpose. The author of *Ancient
Medicine* was a rarity, and the hallmark of modern science, its
experimental method, was equally rare, as has frequently been
noted. Since different methodologies had not yet produced different branches of science, science remained a whole, as well as
basically philosophical: we must observe not only the postulated unity of the natural world, but also must remember that
while our knowledge has been so severely fragmented and com-
partmentalized, in antiquity all fields (medicine, astronomy, geography, biology, botany, ethnography) shared the same methods, purposes, and goals, and even subject matter (again, οὐκ
ἐλάχιστον μέρος συμβάλλεται ἀστρονομίη ἐς ἰητρικήν, ἀλλὰ
πάνυ πλεῖστον, a text worth taking). Third, it is not surprising,
given the postulated interdependence of all things and the as-

sumed unity of knowledge, that the pieces of the world remained as they were for more than two thousand years. The four elements, with their four qualities, gained Aristotle's authority, but would have done quite well without it. We can extend our survey now by looking further into what happened to these elements, again selectively and (I am afraid) superficially.

The Elements

Two more Hippocratic treatises will serve to give a fuller picture of the usefulness of the elements. *The Sacred Disease* (Περὶ ἱερῆς νούσου), another early (end of 5th century?) document professing a familiar scientific enthusiasm, deals with epilepsy not as divinely caused and so requiring a divine cure, but as the result of simple physiology (see chaps. 1–4). Mental illness, not just physical, is viewed in this remarkable work as a matter of pure chemistry. (It is worth noting too that the author is among those few early thinkers to view the brain, rather than the heart, lungs, or diaphragm, as the seat of intellect and emotions—see chaps. 17–20.) The author is representative of the physiology of his time and later, and hence it is useful to see how the elements, qualities, and humors are made to offer a consistent explanation of the sacred disease, and indeed of all madness. The main purpose of the veins (described in chaps. 6–7) is to draw in and disperse air, which goes primarily to the brain, causing thought, and to the abdomen, causing movement. When phlegm, which is cold, descends from the head in amounts beyond the normal, it meets and chills the blood, which is hot (compare the qualities of these humors in the *Nature of Man*): the result is a blockage of the air, either to certain parts of the body (hence spasms of the affected part, and so on) or to the brain (chaps. 8–10).

It is interesting that, given the importance of air circulation for both physical and mental health, the next logical step is taken—logical, that is, if man and the world are consistently viewed as related and interdependent. In chapter 16 the author turns to the winds (of prime importance for medical theorists—e.g., in the *Airs, Waters, Places*—as affecting climate, seasons, local waters, and consequently physiological changes). The north and south winds are strongest and most opposed: the north wind is healthy, in that it separates out the turbid and wet and compacts the air, making it clear and transparent; the south wind does the opposite, moistening and confusing, and "from the cold comes hot, from dry the wet." (We ought to note here an inherent flexibility at this early stage, which allows contradictions which later systematization will iron out: for this author the north wind is cold and *dry*, the south wind hot and *wet*, which serves his purpose admirably; he does not, however, go on to correlate seasonal change into his system, which would involve him necessarily with winter's cold and *wet* and summer's hot and *dry* character. Compare *Regimen II* 38, where the north and south winds do correspond to winter and summer.) The effects of the winds on the brain are similar, naturally: the south wind loosens and dampens it, the north wind compacts and separates out the diseased and wet, cleansing it. The elemental qualities (chap. 17) therefore affect the brain, "whenever it is not healthy but becomes hotter than usual or colder or wetter or drier . . . : and we become mad from the wet" (καὶ μαινόμεθα μὲν ὑπὸ ὑγρότητος), because moisture "moves" (κινεῖσθαι) the brain, causing disturbance in seeing and hearing, just as lack of movement causes sanity. (Again it is worth noting flexibility—or inconsistency: we will see just below that in *Regimen I* it is fire that produces "movement" [κινῆσαι], and water nourishment.)

In all this we can observe the rationalist working out the cause of the sacred disease, and how at each point he returns to the fundamental oppositions: phlegm is cold and blood is hot; the north and south winds are compounded of opposite qualities; the brain, affected by extremes, becomes too hot or cold or dry or wet—the latter causing madness. Now (chap. 18) phlegm and bile engage his attention (just as phlegm and blood had earlier: he gives the impression of a man excited by a variety of ideas, and too busy to work out a consistent whole), phlegm chilling and contracting the brain to produce a rather quiet form of madness, bile heating it to produce noisy and agitated manifestations. The brain is also heated by blood, he adds. Air is the source of health (if inhaled, air goes first to the brain rather than to the body)—τὴν δὲ φρόνησιν ὁ ἀὴρ παρέχεται (chap. 19). Finally, he concludes, regimen, not magic, can cure disease, if one understands how to produce in men the dry and wet, cold and hot. *The Sacred Disease* is of interest as the first rationalizing study devoted to madness and thus affords us the opportunity to observe what tools were available to the medical rationalist. There are the humors, three in number (blood, phlegm, and bile), but used only in pairs, never as a defined triad. There are the qualities, seen as forces in nature (of the winds) affecting the brain, or again as forces in the body, to be controlled by the physician. Of the actual elements he makes no real use, but our final treatise, *Regimen I*, will serve as an example of what the elements themselves could be made to do.

The qualities are of course observable in the human body, and hence are as necessary and prominent in medical diagnosis and treatment as they will be useful in rational theorizing. The elements themselves, however, have no practical use, especially after the traditional four humors (first seen in *Nature*) have established themselves and their qualities. *Regimen I*, then, is interesting as a reversion to "philosophical" medicine, though "mystical" is often a better description of its wilder moments. Our concern, though, will be only to observe the use it makes of the elements, to view their ubiquity from yet another perspective.

The author of *Regimen I* gives himself away almost immediately. After a consideration of his place among his predecessors (chap. 1), he professes the need to know and understand the general nature of man (πρῶτον μὲν παντὸς φύσιν ἀνθρώπου γνῶναι καὶ διαγνῶναι), which is followed later by the call to observe, among other things, "the seasons of the year and the changes of winds, the situation of the land . . . and the disposition of the year," to which he adds the need to know astronomy (ἄστρων τε ἐπιτολὰς καὶ δύσιας γινώσκειν δεῖ, ὅκως ἐπίστηται τὰς μεταβολὰς καὶ ὑπερβολὰς φυλάσσειν καὶ σίτων καὶ ποτῶν καὶ πνευμάτων καὶ τοῦ ὅλου κόσμου). If, by such terms, we are led to expect a synthetic view of the nature of man, his place in and relation to the environment and the universe, we are misled: even in this introductory chapter the author reveals himself as a man of rather confined philosophical vision, concerned primarily with regimen in a limited sense—food, drink, and exercise. However, it is precisely because of this limited focus that those introductory promises are of particular interest: it is almost standard procedure to appeal to the cosmic relevance of one's medical approach.

In chapter 3 the author reveals himself as a mystic of sorts, again a revelation of interest for the terms in which he does it. All men and animals, he claims, are composed of fire and water, elements continually at odds with each other, but neither able to master the other. The power of fire is to move, of water to nourish (τὸ μὲν γὰρ πῦρ δύναται πάντα διὰ παντὸς κινῆσαι, τὸ δὲ ὕδωρ πάντα διὰ παντὸς θρέψαι). Fire is hot and dry, water is wet and cold, but (and here is a neat touch which allows for much of the mystical nonsense to follow) fire contains moisture as well, and water dryness (chap. 4): thus anything is its opposite, and opposites are the same, as we are told in the manner (and after the matter) of Heraclitus, through several chapters. The author returns to more practical considerations in chapter 25 (soul is a mixture of fire and water), discussing generation of male and female in these terms (males, more fiery, are hot and dry; females, more watery, are cold and wet). More complicated still is the system set forth in chapter 32, where six different combinations of fire and water result in six different constitutions, which are fit or unfit at certain seasons or ages, and require certain diets: for example, a mixture of the strongest (ἰσχυρότατον) fire and the finest (λεπτότατον) water produces a constitution dry and warm, sick at the beginning of fire (early summer?), healthy at the beginning of water (early winter?), sick at the prime of life but healthy in old age, requiring a diet of the cold and moist. So too are the ages characterized: children are wet and hot, youths hot and dry, adults dry and cold, the elderly cold and wet (chap. 33). Intelligence too is to be understood in such terms: for instance, the highest intelligence is a result of the combination of the wettest fire and the driest water, and regimen (diet and exercise) can therefore have an affect on one's IQ as well as on one's physical fitness (at great length in chap. 35).

To such a mind, steeped in what amounts to mysticism and seasoned with the prophetic style of Heraclitus, the two opposing elements of fire and water have a great appeal. The humors, however, whether two, three, or four, have an equal appeal to the scientific mind, such as that which produced *The Sacred Disease*, and the humors, it should be remembered, are nothing but the original elements relabelled for use in the medical laboratory. Between these two extreme approaches lies a great deal that obviously appealed to common sense: the more original minds, of course, extended accepted theory, or qualified or contradicted it, as we have been observing, but it is possible to put together a picture of their common point of departure. The more mundane writers, on the other hand, accept, without retailing, what everyone knew, but here again such pieces as they offer show a systematization that was already set and fixed. Thus, by the way of illustration, in *Humors* (Περὶ χυμῶν) 14, summer produces bile, spring produces blood, "and so on" (τἄλλα ὡς ἕκαστα), a phrase that reveals that the seasonal system of humors we saw fully set forth in *Nature* could be assumed as obvious for the reader. The author of *Regimen in Health* (Περὶ διαίτης ὑγιεινῆς) agrees, noting (chap. 5) that winter produces phlegm, summer bile. In fact, his system of regimen (which seems to be pretty standard fare) is based squarely on the accepted seasonal qualities and corresponding humors. In winter, he advises, eat much (especially roasted meat), drink wine as undiluted as possible, to make the body dry and hot; in summer, boiled meat and diluted wine, to make the body cold and soft. Wine is hot and dry, water cold and wet (so too in *Regimen II* 52, ὕδωρ ψυχρὸν καὶ ὑγρόν· οἶνος θερμὸν καὶ ξηρόν): that wine is hot and dry is commonly assumed throughout antiquity. We may be sure that the qualities of the four elements had been fixed long before Aristotle (as, e.g., in *GC* 330b), and likewise that when Galen accepted the four humors and appealed to the authority of Hippocrates in so doing, he took up a system that had never lapsed. Attempts in later Greek medicine to combat "the dominance of humoral theory" (E. D. Phillips' phrase) failed, undoubtedly because the theory explained so much, was related to so much, and was therefore so much a part of popular thought.

Our survey of selected Hippocratic texts should thus alert us to certain ways of thinking, and to certain concepts, which are fundamental not only to 5th-century medicine, but throughout antiquity and in all the natural sciences, due not only to Aristotle's influence (especially in canonizing the elements and their qualities), but also to the obvious fact of the flexibility of the systems we have observed developing, and to the simplicity that insured the place of such systems in popular thought. We need not, I think, follow the development of the elements in other fields, areas that will be more familiar to readers of the *Georgics* in any case than are perhaps the Hippocratic writings, but a few observations may be in order.

I. M. Lonie has recently written on the philosophical origin of the humoral theory most suggestively, and with authority:

> The real problem is therefore how a theory of four constituent humors, the ground of health as well as of disease, arose towards the end of the fifth century. The answer here is simple and unsurprising. If we remember that philosophers from Thales onward had consistently posed the question of what things are made of, and that Empedocles in particular, the most influential figure in biological thought in the fifth century, had described man as well as everything else as being composed of four elements, earth, air, fire and water; if we add to this the tendency in Greek cosmological thought from Anaximander onward to think in terms of equilibrium between opposing powers, and Alcmaeon's theory of health as a particular instance of that equilibrium between opposites, then it would be surprising if some such theory as that of Nat. Hom. or Morb. IV [in which the four humors are phlegm, blood, bile, and hydrops, i.e., water] did not appear in the fifth century. In fact the influence of Empedocles is particularly obvious upon the Sicilian doctor Philistion, who held that man was composed of earth, air, fire and water (Anon. Lond. xx 25).

The importance of Empedocles has long been clear, but Lonie has emphasized that the humors should be regarded as necessary constituents of the human body with both positive and negative

characteristics; that they existed independent of the Empedoclean elements, so that "the philosopher provides the categories
within which the medical scientist can order his experience";
and that "*It is not the recognition of this or that humour as existing
which counts, but the theoretical use to which that humour is put*" (italics his). What we can profitably observe (again) from these reflections is how a particular science (medicine), developing its
own territory and rules, took its guiding principles from philosophy (much to the annoyance of some doctors), but by so doing
assured that the new science would continue not as a separate
entity, but as an integral part of the whole, whether that whole
is to be called philosophy or natural science.

"The hot and the cold, the dry and the wet appear particularly
often, though not exclusively, in [cosmological] theories of a
general type which can be traced back to Anaximander, in
which the relationship between opposed factors is conceived as
one of a continuous, balanced interaction." So writes G.E.R.
Lloyd in an article titled "The Hot and the Cold, the Dry and
the Wet in Greek Philosophy," to which the reader at this point
can turn most conveniently for an examination of "the question
of the origin of the use of these opposites in Greek philosophy"—how far back they go, and to what extent values (positive and negative) were assigned to each of a pair of opposites.
We may mention here that Lloyd puts particular emphasis on
the "*continuous interactions*" (his italics) of opposites in Anaximander (precisely what these opposites were is disputed,
though it is likely that fire and mist included some functions of
the elemental qualities): in our one real fragment of Anaximander, some cosmological opposites (unfortunately, simply referred to as αὐτά) are in a constant state of balanced but hostile
action and reaction (διδόναι . . . δίκην καὶ τίσιν ἀλλήλοις τῆς
ἀδικίας κατὰ τὴν τοῦ χρόνου τάξιν): we have thus a cosmology, rather than a cosmogony. The opposites (τὰ ἐναντία) are
thus real interactions right from this beginning (compare the
Empedoclean Strife), as they are in "the first philosophical text
in which these four opposites appear (Heraclitus fr. 126 DK)": τὰ
ψυχρὰ θέρεται, θερμὸν ψύχεται, ὑγρὸν αὐαίνεται, καρφαλέον

νοτίζεται. We have noted in the medical writings just how important were the interactions and balances of opposites.

Lloyd also notes that hot and cold, wet and dry of themselves have no values, good or bad, positive or negative, but take on values according to use and situation. He concludes, "It is, then, one of the notable features of the use of hot and cold and dry and wet in early Greek speculative thought, that while there was little agreement about their particular application to different problems, the assumption that *some* correlation was to be set up between these and other pairs of opposites was sometimes shared both by those who put forward views based on *a priori* considerations, and by those who rejected those views on empirical grounds." We would thus be wrong to look for a consistent or systematic structure of oppositions in any area or field, or between any writers on the same subject, or even (often) within any single writer (Virgil, I may add, especially): fire, for instance, may be destructive, or may provide the warmth for life or the beginning of everything (as in Heraclitus).

We may sum up our conclusions thus:

(1) Two sets of oppositions coincided with the beginnings of Greek science (philosophy), the elements and the qualities, which can exist simply as primary elements (e.g., Thales' water), or in pairs of opposites (hot and cold), or in any number of pairs (such qualities as bitter and sweet), but which by the end of the 5th century tend generally to become four in number (earth, air, fire, water; hot, cold wet, dry) and associated in various ways (as in Aristotle's final formulation, fire as the dry and hot, etc.). From these, or concurrent with these, develop other systems, such as in medicine the system of humors (at first two or three, but finally four), or such as the systematizations of the geographers and ethnographers (the qualities of lands and their inhabitants as the result of elemental mixtures).

(2) These opposites are interacting continually, either in a state of balance or imbalance.

(3) It is the elements and the qualities that unite the various areas of inquiry and knowledge, supplying the "grand unifying theory" to ancient science, by supplying the philosophical prin-

ciple (ὑπόθεσις) that made it possible to explain diverse phenomena in similar ways, thereby relating them.

(4) The elements and the qualities, having no inherent values,
and being capable of a variety of arrangements and correlations,
are extraordinarily flexible, explaining everything, though involving at the same time inconsistency or even contradiction.

(5) Hence (because of 3 and 4 especially) the elements and
qualities continued to dominate popular thought (though attempts were made by more original thinkers in various fields to
move beyond them or to ignore them—not always success-
fully), until they surface finally in the rigid systematization of
the middle ages.

The VETERUM PRAECEPTA and Failure

The structure of lines 176–203 is clear:

> 176–77: the subject: the *veterum praecepta*
>> 178–86: making the *area*; its *pestes*; failure
>>> 187–92: observe the nut tree for signs of success or failure
>> 193–99: importance of selecting seeds: failure
> 199–203: example of the rower; inevitable degeneration or failure.

"The teachings of the ancients," the wisdom of the ages—comforting concepts, referring to the *usus* that hammered out different crafts (*varias artes*) after Jupiter's intervention (133), when
came the (repeated) different crafts, and work, and want (*tum
variae venere artes. labor omnia vicit / improbus, et duris urgens in rebus egestas*, 145–46). Virgil has no doubt about man's disposition, right from the beginning: "I can tell you many teachings
of the ancients—if you don't refuse from displeasure to learn
slight concerns." *Labor* may have conquered the world, but Virgil speaks as if the reader still retained a Golden Age mentality.

Now, about the threshing floor, which Virgil for some reason
puts at the top of his list of *praecepta*. What Virgil doesn't say is
that a threshing floor is of use on only one occasion—after the
harvest. This neglect in providing such an essential piece of in-

formation should be remedied immediately by the conscientious commentator, because the entire passage assumes the cereal cycle, but in reverse and at a distance, as the outline reveals: from the *area*, to the signs for the crop's success or failure, to the selection of seed for planting. The *praecepta*, then, as Virgil certainly intends us to realize, are in one sense only the preliminary to a beginning, a theoretical first step. The process itself (planting through reaping) is not even mentioned here, but the effort to be expended is enormous nevertheless: intense care in the selection of seed (*tenuis curas* indeed), heroic effort in making the floor, and in both these labors failure is all but inevitable. What does success depend on then? Simply (the central idea of the passage) the nut tree: just observe the extent of its bloom in any year. Here is the whole passage: reduced to this the *veterum praecepta* seem singularly ineffective. We ought to make sure that we understand it properly.

Back to the threshing floor, the finality of the agricultural process: not only is this put first (with seed selection at the end of the passage), but the description of its making is, as Servius observes, a *hysteron proteron*: level the floor with a huge roller, mix it by hand, and add clay as a binder. The labor involved is emphasized by the three gerundives: in the next book (and nowhere else) three similar gerundives will occur in four passages, all emphasizing again immense labor ultimately to prove futile. A further indication of the care and attention devoted to the floor is the etymological play on *area*. According to Varro (*LL* 5.38), the *area* is so called because the cut grain dries there before it is threshed (*ubi frumenta secta, ut terantur, arescunt, area*); and thus Virgil clearly glosses the word later in the book (298), *et medio tostas aestu terit area fruges*. (Servius [Auctus] again preserves a notice, "area est locus vacuus . . . quasi qui exaruerit," on 178.) Now the etymology of (*pinguis*) *arista* was central and important at the very beginning of the book, as we saw, introducing the elemental opposition of fire and water: it is no surprise to find that opposition echoed here, bringing the *area* within its sphere, when the nut tree gives the signs for a poor year: *at si luxuria fo-*

liorum exuberat umbra, / nequicquam pinguis palea teret area culmos
(191–92). At this point the complexity of Virgil's suggestion has
passed beyond what we can, or ought to, paraphrase.

Now we must note a textual difficulty of some importance.
The modern vulgate reads the subjunctive *inludant* at line 181,
making the verb parallel with the preceding *subeant* and *fatiscat*
("build the floor thus lest weeds enter, lest it turn to dust and
crack, then [lest] diverse pests invade"), passing lightly over the
inconcinnity of *tum* correlative with *ne . . . neu. . . .* Equally
well attested, however, is the variant *inludunt*, a present indicative not parallel with the preceding subjunctives and thus, with
tum, introducing a new movement ("lest it turn to dust and
crack. *Then* diverse pests invade . . ."). It is perhaps the unexpected bleakness of this statement that has driven most editors
to prefer blandness and syntactical impropriety: what Virgil
says here is, simply, "work to the point of exhaustion on your
floor, to guard against weeds and cracking: then come insect and
animal plagues to ruin it anyway." Apart from the syntax, and
apart from the characteristic pessimism of the statement, there
are three reasons for reading the indicative here, a glance at
which will take us farther into the passage.

(1) *Tum variae inludunt pestes*: rhythm and sound pattern establish this phrase as part of a recurrent motif, the first appearance of which was at line 145 just previously, *tum variae venere
artes*, and of which the last (for example) will occur at 4.406, *tum
variae eludent species*. This minor musical theme recurs in similar
contexts with similar point and seems to me to be an original
facet of Virgilian art, but for now it will be enough just to observe that the *variae artes* of 145 return here (at least to the ear) as
the *variae pestes*, and that as the *pestes* are then specified as the
mouse, mole, toad, weevil, and ant, so we must realize that the
artes are then specified as work and want (*labor improbus, urgens
egestas*). In any case this theme is too important to find itself sub-
sumed in the *ne . . . neu . . .* sequence.

(2) Likewise are the pests themselves of special importance.
The hyperbole is marked (see Servius on 181, "ultra meritum rei
locutus est"), the climax of which is the clause (184–85) *quae plu-*

rima terrae / monstra ferunt. In the *Georgics*, the stuff of literature is reality: capitalize *terra* of the present reality, and we have the myth referred to less than a hundred lines later, *tum partu Terra nefando / Coeumque Iapetumque creat saevumque Typhoea / et coniuratos caelum rescindere fratres* (278–80). The earth is still producing *monstra*, its agents of destruction.

(3) Finally, the assumption of a full stop after *fatiscat* (180) and the beginning of a new sentence with *tum* (181) brings the movement of the threshing-floor passage in line with that of the selection of seeds at the end: *vidi lecta diu et multo spectata labore / degenerare tamen* (197–98), an equally emphatic statement of the same idea, "expend endless effort, and failure is inevitable" (on the important qualification that follows, "*ni . . .*," there is more just below).

So it is that, just as the threshing floor inevitably is subject to its *pestes*, the laborious selection of seed, by hand, one by one, is subject to failure as well, due to natural degeneration: and this is *before* the seed is even planted, and *after* the ripened grain is harvested. There is hardly a more pessimistic passage in the entire poem, or one in which Virgil himself is so clearly heard: "I have seen . . . I have seen seed carefully selected degenerate nevertheless" (*vidi . . . vidi lecta diu et multo spectata labore / degenerare tamen*, 193, 197–98). One ray of hope still shines, however, for those disposed to follow it: the protasis "unless annual effort selects each largest seed" (*ni vis humana quotannis / maxima quaeque manu legeret*, 198–99). Presumably then, Virgil (so we are reassured) is saying that superior seed established by careful selection can be maintained only by continuing annual selection—if not, it will degenerate (*nisi vi quotannis maxima quaeque leguntur, degenerant*, we can paraphrase). Virgil might have been more precise and could have saved commentators, from Servius on, a great deal of effort (Servius calls the *ni* clause an ἀνακόλουθον). But by putting the apodosis first, and by setting its verb as an infinitive in *oratio obliqua*, with the *tamen* that bothered Servius, he began perfectly clearly with an ambiguity in no uncertain terms—"I have seen seed carefully selected degenerate nevertheless."

Finally, then, we come to the end of the section that began with the *veterum praecepta*, to *vis humana* and to the simile of the rower who, if he pauses for a moment, is swept back downstream. The *vis humana* was that ray of hope we just observed, and those who have taken courage from it will presumably continue to find Calvinistic comfort in a lifetime of rowing steadily against the current. *Vis humana*, like *labor improbus*, continues to be understood by some as an ennobling virtue, and even those of more modern temper who concede to Virgil that his unending effort may be futile have not reckoned with the possibility that this *vis* may be positively bad. *Vis humana*, or the rower's unremitting effort, has been regarded as a redeeming grace, a glory, or a struggle which even if futile is still acceptable, somehow, as part of the pattern of Jupiter's universe, but it may be that *improbus* is an epithet that can be applied to human effort generally: would there be any observable difference, after all, between *labor improbus* and *vis improba*?

On *vis humana* (line 198) Servius reports a comment of Donatus, worth noticing for that authority alone, but which as well seems extraordinarily perceptive: "VIS HUMANA possibilitas . . . aut certe multitudo. tamen verius est, ut 'vis' quasi violentia sit in rebus, quae contra naturam vertuntur in melius: sic enim Donatus sensit, dicens: nisi violentia fiat naturae, omnia in deterius cadunt. *et hoc est, quod ait, labor omnia vicit improbus.*" Servius' first two glosses (which I have quoted for the sake of completeness) may be disregarded immediately as the inevitable dross. The final remark, however, (preserved in Servius Auctus) is worth attention: *vis humana* is the same as *labor improbus*. But Donatus' comment should strike the modern reader as very contemporary: no interpretation I know of has picked up this observation, or suggested anything like it, but if such an interpretation were to be proposed, it would certainly leave itself open to the charge of importing a modern outlook to Virgil's text. "Unless violence is done to nature, everything deteriorates," says Donatus. Virgil and Donatus both know that water flows downhill, that this is the natural order of things, the way of nature: man (the rower) must exert not only effort, but what is in fact violence, violence against the natural order. Not only does this insight make sense of the improbity of *labor improbus*, but it suggests as well that man's effort is a positive evil, a destructive force directed against the natural course. So ends the first half of the book: we must look back over the preceding lines to see whether Donatus' view can apply, and then briefly at other passages in the first two books to see how this negative view of labor and effort affects our understanding of man's place in the natural order (keeping in mind, though, that Donatus' view may not be Virgil's).

Violence (*violentia* seems to have all the negative connotations of the English derivative) has of course been noted as a marked aspect of the farmer's activity, violence which leads to the first instance of the metaphor of the farmer as soldier:

> multum adeo, rastris glaebas qui frangit inertis
> vimineasque trahit crates, iuvat arva . . .
> et qui, proscisso quae suscitat aequore terga,
> rursus in obliquum verso perrumpit aratro
> exercetque frequens tellurem atque imperat arvis.   (1.94–95, 97–99)

(Much still he helps the fields, who breaks the lumpish clods with rakes and drags the wicker harrows . . . , and who stirs up the field's surface after its first plowing and again breaks through crosswise with his plow turned and repeatedly trains the earth and commands the fields.)

We have noted above the details of the development and extension of this metaphor in the following passage—the suggestion of Achilles in the *Iliad*, of fire, destruction, and war. Perhaps this can explain the oddity we noted then, that the farmer, in spite of the association with Achilles and fire, is at the same time the bringer of water to the parched fields (as in fact irrigation in Homer's simile), or (we can say) the agent of the Scamander, civilization, and peace. Paradoxically, the farmer's violence actually helps the fields (*iuvat arva*, 1.95). Progress is the opposition to nature, and vice versa, as Virgil continues (note here *labores*):

> Nec tamen, haec cum sint hominumque boumque labores
> versando terram experti, nihil improbus anser

Strymoniaeque grues et amaris intiba fibris
officiunt aut umbra nocet. pater ipse colendi
haud facilem esse viam voluit . . .   (1.118–22)

(Though these are the efforts of men and oxen skilled in turning the
earth, nevertheless the wicked goose, Strymonian cranes, and endive
with its bitter roots oppose his efforts, and the shade does harm. Father Jupiter himself wanted the road to be in no way easy . . .)

Birds, weeds, and shade oppose the farmer's labors. The section
continues to set forth the reason for this opposition: before Jupiter the earth bore all things freely (125–28); Jupiter's rule produced, of necessity, the arts of civilization (129–46); and, with
labor came the opposition (147–59—the passage ends with the
birds, weeds, and shade with which it began, *herbam* 155, *avis*
156, *umbras* 157).

Virgil gives no reason for Jupiter's action other than that the
easy life was to be no more (*curis acuens mortalia corda / nec torpere
gravi passus sua regna veterno*, 123–24): Virgil is interested in the
fact, not its causes. The key lines present the facts:

ille malum virus serpentibus addidit atris
praedarique lupos *iussit* pontumque *moveri*,
mellaque dec*ussit* foliis ignemque re*movit*,
et passim rivis currentia vina repressit,
ut varias usus meditando *extunderet* artis
paulatim, et sulcis frumenti *quaereret* herbam,
ut silicis venis abstrusum *excuderet* ignem.   (1.129–35)

(He [Jupiter] gave hurtful poison to the deadly serpents, ordered
wolves to hunt and the sea to storm, struck honey from the leaves
and removed fire, and stopped wine from flowing everywhere in
streams, in order that experience, by thought, hammer out the different crafts gradually, seek the blade of grain in plowed furrows,
and strike forth fire hidden in veins of flint.)

Four lines of Jupiter's actions (the first two, what he gives or
does, the next two, what he takes away), then three lines of the
inevitable results (*usus* hammering out the *artes*). It will be
noted, then, that the lines following give examples of this proc-

ess, with the "various arts" repeated in the lines referred to so often already (145–46), in company now with *labor improbus* and *egestas*. Clearly Jupiter has caused *egestas* (*duris urgens in rebus*, the modern condition), clearly *labor improbus* is a parallel condition, and clearly the *artes* and *labor* are closely related facts of existence in Jupiter's world. In the context of opposition between man and his world, certain of the preceding *exempla* are to be noted for the violence inherent. "Then first rivers knew the hollowed alders" (136): sailing is presented as an inversion of natural order, an *adynaton* become real (there is more of this in the second book). Astronomy (137–38), which is the parent of both navigation and agriculture, has two lines, the second of which (*Pleiadas, Hyadas, claramque Lycaonis Arcton*) is a combination of Homeric (Πληϊάδας θ' Ὑάδας τε τό τε σθένος Ὠρίωνος / Ἄρκτον θ', *Iliad* 18.486–87) and Callimachean (Λυκαονίης ἄρκτοιο, *Hymn* 1.41) lines. Such allusion is never gratuitous: the Homeric constellations are to be found on Achilles' shield; the Bear is Lycaon's daughter. Then comes hunting—specifically, though, nooses, deception, surrounding the glades with dogs, lashing streams, seeking the deep (*alta petens*); and then building. The elements of violence are perceptible in these *artes*, to be heard even in the "shrill saw," but should not be overstressed; Virgil intends the Promethean and Sophoclean greatness of the arts of civilization to be recalled at the same time (for the Latin poets generally the *artes*—man's achievement—is double-edged). The whole point of the poem thus far is being restated in this passage: progress in the modern world comes through violence.

For a moment, a look ahead. The "Days" half of the book, concerned with man and the macrocosm, is of course largely prognostic, and the nut tree writ large is the observable universe itself, from which we can predict seasonal changes and the proper times for various activities. The Eratosthenic cosmos ends thus:

hinc tempestates dubio praediscere caelo
possumus, hinc messisque diem tempusque serendi,

et quando *infidum* / *remis* īmpellĕrĕ marmor ⎤
conveniat, quando armatas dēdūcĕrĕ classis, ⎤
aut *tempestivam* / *silvis* ēvērtĕrĕ pinum; ⎦
nec frustra signorum obitus speculamur et ortus
temporibusque parem diversis quattuor annum.   (1.252–58)

(Hence we can predict storms from an uncertain sky, hence the
proper day for harvest and the time for sowing, and when it is fitting
to strike the deceitful sea with oars, when to launch the armed fleet,
or fell the pine in season in the forest; not in vain do we watch the
settings and risings of the constellations and the year evenly divided
by the four seasons.)

Sound patterns (marked specially by the three metrically identical infinitives) tie together the three central lines and moreover
suggest the earlier passage we have just discussed (129–35) with
its similar rhyme and metrical patterns. The reason is clear: the
two passages are intended to be mutually suggestive: 129–35 in-
troduce the rise of the *artes*, which here are central (agriculture
253, navigation 254, warfare 255, building 256). Prediction is a
part of the *veterum praecepta*, associated with the *artes* themselves: but the observation of signs for the success or failure of a
crop, or for impending storm or disaster, while accurate and re-
liable (*nec frustra . . . speculamur*), does nothing for the aversion
of failure.

To continue: the arts of civilization are synonomous with
man's occupations (the topic of the βίοι), which traditionally
can include the farmer, hunter, sailor, merchant, soldier, states-
man, builder.

Dicendum et quae sint duris agrestibus arma,
quis sine nec potuere seri nec surgere messes.   (1.160–61)

(I must mention too what armament the hardy farmers have, without which crops could not be sown, could not grow.)

Again the same opposition, but now with the clear resumption
of the military metaphor for the farmer's life. The farmer's
"arms" (*arma*, however, can mean simply "equipment," it
should be remembered—thus there is a bit more word play in-

volved in Virgil's *arma* than is suggested by the English "arms")
produce harvests of cereal and wine: Eleusis (Ceres and Celeus)
and Bacchus in these mannered lines (162–66) suggest again the
progress to be won through arms. Domination and the effort of
violence is heard again (*continuo in silvis magna vi flexa domatur /
. . . ulmus*, 169–70—the conquest of the elm has a significance
we will see later): the plow produced by such violence takes an-
imate form, but rather than being a product of Virgilian human-
izing, appears as a monster, and its parts—including its eight
feet (of length, actually), its teeth on its double backbone—are
those of an unimaginable chimaera. With this prepared in advance, the *divini gloria ruris* awaits the worthy farmer. On this, a
word of caution: *gloria* is a rather special Roman abstraction, the
reward for *virtus*, generally achieved through military distinction (of which *honos* can be the civilian equivalent). Rigid definition of the word is not called for, but in the developing context, and specifically here in the section concerned with the
farmer's arms, *gloria* is most likely to have a precise military connotation—the fame acquired by *victory over* the divine
country.

The "Works" half of the book presents a consistent unity: the
farmer's *labor* is an act of violence against nature, necessary,
however, for progress in the face of nature's opposition; the
course of nature, for man, is degeneration, inevitable as the flow
of water downhill, a process started by Jupiter. Virgil does not
moralize about, or draw conclusions from, these facts, but there
are certain suggestions that arise from his arrangement of facts:
the ultimate futility of experience (the *veterum praecepta*) and
endless effort.

Ceres and the Acorn

Several important connections are made through the figure of
Ceres (who appears by name outside of Book 1 only at 2.229).
She is of course prominent in the invocation (1.7), for by her gift
the earth exchanged Jupiter's (Chaonian = of Dodona) acorn
for the rich ear of grain. This is the first important connection,
certain implications of which have already been discussed:

Ceres' grain is an improvement over a diet of acorns, which is here attributed to Jupiter (as again at 2.67, *Chaoniique patris glandes*), and for the present we simply accept this as progress. Progress demands violence: the farmer helps his fields by employing violent methods, like a military commander training his troops, and on him Ceres smiles (1.94–99, discussed above); and the farmer's *arma* are directly associated with Ceres, the Eleusinian mother (1.160–66, also discussed above). Again (as we have just seen) this complex of progress, violence, Ceres, and Jupiter's acorns occurs immediately after the appearance of the *artes*, *labor* and *egestas* (1.145–46):

> prima Ceres ferro mortalis vertere terram
> instituit, cum iam glandes atque arbuta sacrae
> deficerent silvae et victum Dodona negaret.   (1.147–49)

> (Ceres first taught mortals to turn the earth with the plow, when already acorns and arbutes were exhausted in the sacred wood and Dodona denied her fare.)

Ferrum is a metonomy to be noted in the *Georgics*, suggestive of violence and the modern iron age. Jupiter was behind this, we are to infer, somehow causing a deficiency in either the production or the quality of acorn and arbute (both used by Virgil's own countrymen as pig fodder—see e.g. Menalcas at *Ecl.* 10.20), and unless the farmer incessantly presses the battle against his natural enemies (*mox et frumentis labor additus, ut mala culmos / esset robigo . . .* , 150–57, ending with the birds, weeds, and shade with which the passage had begun), he will again be forced to feed on acorns, in the wilds (*concussaque famem in silvis solabere quercu*, 159).

Thus, in the first half of the first book Ceres is consistently represented as the progress she has taught. In the second half she appears in two passages, central in one, dominating in the other, and in each the connections made through her are important.

The second ("Days") half of the book has again an obviously bipartite structure—the "Days" section proper (204–350) and the "Signs" (351–514). The first section ends with the great storm and the festival of Ceres, and the second with the civil war and Augustus. For the present we will look only at this first section and Ceres. Its structure is clear:

204–30: the "Days" must be observed: work appropriate to spring and fall

┌ 231–58: the zones of heaven and the four seasons of the solar year
└ 259–75: work to be done even on days of cold rain and on holidays
┌ 276–86: the month, or lunar days
└ 287–310: work to be done at night; winter activities and ease

311–50: storms of spring and fall; Ceres.

What is really quite clear about this structure is that there is no other way to see the pieces: the usual paragraphing and structural analyses all agree. Less clear, it would seem, is the relation of the pieces to each other: what is the logic of development here, the contrasts or balances between these paragraphs? Just below the surface we can see a movement that seems to make real sense. The primary division is one recognizable from Varro: *et quoniam tempora duorum generum sunt, unum annale, quod sol circuitu suo finit, alterum menstruum, quod luna circumiens comprendit, prius dicam de sole* (*RR* 1.27). (Whatever else the strange Hesiodic panel of the lunar days achieves, it certainly has an important structural function. Varro's discussion of lunar periods (*RR* 1.37.1–3) is brief, unhelpful, and redolent of rural superstition.) From this position, now, the lie of the land is much clearer. Following the panel of the year as ruled by the golden sun (231–58) comes—a surprise—what to do in periods of cold rain (*Frigidus agricolam si quando continet imber*, 259) or holidays: even on such days works involving some violence may be done, works appropriate to the sun's fiery temper (the characteristic language of violence is there to be seen—for instance, the last line of the "cold rain" section, *nunc torrete igni fruges, nunc frangite saxo*, 267; or, for instance, *insidias avibus moliri*, 271, with its military metaphor). Just as we might now expect, the mystical and yet folksy lunar diary is followed by works better done in the chill damp of the night: the first four lines (287–90) are full of this by now obvious opposition (*gelida nocte, inrorat, arida prata, lentus umor*). Real farmers, however, spend most of the night asleep (hence the early morning's dew seems to be the nearest Virgil can get, for agricultural purposes, to the night's cold damp), but it doesn't much matter: what Virgil really wants to present is the season of cold and wet, and thus (after the first four lines) winter night becomes the subject (*hiberni luminis*, 291), then winter itself for the rest of the section, ending *cum nix alta iacet, glaciem cum flumina trudunt* (310).

It is important to see the structural development of this part of the book (the first half of the second half, if you will), because only by seeing its thematic balance (solar and lunar) and contrasts (here winter and summer, but in the outer panels spring and autumn) do we appreciate and understand the essential point. Thus, all of a sudden, as the moon's night turns to a winter's night and then to winter, it is summer with its blazing heat:

at rubicunda Ceres medio succiditur aestu
et medio tostas aestu terit area fruges.
nudus ara, sere nudus: hiems ignava colono.   (297–99)

(But ruddy Ceres is cut in mid-summer's heat and the threshing floor grinds the grain parched by the same heat. Strip when you plow, when you sow: winter is the farmer's lazy time.)

Just as in the preceding lines warm moisture predominated (as noted just above in the first lines 287–90, or just preceding these lines, *aut dulcis musti Volcano decoquit umorem / et foliis undam trepidi despumat aeni*, 295–96), so here the dry heat of summer. Ceres is thus brought within the context of the elemental physics of farming that runs so consistently through this first book: the threshing floor, prominent and important before (beyond normal expectation or didactic requirement), is again glossed etymologically (recall Varro's *ubi frumenta secta, ut terantur, arescunt, area* and Servius' *area est locus . . . qui aruerit*). Now, though, the effort that Ceres taught together with the lesson of inevitable failure finds a balance in the opposite season, just as the moon (moist and cold astrologically) balances the sun.

Winter is the lazy time, the genial season (300–302). There is no agricultural exertion, no sailing (303–305): in fact, no *artes*, or *egestas* for that matter. This may be the closest the real world can come to the happy life before Jupiter, as Virgil suggests without a doubt: *sed tamen et quernas glandes tum stringere tempus / et lauri bacas oleamque cruentaque myrta* (305–306). The opposition of Ceres and the acorn is by this time loaded with suggestion, and with one ambiguity as yet unresolved: is the gathering of acorns intended to summon up a Dickensian scene of warmth and cheer around the roaring fire, chestnuts (the modern equivalent, I suppose) roasting? or, as Virgil clearly had it before ("unless you work incessantly, you will have to appease your hunger with acorns in the woods," 159), do these acorns suggest again a less than ideal reality—pig fodder, bluntly? There is room for doubt, but I think the point here is simply that winter, the opposite to all that Jupiter's regime connotes, is to be taken at face value: it is a happy time, precisely because nothing grows that requires the farmer's labor. The olive is conspicuous (along with the acorn, laurel, and myrtle), a fruit requiring pointedly little attention (from the farmer, and therefore from Virgil in the second book) and the tree of peace (the six-line section on the olive ends *hoc pinguem et placitam Paci nutritor olivam*, 2.425). Hunting, the other winter activity (307–9), is similarly double-edged: it has of course no place in golden age co-existence, and has previously been suggestive of the mutual hostility between man and nature (recall the birds as pests, 119–20 and 156, or the *insidias avibus* just previously at 271), but again the idea of hunting as pure sport seems to predominate here. There is, in this winter scene, no suggestion of the Golden Age motif at all: this is the primitivism of the anthropologists rather than the Golden Age of the poets, the only difference being that Virgil presents this hunting and gathering as a possibility in his own day. The context is realistic, and through Ceres and the acorn primarily connections are made and suggested which propose an alternative to Jupiter's world of toil and failure: congeniality and peace. Whether this mirror image is desirable or attainable isn't for the moment the question: that will await further development and other connections.

The inner panels of this section of the book present a coherent balance: the sun and its seasons, demanding work even on days

88

of cold rain and on holidays; the lunar month, the night and the winter (both cold and wet), contrasting in every way with summer's heat, with further suggestive contrasts supplied by the sudden intrusion of Ceres (at line 297). The outer panels present the same motifs, and again Ceres is prominent.

We must watch the risings and settings of Arcturus (as Servius understands *Arcturi sidera*), and the days of the Haedi, and Draco (which doesn't rise or set), just as much as the sailor must (again, the *artes* and occupations of civilization are all that Virgil intends to remind us of by this mention of sailors—nothing more fanciful than this). As this opening passage (204–30) proceeds, spring and fall alternate repeatedly, as the times of plowing and sowing, naturally enough according to the real agricultural calendar. It is a passage interesting in its richness of detail, none of which may we linger over, but its overall purpose is clear: spring and fall as the beginnings (plowing and sowing— see Servius on 229 for some relevant ancient speculation about the passage), just as Taurus "opens" the year (*aperit* 217 = *Aprilis* < *aperire*—so e.g. Varro, *LL* 6.33, *quod ver omnia aperit, Aprilem*, or Ovid, *Fasti* 4.87–90, *nam quia ver aperit tunc omnia . . . Aprilem memorant ab aperto tempore dictum*). Attention is focused on hopeful expectation (*anni spem*, 224), and there is no mention (beyond the rather negative suggestion at 225–26) of harvest.

The final passage of the section (311–50) begins with a resumption of these ideas:

> Quid tempestates autumni et sidera dicam,
> atque, ubi iam breviorque dies et mollior aestas,
> quae vigilanda viris? vel cum ruit imbriferum ver,
> spicea iam campis cum messis inhorruit et cum
> frumenta in viridi stipula lactentia turgent?   (311–15)

(Why should I mention the storms and stars of autumn and, when now days are shorter and summer is more gentle, what men must watch out for? or when rain-bearing spring rushes on, when now the spikey harvest bristles in the fields and when the milky grain swells on the green stem?)

Spring and autumn, but now as the times of harvest, and now as the times of storms. Virgil continues with storms he himself has seen, often, that have caused the utter destruction of crops ready for the reaper:

> saepe ego, cum flavis messorem induceret arvis
> agricola et fragili iam stringeret hordea culmo,
> omnia ventorum concurrere proelia vidi,
> quae gravidam late segetem ab radicibus imis
> sublimem expulsam eruerent.   (316–20)

(Often, when the farmer was leading the reaper to his tawny fields and was already stripping the barley from the brittle stalk, often I have seen all the winds in battle rush together, which tore out the crop heavy far and wide wrenched aloft from its deepest roots.)

That such battles of the winds occur specifically in spring and fall is not a matter of circumstance. The emphasis on these two seasons in the opening passage, as we have thus seen, demands our attention here. We have previously seen that there is a good physical explanation for storms at these times: when either winter (cold and wet) or summer (hot and dry) changes into the other, periods of imbalance and strife inevitably result (*tempes tates*, 311, plays with the root of *temperies*, κρᾶσις). Servius (on 311) still had the key to the passage: "verno et autumnali tempore fiunt tempestates, quando nec plena aestas est nec plena hiems: unde medium et confine utriusque temporis ex coniunctione rerum contrariarum efficit tempestates" ("Storms arise in spring and autumn, since neither is full summer or full winter: therefore what is between and neighboring each of those (latter) seasons creates storms from the meeting of opposing forces"). In the opening passage there had been a tone of somewhat fearful hope, of haste before a gathering storm (*dum sicca tellure licet, dum nubila pendent*, 214); now the storm breaks.

Learn the stars and constellations and observe their seasonal risings and settings for the times to plow and sow. Know the *veterum praecepta*, observe the nut tree. Again Virgil has no need to underline the futility of experience. The *veterum praecepta* passage (176–203), the final passage of the first half, is a miniature

complement to the larger section (204–350) we have been discussing: that had concerned operations *after* the harvest (the
threshing floor) and *before* sowing (selection of seed), on either
side of the predictive nut tree, and failure was all but inevitable;
here we are concerned with the sowing and reaping and with
predictions from observations of the cosmos, and disaster almost inevitably follows. The differences are only a matter of
scale (between the heavens and the foliage of a single tree, between the raging storm in which Jupiter himself participates and
the moles, weevils, and toads), but the effort and the conclusion
are identical.

> in primis venerare deos, atque annua magnae
> sacra refer Cereri laetis operatus in herbis
> extremae sub casum hiemis, iam vere sereno.   (338–40)

> (Above all, worship the gods and pay to great Ceres her annual rite,
> with sacrifice in the lush grass at the close of winter, finally, now in
> calm spring.)

Can we believe that Virgil meant this sudden intrusion of faith
to be taken seriously as man's hope and salvation? Roman religion offered notoriously little in the way of such consolation,
but our answer must come from the poem itself. Here again we
should first hear Servius (on 338): "post haec cognita da praecipue operam sacrificiis, quibus tempestates et pluviae possunt re-
pelli. et mire hoc statim subiunxit, quia occurrebat: quid pro-
dest tempestates videre?" (" 'After these reflections, pay
particular attention to sacrifices, by which storms and rain can
be repelled.' It's strange that Virgil added this right here, because the thought must arise, 'How does it profit us to foresee
storms?' ").

What good does it do to be able to predict disaster? What occurred to Servius at the end of line 337 must occur to every
reader. (Note that Virgil nowhere suggests the stock answer
usually given by, for instance, astrologers, that by foreknowl-
edge one is more capable of bearing disaster.) But I find it
strange (*mire* indeed) that Virgil would be supplying such an answer as seems to follow—*in primis venerare deos.* Virgil is far

from being a poet of faith, even had the forms of Roman religion supplied him with faith. Were this the answer, it plays a surprisingly small role in the rest of the poem (or for that matter in the *Eclogues* or the *Aeneid*): if Virgil is saying here, so suddenly and resoundingly, "Give particular attention to sacrifice and rite, by which storms and rain may be averted" (as Servius takes it), then why does the poem continue for three and a third books more, in which this answer is hardly suggested again, and in which there is so overwhelmingly much at odds with the spirit of faith? A religious attitude does not concern itself with Virgil's concerns, nor express itself as Virgil does. The point does not need to be labored, except that everyone seems to agree with what Virgil appears to be saying: worship the gods, follow the forms of that old-time religion. Yet this admonition follows (please note) as a *complement*—not a corrective—to the three lines preceding, *hoc metuens caeli mensis et sidera serva* (335–37): if prediction cannot avert disaster, then how can religious rite do so, which Virgil presents as a parallel to prediction, not as an alternative? And, to get right down to it, are we seriously to imagine Virgil telling us that religious observance will avert the deluge? annually? from my farm, though perhaps not from my careless or irreligious neighbor's?

Two motifs dominate these lines, both of which should convey clearly enough what Virgil intended: spring and Ceres, together, are eloquent. The festival itself is an eclectic conflation of the Ambarvalia (29 May, probably) and the Cerealia (12–19 April), with perhaps a suggestion of the Vinalia (23 April), a generality rather than a specific description, indicating that we should understand the passage in a general context rather than in the light of a specific festival or rite. Spring receives more emphasis than one might expect: the dates of the festivals Virgil seems to suggest are congruent, the season is precisely indicated (*extremae sub casum hiemis, iam vere sereno*, 340) and described (*tum pingues agni et tum mollissima vina, / tum somni dulces densaeque in montibus umbrae*, 341–42, pointedly with the close translation of Hesiod's τῆμος πιόταταί τ᾽ αἶγες καὶ οἶνος ἄριστος, *WD* 585). If we know anything by this point, we know better than to accept the seductive allure of season or deity. Spring in the real world is far different, as physics and meteorology have repeatedly made clear, and as we heard last at the very beginning of this passage (*Quid tempestates autumni et sidera dicam . . . vel cum ruit imbriferum ver*, 311–13). *Nudus ara, sere nudus*: in the real world of labor, where is the sweet sleep of spring? The real world is Jupiter's, in which Ceres' gift involves a life far different and more dangerous than the idyllic scene here: *si bracchia forte remisit, / atque illum in praeceps prono rapit alveus amni. Vis humana quotannis* and *violentia* are here set aside for a moment, but they can hardly be forgotten, simply because it is Ceres who dominates the scene, whose festival this is.

One detail indicates that this is the same Ceres as before, summoning up the same connections and eliciting from the reader the same reactions. Usually Ceres, in art and poetry, bears as her attribute a garland of grain (see Bömer on Ovid, *Fasti* 4.616, [*Ceres*] *imposuitque suae spicea serta comae*; Tibullus 2.1.4, *et spicis tempora cinge, Ceres*). Here, and perhaps only here (though I cannot speak with certainty on this point), she is associated with a garland of oak leaves. Whether this is of Virgil's devising or not, it is both unusual and obvious (Servius noted that it called to mind man's *victum priorem*).

Prognostication and religious observation are parallel, not alternatives. Ceres is appropriate to the generalized festival in this book, just as Bacchus will be in the next (380–96), but she is far from being a figure of joy and hope. Her associations are consistent: progress, again, is not an ummixed blessing, and degeneration, destruction, and disaster are ultimately inevitable.

Some Observations

At this point we have offered far more description and detail than synthesis, general interpretation, and conclusions. We have neglected entirely some large and important sections of the first Book, but have discussed at length some ideas, from a circumscribed area of an early period of Greek thought, that may well seem irrelevant to Virgil. To some of the neglected sections we will return later, as Virgil returns for further development of these themes and ideas; and as he gradually forms clearer patterns from the details presented in this book, weaving and reweaving with the same threads, so I hope that our attempt to follow some of these threads will eventually produce the synthesis of interpretation which is at this stage simply not possible. It may be helpful, however, to review and anticipate a few important points and connections.

Virgil first established a scientific basis for his poem. (There is always the risk of forgetting that this is a poem and that Virgil is a poet: his science is, of course, reworked through the poetic imagination and is hardly pure—Lucretius, in comparison, is a pure scientist.) Virgil's science is based on the elements and qualities, by means of which antiquity, from the earliest Greek thinkers on, could, and commonly (and popularly) did, explain all aspects of the physical world. Inherent in the elements and qualities are oppositions (water and fire, hot and cold, wet and dry), which can as well be resolved and balanced. This is the marvelous simplicity of Virgil's science: conflict and resolution, opposition and balance, war and peace, to be presented through, and explained and understood by, the four elements.

Science is knowledge, and knowledge is power and control. The *pinguis arista* represents man's scientific achievement, his learned ability to resolve the elemental oppositions of nature, to create an artificial balance, and thereby to produce what we call civilization, through the arts of civilization. The acorn, thereby, is replaced by the ear of grain.

However: the apparent simplicity of complete understanding is (to be) another of life's grand deceptions and, as well, a gulf emerges between understanding and the power to control. The farmer's creation (*na-tura*, his farm) is after all subject to the storms arising beyond the *termini*, as well as to the pests and plagues within, and, as he will learn, prediction is not protection. Storm and civil war alike force one back to the ultimate unscientific resort, *in primis venerare deos.*

This is Virgil's opening book, as I understand it. Knowledge has appeared in many forms (from the pure science of Hippocrates, Empedocles, or Pythagoras to the *veterum praecepta* of the stereotype of the Vermont farmer), and it and its achievements have been seen both as supreme achievement and inevitable failure. Conflict is everywhere, sometimes splendidly resolved, sometimes (and finally) culminating in chaos and destruction. Virgil's view has been universal and has encompassed a sweep of time that recedes to an obscurity even beyond Jupiter's arrival. The next book will focus (for the most part but not entirely) on the farmer's world as it exists today and on man's present condition. Knowledge and conflict will still be Virgil's subject, and both, of course, will involve the constant interplay of his elements.

CHAPTER THREE

BOOK II

Trees Wild and Cultivated

The basic opposition of Ceres and the acorn is still present in the second book, though somewhat altered to fit a different context. The first book is concerned with man in his immediate environment and in the universe, and considers as well certain changes that affected an idealized past: Ceres is thus part of a transition from that past to the present, and as well a fact of the present condition. The second book is concerned more (though hardly exclusively) with this present condition and with man's efforts to deal with it; its focus is narrower in space and more immediate in time. To paraphrase Virgil, the first deals with the fields and their *natura*, their ability to produce (*Quid faciat laetas segetes*, 1.1; *Hactenus arvorum cultus*, 2.1) and, larger still, with their cosmic setting (*quo sidere terram / vertere*, 1.1–2; *et sidera caeli*, 2.1), and the second more directly with the products of the fields (*ulmisque adiungere vitis / conveniat*, 1.2–3; *et super arboribus*, 4.560). The greater universality of the first book, both temporal and spatial, is thus reflected in Ceres' grain and Jupiter's acorn. In the second book Virgil works with county maps rather than with a globe, and is concerned with current production figures rather than with historical rates of growth and decline; he now looks to the larger world and the past only as they seem relevant, rather than making them the subject and focus of his study.

The present condition is of course simply another name for history's final stage: trees that are cultivated and trees that are

(95)

wild are other manifestations of our basic opposition (and, obviously, this second book is concerned with trees rather than
grain). The second book accepts what the world has become:

> nunc te, Bacche, canam, nec non silvestria tecum
> virgulta et prolem tarde crescentis olivae.   (2.2–3)

> (Now my subject is you, Bacchus, and with you, as well, the forest
> thickets and the generation of the slow-growing olive.)

The prominence of Bacchus (both in this eight-line invocation
and in the rest of the book) has totally obscured for modern
readers the distinction, of fundamental importance, that was
clear in antiquity: the litotes *nec non* is no empty rhetorical device, but emphasizes the essential opposition between trees
(such as the vine) that are useful, productive, and therefore subject to cultivation, and those on the other hand that are unproductive and therefore not cultivated. Servius recognized this
distinction when he glossed *virgulta* with "id est infecundas ar-
bores"; he continued with a somewhat vapid remark ("quibus
praecipue in Italia vites cohaerent") that may be explained by his
having before him, as he composed and conflated his material,
some reference to the beginning of the poem, *ulmisque adiungere
vitis / conveniat* (1.2–3), where (as I hope will become clear later)
the elm and the vine represent the wild and the cultivated (as
well as, of course, one method of viticulture). There are two
subjects of this book, not one (although one of them receives,
naturally enough, most of Virgil's attention and all of the attention of modern readers). The wild and the cultivated are the
present reality, or the final stage, of the historical process represented by the acorn and Ceres. After the short invocation,
Virgil gets directly to the point.

> Principio arboribus varia est natura creandis.
> namque aliae nullis hominum cogentibus ipsae   (10)
> *sponte sua* veniunt . . .
> pars autem *posito* surgunt *de semine* . . .   (14)
> pullulat *ab radice* aliis densissima silva . . .   (17)
> hos natura modos primum dedit, his genus omne   (20)
> silvarum fruticumque viret nemorumque sacrorum.
> sunt alii, quos ipse via sibi repperit usus.

(First, nature has various ways of reproducing trees. For some come forth voluntarily of themselves, without man's intervention . . . : some grow from fallen seed . . . ; in other types a thicket shoots up from the roots . . . Natural growth first produced these ways, by these all sorts of forest trees, and shrubs, and the trees of the sacred groves flourish. But there are other ways which man's experience has discovered by rational trial.)

This basic distinction is taken directly from the beginning of the second book of Theophrastus' *History of Plants*: αἱ γενέσεις τῶν δένδρων καὶ ὅλως τῶν φυτῶν ἢ αὐτόμαται ἢ ἀπὸ σπέρματος ἢ ἀπὸ ῥίζης. Theophrastus continues to list five further ways of reproduction, which in fact correspond (more or less) to Virgil's man-invented ways, lines 22–34; he then remarks that spontaneous reproduction is the first, but that reproduction from seed and root would seem most natural (φυσικώταται) and thus should also be considered spontaneous (αὐτόμαται), whereas the other methods are a matter of horticultural craft or choice (αἱ δὲ ἄλλαι τέχνης ἢ δὴ προαιρέσεως). Virgil invites comparison with his authority.

What stands out from such a comparison is first the clarity and emphasis with which Virgil distinguishes between nature and man. In Theophrastus this distinction is assumed as a simple fact and a convenient division, not in itself worth particular attention: his second book is devoted to reproduction of cultivated trees (περὶ τῶν ἡμέρων), the third to uncultivated (περὶ τῶν ἀγρίων). Virgil, though, sets man against nature: trees that reproduce spontaneously do so "without man's intervention," without compulsion (*nullis hominum cogentibus*). Second, as this phrase also reveals (*cogere* is not an altogether colorless verb), man's methods involve a force that borders on actual violence. Theophrastus' technical γένεσις ἀπὸ παρασπάδος ("from a shoot," though the Greek suggests "a tearing away") becomes in Virgil the work of someone "cutting (ripping) shoots from the delicate bodies of mothers" (*hic plantas tenero abscindens de corpore matrum / deposuit sulcis*, 23–24). Virgil replaces Theophrastus' technical terms with vivid representations of the actual acts ("procedures" is too precise a term): burying, bending the living limb, forcing roots from cut bark—simple procedures still to be found in every handbook, but notable (simply because so common) for the forceful detail given them here. It will not be enough to refer this vividness to Virgilian sympathy.

This opening section concludes (though it is hardly possible, or necessary, to decide whether lines 35–38 are a conclusion or the beginning of a new paragraph) with a familiar theme:

> Quare agite o proprios generatim discite cultus,
> agricolae, fructusque feros mollite colendo,
> neu segnes iaceant terrae.

> (Wherefore come, farmers, and learn the methods of cultivation appropriate for each type, and by cultivation tame the wild fruits, that the earth not lie idle.)

Here, first, is the subject of today's lesson: different trees (*generatim*) are reproduced best in different ways, as Theophrastus described. But for Virgil the real matter is the taming of the wild (*feros* = τὰ ἄγρια), lest the earth lie in idleness. This, of course, was precisely what Jupiter had in mind when he set the world on a new course:

> pater ipse colendi
> haud facilem esse viam voluit, primusque per artem
> movit agros curis acuens mortalia corda,
> nec torpere gravi passus sua regna veterno.   (1.121–24)

> (Jupiter himself wished the path of progress to be in no way an easy one, and first roused the fields through the arts and sciences, whetting men's minds by worry, not suffering his kingdom to lie in sloth with the lethargy of age.)

The *artes, usus, experientia* reappear necessarily, those methods *quos ipse via sibi repperit usus* (2.22): the slight difficulty of *via* is expressive (Servius' gloss "ratione" is correct, but the more literal meaning "way" should be heard here as well in the context of 1.122, just cited—the expressive ambiguity of the word at 1.41, *ignarosque viae . . . agrestis*, is similar).

What the first book represented (in part, at least) as an historical process, the second book will develop as a present condition: it is worth repeating this connection between the two books, for Virgil seems to stress it here by the strong reminder of the key terms used throughout the first book. Ease, the earth's free bounty, torpidity; Jupiter's action; the *artes*, the struggle (*labor*) against the earth and its *pestes, egestas* and failure. We are warned at the beginning of Book II to observe the same forces: *nunc te, Bacche, canam, nec non silvestria tecum/virgulta . . .*

★

The beginning of the second book may be outlined as follows:

1–8:   Prologue, statement of subject: Bacchus and *silvestria virgulta*

9–38:   Theory: natural reproduction and man's methods

39–46 (= 8 lines):   Address to Maecenas

47–72:   Theory: natural reproduction and man's methods

73–82:   How to do it: methods of grafting

Several features of the opening of the book are notable, and, since notable, are pointers to Virgil's purposes. To begin with, the first two didactic sections (9–38, 47–72) are identical in content. The only difference between them is that the second lacks the simplicity of exposition of the first: Virgil repeats the three natural ways of reproduction, but, after each, man's methods are intruded, and the section ends with a mishmash of wild and cultivated trees. Since the material presented is standard arboricultural fare (directly from Theophrastus, as we have just noted—though undoubtedly older still), and since Virgil's first exposition is so clear and spare, the apparent confusion of the second section, in addition to the fact that it is a blatant repetition, ought to indicate something of importance.

Obviously, the repetition serves the same purpose as the vividness of language so marked in the first passage: Theophrastus' scientific division is something far different for Virgil. Another feature of these two sections is relevant. In the first, the only trees named occur in the description of natural reproduction and are of course wild: osier, broom, poplar, willow (spontaneous); chestnut and oak (from seed); wild cherry, elm, and laurel (from roots). When man's methods are listed, no trees are named, except for the indirect reference to the olive (*radix oleagina*, 31), until the grafted mutations (apple, pear, and plum) mentioned at the very end. (We may note in passing that the mention of both the specific *aesculus* and generic *quercus* in lines 15–16 is surprising—"Die Nennung von *aesculus* . . . und *quercus* nebeneinander überrascht," says Richter—but perfectly comprehensible in the light of the development, throughout the previous book, of the opposition of Ceres and the acorn: the mention of Jupiter's oracle serves to help set this theme in its new context—the wild and the cultivated.) In the next section, however, no trees at all are named in the first sixteen lines, but then they come in a bewildering profusion of wild and cultivated: olive, grape, myrtle, hazelnut (καρύα in Theophrastus, a wild tree, *HP* 3.2.3), ash, poplar, oak, palm, fir, nut, arbute, plane, apple, chestnut, beech, mountain ash, pear, oak, and elm. These ten lines (63–72) are as extraordinary as any Virgil ever wrote. I have listed the trees which occur in them to emphasize both the number (there are nineteen) and the unexpectedness of the mix, but since the passage does not seem to have aroused the imagination of modern readers as I think Virgil intended, and since the point is so essential, I will be explicit.

The Italian farmer paid no more attention to wild trees than does his modern counterpart in either Tuscany or Vermont. Effort is expended on fruit (and fruitful) trees—the effort, for instance, of rooting slips, of setting out the rooted plants in nurseries, and finally of establishing the young trees in orchards, with the additional effort of grafting varieties onto established stock: all of this, as of course Virgil relates in selected detail, is the business of the arboriculturist, to whom oaks, maples, and beeches are of no concern whatsoever (forester is a modern occupation). In antiquity the woodcutter or the lumberer took what he wanted and left—left the forest, that is, to get along as best it might, if at all (the economics of European deforestation need not concern us here). The very division of trees into wild and cultivated assumes these circumstances as long established facts of rural life: fruitful trees required cultivation, wild trees (which are of course useful in a number of ways—for lumber or fuel, or for their nuts for human consumption or for pig fodder, and so on) aren't worth bothering with and will in any case take care of themselves pretty well.

Which things being so, and which things being patently clear to even the most urban of Virgil's readers, the mix (or mess) of the nineteen trees listed in lines 63–72 ought to be rather unnerving. Servius thinks it worth noting, on 63, "et iam redit ad eos modos, quos invenit industria," but unfortunately he does not go on to ask why those methods which technology devised should be applied to (for instance) fir, arbute, plane, ash, oak, or elm: and if ever sheer nonsense called for explanation, this is it.

Part of this may not be such nonsense as most texts have:

> sed truncis oleae melius, propagine vites
> respondent, solido Paphiae de robore myrtus;
> plantis et durae coryli nascuntur et ingens
> fraxinus Herculeaeque arbos umbrosa coronae,
> Chaoniique patris glandes; etiam ardua palma
> nascitur et casus abies visura marinos.   (2.63–68)

(But olives are better propagated from lopped pieces, vines from slips, the Paphian myrtles from the solid wood; from cuttings the hard hazels are born, and the native ash and the shady tree of Hercules' crown, and the acorns of the Chaonian father; (so) even the lofty palm is born, and the fir, destined to witness disaster at sea.)

Most editors read *et durae* in line 65 (so the Medicean MS, the only ancient MS to give these lines) and punctuate with a full stop preceding the line; commentators are then forced to explain the *nascitur* of line 68 with "scilicet *plantis*," just as the *nascuntur* of 65 must be taken, as if the verbs were equivalent to *crescit* or *crescunt*. Mynors, however, reads *edurae* (an ancient variant mentioned by Servius, and certainly *difficilior*) and punctuates with a full stop after *coryli*:

> Paphiae de robore myrtus,
> plantis edurae coryli. nascuntur et ingens . . .

Certainly the resulting periodicity is both more elegant and more decisive, but now what does *nascuntur* mean? (The question ought to have been asked of *nascitur* previously—to understand *plantis* is not really very satisfying.) *Nascuntur* is now emphatically placed at the beginning of its sentence, which makes any weakness or vagueness of meaning ("There are born . . .") even more intolerable. "Born" in what sense? The only sense possible is the one inherent in the Latin root of the verb, recognized in fact by Servius in his comment on line 49 just above, *quippe solo natura subest*: "quia . . . naturaliter rerum omnium mater est terra . . . nam natura dicta est ab eo, quod nasci aliquid faciat" (" 'of course the power of growth lies hidden in the soil': since . . . naturally the mother of everything is earth . . . For the word *'nature'* is derived from its causing something *to be born*"). *Nascuntur* then means "are products of nature," similar to the English "Poets are born, not made." The list of trees, then, begins with the important distinction: the olive, vine, myrtle, and hazelnut are responsive to cultivation; the natural (for *ingens* suggesting "native" or "natural," see below) ash, poplar, oak, palm, and fir are products of nature.

The confusion introduced by most editors, and glossed over (if noticed at all) by commentators, is one that Virgil actually promoted. At this point another reason for the repetitiveness of this section becomes clear: Virgil suddenly extends the farmer's sphere of action from cultivated trees to all trees, even the wild. This is quite clear now, even at the beginning:

> Sponte sua quae se tollunt in luminis oras,
> infecunda quidem, sed laeta et fortia surgunt;
> quippe solo natura subest. tamen haec quoque, si quis
> inserat aut scrobibus mandet mutata subactis,
> exuerint silvestrem animum, cultuque frequenti
> in quascumque voles artis haud tarda sequentur.   (47–52)

(Those which voluntarily raise themselves into the shores of light arise unfruitful, yes, but vigorous and strong: for of course the power of growth lies hidden in the soil. Nevertheless these too will put aside their forestral character, should someone graft them or entrust them, transplanted, to deep-dug trenches, and with continual attention they will not be slow to obey any craft you wish.)

Theophrastus is the authority again: wild trees are stronger, more vigorous (καὶ ἰσχυρότερα τῇ φύσει, *HP* 3.2.1: *laeta et fortia surgunt*) because of the productiveness in the earth itself (and in *quippe solo natura subest* Virgil may be playing with Theophrastus' τῇ φύσει). Totally unexpected, however, is what follows: *tamen haec quoque, si quis. . . .* The unusual fifth- and sixth-foot cadence introduces the extraordinary statement that these trees, too, nevertheless (*tamen*), are to be cultivated, will change their character, and will readily respond to any art whatsoever. This is where Virgil parts company with the writer of an agricultural handbook: not only is his advice quirky (not unlike that of the talk-to-your-houseplants cultists) and actually wrong according to ancient theory, but also totally impractical and unreasonable, as we have seen. *Caelum non animum mutant* is a cliché of long standing: character is not as easily altered as Virgil implies when he says, *exuerint silvestrem animum. Silvester*, too, is a key epithet in this book, from the *silvestria virgulta* of line 2 to the *bacis silvestribus* (183) and the olives, *oleae silvestris . . . truncos* (302), always in these instances denoting the wild tree. Here (line 51) Servius again sees the point, when he glosses "their forestral character" with "natural harshness and barrenness": "SILVESTREM ANIMUM naturalem asperitatem et infecunditatem." (In the *Georgics* the adjective occurs only in this book, with the exception of 3.411, though at 2.374, *silvestres uri*, it is not used of uncultivated trees.) The contrasting mention of the *artes* needs only be noted; connected themes from the previous book are suggested too by the idea of the degeneration of fruit (without man's intervention), the spoil of birds (man's occasional opponents): *pomaque degenerant sucos oblita priores / et turpis avibus praedam fert uva racemos* (59–60).

The clearest theme from Book I, though, is in the lines immediately following:

scílicet ómnibus ést labor ímpendéndus, et ómnes
cogendae in sulcum ac multa mercede domandae. (61–62)

("Of course on all these effort must be lavished, and all must be forced into their trenches and subdued at great cost.")

Along with the theme of *labor*, Virgil picks up a musical motif from a related passage in the first book, one which will recur three more times in this book and not again. The musical metaphor is apt and precise: rhythm and sound, as much as meaning, connect the lines *tum variae venere artes* (1.145), *tum variae inludunt pestes* (1.181), and *tum variae eludent species* (4.406), as we saw. So are these two lines connected by the three gerundives with 1.178–79, describing the effort involved in making the threshing floor, and with lines to follow. The effect of the sound produced by the coincidence of word accent and verse ictus in most of the gerundives is purely musical. That the effect was intentional, and not to be missed, is certain from the fact that line 61 is remarkable for the total absence of conflict of accent and ictus, as such to be seen alongside such lines as *ímpius háec tam cúlta nováolia míles habébit (Ecl.* 1.70) and, with totally different effect, *spárgens úmida mélla sopóriferúmque papáver (Aen.* 4.486). Effort to be expended (*impendendus*), with compelling force (*cogendae*) and domination (*domandae*), is not only a repeated theme, but a repeated musical motif to occur again. (I know of no other poet to use pure sound—that is, music—as a recurring motif in such a way.)

The restatement of the theme of *labor* and the recurrence of the musical motif serve to underline the unusual assertion Virgil made just previously in this passage: the repetition *omnibus . . . omnes . . .* hammers home the insistence that *all* trees, wild as well as cultivated, require and even demand man's efforts and domination. The final effect of these two theoretical passages here at the beginning of the book is flatly to contradict experience (Theophrastus) and reason: the first states the accepted theory and reasonable practice in the matter of wild and cultivated trees; the second, seeming at first to restate the matter in the same terms, is in fact an extraordinarily vivid, verbally dramatic refutation and inversion of what preceded. Man's control is to be extended over nature itself. The present is a further stage in a process begun long ago: *labor omnia vicit / improbus . . .*

The Art of Grafting

Virgil's instruction to the farmer is, as we have seen, selective, and it is just as instructive for us to pay attention to what he has selected and why. Here in these first 82 lines of the book, where the general topic is reproduction, the focus is on grafting, both at the end of the first theoretical section (32–34) and at the end of the second (69–72); and the first section of practical instruction (73–82) is devoted to grafting. What Virgil says about this craft is as strange as anything we have noted thus far in the book, but the strangeness of it, though observed by a few historians of agriculture, has been totally lost on interpreters of the poem.

The grafts mentioned by Virgil are: apple onto pear, plum onto cherry (32–34); walnut onto arbute, apple onto plane, chestnut onto beech, pear onto ash, oak onto elm (69–72). With the doubtful exception of the first, all these grafts are impossible. Without exception all are impractical or grotesque.

The impossibility of grafting an oak with a pear need not be argued here in detail, but otherwise what he says about this craft does need to be recognized, and the significance of his misstatement of fact needs both emphasis and reflection. To put it simply, modern theory and practice can be stated thus: grafting between families is impossible, between genera (intergeneric) possible though difficult and often unsuccessful, and between species (intrageneric) generally successful. We can thus say immediately that six of Virgil's seven examples are impossible (though chestnut and beech both belong to the family Fagaceae). Concerning the graft of apple onto pear, there must remain some uncertainty: both belong to the same family (Rosaceae), and since Linnaeus, who considered that both belonged to the same genus (*Pyrus*), there has been doubt as to whether the two belong to separate genera; in any case, successful grafting of apple and pear must be regarded as possible though very unlikely.

Did Virgil, however, believe that such grafts were possible? One splendid example can be given, simply for illustration: Pliny (*NH* 17.120) claims to have seen (*vidimus*) a tree at Tivoli grafted with every sort of fruit—walnuts on one branch, "berries" on another, grapes, pears, figs, pomegranates, and apples. That such experiments were made can be assumed; that no such grafts lasted more than a few days can also be assumed. Of this tree, significantly, Pliny adds, *sed huic brevis fuit vita* (he was not fooled, he lets us know). Other reports of impossible grafts may be collected, but the point is this: all such reports are later than Virgil, and some are quite obviously the direct result of these lines. Conversely (the point is worth restating), Virgil is the first to make claims for grafts that we know could never have been accomplished.

Since the significance of this point needs some explanation (the point itself has been barely recognized), it is probably worthwhile to sketch in the arboricultural background for grafting, which Virgil, I think, could have assumed to have been familiar to his readers. In antiquity (as now) grafting was the only practical method of reproducing varieties of fruit trees. The two other methods have obvious drawbacks. A tree grown from seed will not produce fruit true to type, but will degenerate or revert to the "wild," losing the characteristics of the original variety; reproduction from seed is also a lengthy process. A tree grown from a slip or cutting also requires a long time to mature, may as well be less strong and vigorous, and in some instances too may suffer degeneration; this method, however, is most often practical and common when time is not crucial and a number of new trees are needed. Grafting, however, is the fastest way of obtaining fruit of a different variety (today, for instance, apple trees grafted with three or four varieties are offered in every nurseryman's catalogue), and as well the best way to assure vigorous stock (again for example, modern hybrid tea roses are for this reason all grown from grafts).

Grafting, then, was and is the only method of reproduction when the variety of the fruit was important (and varieties were then extremely important: Pliny—according to K. D. White in *Roman Farming* (p. 262)—knew 71 varieties of grapes, for instance, 39 of pears, 23 of apples, and 29 of figs; cf. Virgil's catalogue of varieties, especially of grapes, *Geo.* 2.83–108). For Virgil's readers the idea of grafting an elm with an oak would have seemed a fit occupation for a madman. Even the graft of pear and apple would have seemed pointless, and in fact was probably regarded as futile: Varro, in his brief discussion of grafting, assumes as a rule that both scion and stock be of the

same *genus* (*si eiusdem generis est, dumtaxat ut sit utraque malus,*
1.40.6). Only an occasional curious amateur, or practical joker
(as perhaps was responsible for Pliny's monster) would ever
have considered fooling with the graft of apple and pear—and,
we can be sure, with a very slim chance of success.

To recognize these grafts as impossible is in fact to see Virgil's
purpose. I have elsewhere discussed the background of this passage. Close at hand is Damon's *adynata* in *Eclogue* 8, at the conclusion of his song:

> nunc et ovis ultro fugiat lupus, aurea durae
> mala ferant quercus, narcisso floreat alnus,
> pinguia corticibus sudent electra myricae (52–54)

(And now let the wolf of his own run from the sheep, let hard oaks
bear golden apples, let the alder flower with narcissus, let tamarisks
sweat rich amber from their bark.)

Ultimately these lines reflect a similar announcement of suicide,
Daphnis' final words in Theocritus' *Idyll* 1: "You brambles and
thorns, bear violets; let the beautiful narcissus flower on the jun-
iper; let everything be upside down; let the pine bear pears"
(1.132–34). There are several points to take note of here. First,
there is no doubt that Theocritus' Daphnis is the model for Virgil's Damon in these lines. There is no doubt as well that the
convention of the *adynata* is employed by both poets in one of its
most basic applications—to represent a world gone wrong for
the desperate lover. Furthermore, it has been observed that botanical *adynata* are very rare—so rare, in fact, that Theocritus'
precedent was for Virgil virtually unique in verse.

Neither Daphnis nor Damon, however, is a practical farmer,
and neither of them of course is thinking of grafting. There was
another precedent important for Virgil when he was writing of
grafting at the beginning of *Georgics* II, but which he also must
have had in mind when he composed the *adynata* in *Eclogue* 8.
Varro discussed grafting briefly in the first book of the *De Re
Rustica* (published in 37 B.C.—a date consequently of significance for the dating of the *Eclogues*). He considered what trees
may be grafted, when, and how, and then wrote, to illustrate,

non enim pirum recipit quercus, neque etiamsi malus, pirum "For example, an oak does not take the graft of a pear, nor, even if (it is) an apple, does it take the graft of a pear" (1.40.5—*caveat lector*: I give Varro's text with an emendation which gives a sense, as in my translation, which is just the opposite of what is to be found in other translations, and editions, of Varro). Varro's illustration first presents us with an accepted absurdity (an oak grafted with a pear), then with what might seem possible (apple with pear): Varro goes on to stress that scion and stock must be of the same genus.

The sequence of precedents is now clear:

> Theocritus' Daphnis: pine bearing pears
> Varro (independently): oak/apple grafted with pear
> Virgil's Damon: oak bearing (*ferant*) apples
> Virgil (*Geo.* 2): pear bearing grafted apples (*ferre insita mala*).

It is thus the one graft that might seem (and could thus barely be) possible that shows most clearly Virgil's purpose—the impossibility of these transformations of nature. Here is another example of a common practice in the *Georgics*: a literary topic or convention that becomes a reality, an allusion or illusion made real in the farmer's world; the poetic *adynaton* ("let the pine bear pears") has become a real impossible (a pear bearing grafted apples).

Further, the complete list of monstrous alterations—pointless, as well as futile, as we observed before—is summed up by Virgil at the end of the passage:

> nec longum tempus et ingens
> exiit ad caelum ramis felicibus arbos,
> miratastque novas frondes et non sua poma. .   (80–82)

(Nor is it long before the monstrous tree reaches forth to heaven with productive branches, and wonders at its strange leaves and fruit not its own.)

The words lend themselves to a double construction. One can see a happy smile on the face of this anthropomorphized tree, or one can see it shrinking in disbelief (*miratast*) at the perversion worked upon it, at its mutation (*novas frondes et non sua poma*—cf. (*pirum*) *mutatam*, 2.33). Again, *ingens* seems a key epithet, meaning here "unnatural" (see below). Servius records a telling summation in his brief comment on line 82, "ingens phantasia."

Virgil's art of grafting, then, consists of what is simply not possible on any real farm, and indeed is a poetic *adynaton*—the representation of an order inverted, a world gone totally wrong—come alive in the Italian countryside. The product of this art is the monstrous and unnatural. *Labor* has subdued all, not only what is man's (the cultivated) but nature's as well (the wild), and the book's main injunction to farmers has already been carried out (*fructusque feros mollite colendo*, 2.36): swine *have* (*fregere*) crunched acorns under the elms, a tree *has* (*exiit*) grown and *has* (*miratast*) wondered at its unnatural leaves and foreign fruit. Again, Virgil's focus is now the present condition, the final stage of the historical process previously considered.

Laudations and the Lie

Thus far in the discussion of the beginning of Book II I have followed lines resulting from two observations that are demonstrably central to Virgil's plan. First, that wild trees are to be given attention equal to that obviously given to the cultivated: Virgil's close reading of Theophrastus, as well as his own emphasis on the wild from the opening words (. . . *nec non silvestria tecum virgulta*), make this clear. Second, it ought to be just as obvious (as I believe it once was), that Virgil's examples of grafting (which are now read without the slightest perturbation) are impossible, unnatural, and blatantly unthinkable perversions of the wild (as well as of the cultivated); the most rudimentary awareness of horticulture, ancient or modern, is enough to alert us to the enormity (not too strong a word) of the poet's creations.

To say that we see a pear tree bearing apples and a cornel cherry growing red with plums is to state an untruth, and should be recognized as such. It would be naive to think that Virgil didn't realize what he was saying here. Our response must start from the simple awareness of the lie that runs throughout these lines on grafting, which after all summarizes and exemplifies the farmer's art here: any other response will be inadequate and improper. Once we are aware that Virgil has constructed an elaborate lie, we can then ask why, or who has perpetrated the deception and who has been deceived, or whether the untruth is one that will turn out to be paradoxically true after all, or any number of such questions. But unless we see that Virgil has told a lie, none of these questions will arise, and, what is worse, we will have accepted an entirely erroneous view of the poem, the very opposite of what Virgil expected his readers to accept.

I would like to proceed now with this in mind, the awareness that Virgil tells lies. Putting it so flatly will at least serve to make the point, to sharpen our awareness, and to assure that our next response will be an appropriate one. "The Virgilian Lie" may be a more dignified heading, but I am not sure it would be any more accurate than to say simply, "Virgil tells lies." He has warned us as clearly and loudly as he could, in these opening lines and will warn us again and again. We may see the warnings in each of the three "digressions" in the book, the Praise of Italy, the Praise of Spring, and the Praise of Country Life. Since each of these passages have had far more than their share of comment and explication, I will discuss them only briefly, with the sole purpose of watching for The Virgilian Lie.

The Praise of Italy (136–76) is neatly integrated into the thematic development of the book. It is preceded by almost equal sections on the diversity and variety of plants (especially of grapes) and on the diversity of lands, each with their own nature and therefore with their own plants (*nec vero terrae ferre omnes omnia possunt*, 109). That each land, with its elevation and physical relief, its water, and its winds or air, has its own annual temperament and seasonal characteristics that form and affect every living thing including its human inhabitants, is an assumption as old as the *Odyssey* (for example, the strangely "scientific" ring to the description of the potentially productive but uncultivated island lying off Polyphemus' land (9.116–41), and as long-lasting and far-reaching as it is old. It is a constant in geographical writings, is best known in Herodotus (where it is the fundamental assumption for establishing the basic character of the eastern peoples, as well as underlying his more purely geographical discourses), is the principle for so much of the early Hippocratic corpus (best illustrated by the *Airs, Waters, Places*), and is never far removed from Greek and Roman thinking about the character of peoples (which means, frequently, of cities or towns). The subject has been thoroughly investigated. We have touched on the idea previously in the *Georgics* and will return to it again. Here we need only note that the background Virgil assumes is Greek: in illustrating "the diversity of lands" he looks to the East and northern Africa primarily, Arabia and India particularly, with echoes of Herodotus, and more directly of Theophrastus; the extremes of the world are viewed as precisely that—imbalances of elements which imply consequent imbalances of character.

For Greeks, of course, Greece is assumed to be temperately situated and therefore enjoying a well-balanced climate. The later tradition granted this virtue to Italy, and the *laus Italiae* became a set piece (a Posidonian original has been posited). Servius noted (on line 136), "now begins the *laus Italiae*, which Virgil relates according to rhetorical principles (*secundum praecepta rhetorica*): for he says that Italy has everything good and is without everything bad (*carere malis universis*)." Varro's *laus Italiae* (*RR* 1.2) was obviously a precedent for Virgil, but is, it should be noted, restrained and almost flatly factual by comparison. Dionysius (Virgil's contemporary) also keeps his praise (*Rom. Ant.* 1.36–37) well within the bounds of fact, though he begins with mention of the myth of Saturn's reign in Italy; and Strabo (6.4.1) is coldly scientific. An unbiased first impression must admit that Virgil not only has written *secundum praecepta rhetorica*, but has gone far beyond the confines of both propriety and truth.

★

At this point we must digress slightly to discuss the lemon tree of Media, the *felix malum*, which Virgil makes the transition from the diversity of lands to the Praise of Italy. This short passage (126–35) is the first of four related etymologies, elaborate aetiologies which serve to establish themes of major importance. (There are, of course, other etymological aetiologies of considerable importance in the poem, such as the *arista* complex at the very beginning, but these four are similar in structure as well as observably related in theme.) We will discuss each in its own context, noting now only the relation of the four to each other. The lemon tree anticipates the *amellus* in Book 4 (271–80), as Servius saw—or found in an older note: "plene hanc herbam, ut etiam supra arborem felicis mali, exsequitur: nam dicit ubi creetur, qualis sit, quid possit" ("he discusses this herb in detail, as also the lemon tree (above): for he mentions where it grows, what sort of plant it is, and what it can do," (on 4.271, with a similar comment on 2.134). Both passages, then, were related in antiquity, and both were recognized to be of a type appropriate to technical descriptions of formal botany, giving habitat, character, and use. In the third book occur the other two major etymological aetiologies, the *asilus* (3.146–53) and the *hippomanes* (3.280–83). Three of these are plants; the fourth (the gadfly) is treated similarly and (as we will see) is of a literary pedigree of such prominence that it may well have served in Virgil's mind as the prototype of the other three.

The relation of these passages can be seen schematically from the table (opposite), which simply sets forth, under the botanical handbook headings recognized by Servius, certain relevant features (there are, of course, other details which relate these passages to each other and especially to their own contexts). It is clear from the shared characteristics (as well as from the formal etymologies that we have not yet noted) that Virgil composed each of these passages with an eye to the others, that we should look for some significance in whether each is Italian or foreign, and that two are beneficial (an antidote to poisons, a panacea for plague), two are destructive (inducing madness, sexual *furor*). With this general scheme in mind, we can turn again to the lemon tree:

Media fert tristis sucos tardumque saporem
felicis mali, quo non praesentius ullum,

	HABITAT	CHARACTERISTICS	USE
The lemon (2.126–35)	Foreign (Media)	*tristis sucos, tardum saporem; ingens*	Curative, used as an antidote to poisons of *novercae*
The *asilus* (3.146–53)	Native (southern Italy)	*asper, acerba sonans*	Harmful, sent by Juno against herds
The *hippomanes* (3.280–83)	Foreign (by implication— locale not specified)	*lentum virus*	Harmful, used as a love-charm by *novercae*
The *amellus* (4.271–80)	Native (northern Italy)	*asper in ore sapor; ingentem silvam*	Curative, used by shepherds, on altars of gods

pocula si quando saevae infecere novercae
[miscueruntque herbas et non innoxia verba,]
auxilium venit ac membris agit atra venena.   (130)
ipsa ingens arbos faciemque simillima lauro;
et, si non alium late iactaret odorem,
laurus erat; folia haud ullis labentia ventis,
flos ad prima tenax; animas et olentia Medi
ora fovent illo et senibus medicantur anhelis.   (135)

(Media bears the bitter juice and lingering taste of the "healthy apple," than which, if ever wicked stepmothers have poisoned your
drink [and mixed their herbs and harmful spells], no aid comes more
readily and drives the deadly poison from your limbs. It is an indig-
enous tree and most like the laurel in appearance—it would be a laurel, if it did not have a different, far-spreading perfume. Its leaves seldom drop, no matter how strong the wind; its flower is especially
tenacious. The Medes use it as a mouthwash and to cure shortness of
breath in the aged.)

Why Media? First, of course, because it is appropriate in a catalogue of eastern lands, in a demonstration of the common topic
(beginning with line 109) *nec vero terrae ferre omnes omnia possunt*,
and continuing with the superiority of Italy to the fabulous East:
*haec loca non tauri spirantes naribus ignem / invertere satis immanis
dentibus hydri, / nec galeis densisque virum seges horruit hastis* (140–

42). Ostensibly and initially, at least, the contrast is between the natural fertility and temperate climate of Italy and the monstrous and unnatural productivity of eastern lands. But the fire-breathing bulls and the armed men sown from the dragon's teeth are of course those of Aeetes, whom Jason subdued with Medea's help, the witch with her drugs and poisons, the savage stepmother. Long before Virgil the tradition existed that Media was named from Medea's son Medus; Herodotus, among others, had reported this connection (see the commentary of How and Wells on 7.62 for references), and the tradition was sufficiently alive and well for "Probus" to repeat in his comment on line 126 here, "Pars Parthorum Media est appellata a Medo, filio Medeae et Aegei, ut existimat Varro, qui quattuor libros de Argonautis edidit."

The association of Media and Medea, then, provides a second reason for this aetion, as well as the best reason for the authenticity (?) of line 129: Medea's land provides the antidote for the savage stepmother's poisons. Theophrastus had the core of Virgil's description, when, after saying that Asia has its own flora and fauna, he gave as an example τὸ μῆλον τὸ Μηδικὸν ἢ τὸ Περσικὸν καλούμενον; and added, χρήσιμον δ᾽ ἐπειδὰν τύχῃ ⟨τις⟩ πεπωκὼς φάρμακον ⟨θανάσιμον⟩ . . . καὶ πρὸς στόματος εὐωδίαν . . . ποιεῖ τὴν ὀσμὴν ἡδεῖαν ("The apple known as the Median or Persian: useful whenever one happens to have drunk a deadly poison . . . and, as regards oral hygiene, it makes the breath sweet," HP 4.4.2–3). The supposed curative powers of the lemon, then, provided Virgil with other details. The lemon is "very like the laurel," perhaps (beside certain other characteristics) because the laurel is the tree of Apollo (as Healer). Certainly Virgil's prime concern is healing, since healing provides the etymology, as again Servius recorded (on 126), "arbor, ferens mala, quae medica vocantur: quam per periphrasin ostendit, eius supprimens nomen." The name is suppressed in the learned manner, but is provided by the glosses that stand at the beginning and end of the passage: Media . . . (126), . . . Medi (134), . . . medicantur . . . (135). A further gloss is provided by the attribute felicis (mali), which Servius (on 127) explains as "fecundi

. . . aut certe . . . salubris: nulla enim efficacior res est ad venena pellenda." If we allowed the old pun on *malum* "apple" and *malum* "evil," we then have in *felicis* a gloss from the opposite: precisely this seems to be Virgil's point in all the details of this complex action—that there is in the monstrous and unnatural East the antidote itself for its own (traditional) evil.

One last detail. Those who have supposed this tree to be other than the lemon have been misled particularly by one word, *ingens* (*ipsa ingens arbos*, 131): lemon trees are hardly "huge," as Virgil would have known as well as any one. We have just seen, though, that Virgil used the adjective of the grafted tree "wondering (in horror) at its strange leaves and fruit not its own" (80–82), where the contrast between the tree's *ingenium* and its foreign branches was clearly the point in calling it *ingens*. As was first noted by J. W. Mackail in 1912, *ingens* in Virgil frequently means "native" (so used, for instance, of the river Mincius at *Geo.* 3.14), and more often has the play (Virgil's own?) on the noun *ingenium*, which we can see in the grafted tree "with its own character," and which we will see elsewhere in the poem. The pun here seems to support, and extend, the fundamental purpose of the passage: the lemon tree is a "native product" of Media and has the same character (*ingenium*) as the inhabitants of the land (Medea), but with a difference we can observe in concluding. The tree's special character is to heal (and hence its name *medica malus*, which Virgil purposely leaves for the reader to supply), and it is in fact the East which produces this marvel, one beneficial and natural. The idea of the East as monstrous and unnatural has in fact been inverted, or even confounded. It is this inversion, so beautifully presented by the short excursus on the fruit of this tree, the *felix malum*, which serves as the transition to the *laudes Italiae*.

★

The *laudes Italiae* is concerned first with the nature of the land itself (136–54), then with the works of men (*adde tot egregias urbes operumque laborem* . . . , 155–76). The transition from the lemon of Media and Medea is effected by the suggestion of Aeetes' dragons' teeth and the armed men who sprung from the plowed earth to face Jason (140–42): no such monsters exist in Italy, which instead has grain, wine, olives, and herds (143–44). This is fine—as far as it goes. We observed above, however, the transformation worked by Virgil on the stock theme of the wicked witch of the East; the lemon (the *felix malum*, as he perversely calls it) by etymological association became in fact the antidote (*quo non praesentius ullum . . . auxilium*) to the poison of stepmothers and a general cure-all (*Media* at the beginning, *medicantur* at the end). General considerations of the themes of the poem, and of this passage specifically, will allow reference here to the fields of Pharsalus and Philippi, made fertile with Italian blood, and the prediction of a harvest to come from those fields, when the farmer with his plow and rakes will unearth javelins, helmets, and huge bones (1.489–97). Past (the myth of Medea, Jason, and eastern savagery), present (Virgil's contemporary Italy, *haec loca* 140, *hinc . . . hinc* 145–46), and future (*scilicet et tempus veniet*, 1.493) are united in such a way as to imply that the present must in some way reflect both past and future: a few lines later we find that this land did indeed bear warriors (*haec genus acre virum . . . extulit*, 167–69, with tribes and individuals mentioned by name).

So begins the Praise of Italy, with a confounding of its ostensibly naturalistic and pacific nature, parallel with, and working directly through, the confounding of the ostensibly fabulous and warlike character of the East. Whatever suggestions the next line may have (*sed gravidae fruges et Bacchi Massicus umor / implevere*, 143–44), I am not at all sure; but there is no doubt that the complement (*tenent oleae armentaque laeta*, 144—the unusual hiatus may strength the contrast) sets the tree of peace (so 2.425, *et placitam Paci nutritor olivam*) against the *armenta* (for the obvious verbal play, as well as the connection of Italy with *armenta*, compare the first sighting of Italy at *Aen.* 3.537–40, the four snow-white horses on the shore, greeted by Anchises with the words, *bellum, o terra hospita, portas: / bello armantur equi, bellum haec armenta minantur*: the association will be an important element of the next book of the *Georgics*). Immediately in fact (145–48) comes the *bellator equus*, and the *albi greges* and the bull, *maxima victima* of the Roman triumph (with a glance ahead to the important motif from Aratus that occurs at the very end of this book, the impious (bronze) age that first fed upon their bullocks, *caesis iuvencis*, 2.537). In the first thirteen lines there is little that does not in fact point directly to Italy as a land of war. The first half concludes with lies that come in quick succession:

149, *hic ver assiduum atque alienis mensibus aestas*: Servius, "verna temperies; nam ver adsiduum esse non potest." We do know about Italian winters, of course, and we hear about them elsewhere in the poem. The motif, however, is part of the Golden Age/Isles of the Blessed landscape.

150, *bis gravidae pecudes, bis pomis utilis arbos*: Servius, troubled with the twice-bearing flocks, finds justification in *Ecl.* 2.22 (*lac mihi non aestate novum, non frigore defit*), not realizing that Corydon's words ought to be writ in wind and water. Menelaus in his travels had heard of flocks in pastoral Libya (significantly enough for Virgil's Libya in Book 3) which bore thrice annually (*Od.* 4.86), and Hesiod's Isles of the Blessed are thrice fruitful (*WD* 172–73). In the real world lambing time is an annual occurrence and fruit trees bear just once. For Virgil's readers, knowing nothing of the supermarket's bounty, these were facts.

151, *at rabidae tigres absunt et saeva leonum / semina*: Quite true. In the first stage of Virgil's reversion to the Saturnian Age, however, herds will no longer fear great lions (*Ecl.* 4.22), which is why they are absent from Italy here.

152, *nec miseros fallunt aconita legentes*: Much ingenuity has been spent on this puzzle since Servius, who noted the falsehood ("mira arte usus est, ut excusaret rem, quam negare non potuit; nam aconita nascuntur in Italia") and explained it away by saying, "sed ea [aconita] non obesse dicit, quia sunt omnibus nota." Here is a further lie needing no further explanation, other than to point out that *fallunt* is due to *Eclogue* 4, the *fallax herba veneni* (of line 24) that disappears as the Saturnian Age returns.

153–54, *nec rapit immensos orbis per humum neque tanto / squameus in spiram tractu se colligit anguis*: Servius, again noting the falsehood and groping for a way out, says, "sunt quidem serpentes in

Italia, sed non tales, quales in Aegypto aut in Africa." Virgil again
tells a lie, relying again on the reader's awareness of *Eclogue* 4 (line
24, *occidet et serpens et fallax herba veneni*). When Jupiter put an end
to the Golden Age, he gave poison to snakes (*Geo.* 1.129).

This succession of lies, then, has the obvious purpose of establishing Italy as an ideal land, comparable to Saturn's Golden
Age or the Isles of the Blessed. To say that Italy enjoys eternal
spring and unceasing plenty, devoid of all evils (savage animals,
poisonous plants, snakes) is an acceptable way to make this analogy—poetic license, after all, and only the most literal-minded
dullard would insist on factual botany or natural history. But
what follows is what we might call a Lie of the Second Convo-
lution: the Italian character, as was suggested earlier, is nothing
if not well grounded in war.

Adde tot egregias urbes operumque laborem (155): the rest of the
laudes Italiae is devoted to the works of civilization—cities,
towns with steep fortifications, rivers flowing beneath ancient
walls. The mention of both Italian seas and lakes leads only to
the topic of human force brought against nature, Octavian's Lu-
crine harbor (*an memorem portus Lucrinoque addita claustra / atque
indignatum magnis stridoribus aequor*, 161–62, suggestive of the old
exemplar of Xerxes' hubris at least, as well as part of a familiar
contemporary pattern of sea vs. all-too-arrogant building. Sil-
ver, bronze, and gold flow in streams (165–66): there was no significant mining of precious metals in Italy, as Virgil knew perfectly well; and in any case such wealth is again a familiar mark
of modern degeneration. The passage ends (taking us back to
Aeetes' fields) with the list of Italy's *genus acre virum* (167–72),
first the most warlike of its peoples, then individuals, concluding with *Scipiades duros bello et te, maxime Caesar*, "you who
now, as conqueror in farthest Asia, turn the unwarlike Indian
from the Roman citadel" (*imbellem avertis Romanis arcibus In-
dum*). Again much ingenuity has been expended. Octavian had
been nowhere near India and showed no inclination for such a
trip, but enthusiasm can excuse the hyperbole. More serious is
the simple epithet *imbellem*, for which Servius collected several

glosses and an obvious question ("ceterum quid grande, si imbellem avertis?") and for which in this line the lexicon of Lewis
and Short offers a singular definition ("deprived of warlike spirit
by defeat"—actually a Servian explanation). At this point is
there any reason to exercise ingenuity to explain away or excuse
a falsehood? Octavian never considered India, and the Indian
never launched an expedition against the Capitol; *imbellem* is
perhaps the most accurate detail in these lines. The passage
ends, as it had begun, with a geographically comprehensive
view, the extremes of earth (*extremis . . . in oris*) contrasting
with the tempered center: in this the very essence of the Lie.
Salve, magna parens frugum, Saturnia tellus / magna virum. I suspect that part at least of Virgil's point in concluding this passage
with the claim of an Ascraean poem (*Ascraeumque cano Romana
per oppida carmen*, 176) was the Muse's pronouncement to Hesiod, "ἴδμεν ψεύδεα πολλὰ λέγειν ἐτύμοισιν ὁμοῖα, / ἴδμεν δ᾽,
εὖτ᾽ ἐθέλωμεν, ἀληθέα γηρύσασθαι" ("We know how to speak
many things like the truth, and we know, when we wish, how
to speak the truth," *Theog.* 27–28).

Moving on rather quickly to the next "digression," we can be
brief and general. The relevance of the Praise of Spring (315–45)
has been questioned. It seems, initially at least, organic in its
context: winter is no time for plowing, seeding, or planting out
(315–22): spring, or fall, are best, seasons between unalleviated
cold and heat (*cum rapidus Sol / nondum hiemem contingit equis, iam
praeterit aestas*). The rest of the panel, though, is concerned with
the traditional Marriage of Sky and Earth (323–35), the ἱερὸς
γάμος, a quasi-religious concept of great antiquity, and then
with Spring as the creation of life from earth (336–45), a quasi-
philosophical idea. Yet surely Virgil is not simply stressing
spring (or fall) as the best time for planting, or saying that spring
is indeed a pleasant time of the year, or speculating dreamily on
creation theologically or philosophically.

The didactic opening is worth attention: it is not simply
spring that Virgil has in mind, but spring *and* fall, and, what is
more, these seasons as opposed to winter (to which the first four
lines are devoted) and summer (in the last line, 322, of the intro-

ductory movement, again with winter). Likewise, the North and South winds in lines 333–34 again mean winter and summer, opposed to the spring Zephyr (330), and anticipating the south-east Eurus with its "wintry blasts" (339). Finally, the passage closes with a clear, almost prosaic statement of the peace (*quies*) of spring between cold and heat (*frigusque caloremque / inter*): that is, the *indulgentia caeli*.

The beginning of the passage and the conclusion clearly present a contradiction to what we have previously heard of spring and fall. Most notably, the great storm of the first book (311–50) assumes at the start that spring and fall are the most dangerous times of the year (*Quid tempestates autumni et sidera dicam . . . vel cum ruit imbriferum ver*, 1.311, 313), an assumption grounded in scientific concepts as we noted earlier. The most convenient characteristic of the four elements and their qualities is how easily and thoroughly they lend themselves, in various mixtures, to balances and imbalances, to be found in microcosm and macrocosm alike, in the universe, on earth, and in the human body. The zones of heaven and the corresponding zones of earth consist of extremes and temperate balance: the Eratosthenic world view at the beginning of the second half of the first book both anticipates and explains the great storm, because in the commonest view winter and summer are the seasons when there exists a steady domination of wet/cold or dry/hot, while spring and fall are times of transition and therefore of conflict. Medical theory, therefore, finds spring and fall as the most dangerous seasons (for instance, the later "Hippocratic" treatises *Regimen in Health* and *Nature of Man*, which develop systematically the correspondences between the four elements and their qualities, the four seasons, and the four humors of the body—along with sex, age, and much else).

All of this we have surveyed previously, but we can go further into Virgil's use of these basic assumptions in the digressions of Book II. In the discussion of the *laudes Italiae* above, one important fact was omitted. The geographical background, developed by the Greeks, established a balance between north and south (traditionally Scythia and Libya), east and west (less subject to neatness of ethnographical description), as we did note; and this idea of εὐκρασία was transferred as *temperies* to Italy and is its most prominent characteristic in the *laudes Italiae* of Varro, Dionysius, Strabo, and Pliny. What is therefore remarkable is that in Virgil's *laudes Italiae* there is *no suggestion whatsoever* of this idea, though it is always there, as a given, just offstage. The explanation is simple: the picture of Italy as a land of balance and peace (its Saturnian character) is being contravened, and hence Virgil will have no direct mention of that necessary given, *temperies*.

What was never suggested in the denial of Saturnian Italy is prominent in the Praise of Spring: here Virgil never for a moment obscures the scientific premises of his poem. The result is that the religious and philosophical ideas of the ἱερὸς γάμος and the Spring of the Creation are rendered as questionable as Saturnian Italy. The first lines suggest inevitably spring and fall as the times of storm in the real physical world; throughout, references to winter and summer, or winds, or the elemental qualities, inject reminders of reality into the other-worldly descriptions of idealized spring, culminating in the *quies* of the conclusion, supposed to exist between heat and cold. The dreamlike quality of the passage, beautiful and moving, undercut by flashes from the real world, is a construction very similar to a spring earlier in the poem. The great storm of Book I suddenly yields to a vision of peace:

> in primis venerare deos, atque annua magnae
> sacra refer Cereri laetis operatus in herbis
> extremae sub casum hiemis, iam vere sereno.
> tum pingues agni et tum mollissima vina,
> tum somni dulces densaeque in montibus umbrae.   (1.338–42)

(Above all worship the gods, and perform annual rites to great Ceres, sacrificing in the grass at winter's final end, now in calm spring. Then are lambs fat and then is wine most mature, then sleep is sweet and the shadows on the hills are full.)

We previously noted this stunning *non sequitur* and its importance in the context of Ceres. Again we may wonder whether the reference to Hesiod (line 341 = *WD* 585 τῆμος πιόταται τ' αἶγες καὶ οἶνος ἄριστος) is again intended to suggest the poet as the Muses' purveyor of many lies like the truth, as well as of the truth itself. We can recall, too, that one of the characteristics of Saturnian Italy, just a few lines previously, was in fact eternal spring, *ver assiduum* (2.149). Virgil knows that Spring, like the Golden Age, may represent a hope, an ideal abstraction, but that it can be no reality, that spring in the farmer's calendar and in the real world is a time of danger and of conflict more likely to result in destruction than in generation and growth.

The last digression, the Praise of Rustic Life (458–540), comes on with an abruptness that had been remarked upon in antiquity (Servius apologizes for it, "non est abruptus transitus ad laudem vitae rusticae, nam ad superiora pertinet," etc.). This third great lie is, or should be, patent; the first section (458–74) is a catalogue in which every item has received prior attention—refutation in advance. Again, as in the two previous digressions, reality is opposed to an idealized conception.

> O fortunatos nimium, sua si bona norint
> agricolas! quibus ipsa procul discordibus armis
> fundit humo facilem victum iustissima tellus.   (2.458–60)

> (O happy farmers—even too happy—if only they know their own blessings! for whom, far from armed discord, the just earth itself pours forth from the soil an easy sustenance.)

Servius' comment on line 460 indicates again an ancient controversy: " 'iustissima tellus' quomodo, si alibi dicit ⟨1.279⟩ 'Coeumque Iapetumque creat saevumque Typhoea'?" ("How can the earth be 'just,' if elsewhere Virgil writes 'it begat the monsters Coeus and Iapetus and savage Typhoeus'?"). (The question is then solved in a rather silly way.) *Procul discordibus armis*: the *duris agrestibus arma* have been prominent, both metaphorically and as a reality, throughout the poem. *Fundit humo facilem victum*: what of *labor*, especially of the never completed round of toil most recently and most vividly described in lines 397–419? As the section continues, such idealization (e.g., *secura quies, nescia fallere vita, otia,* 467–68) occurs in a succession of stock clichés: caves and grottoes, lowing cattle, sweet sleep under a tree, sturdy country folk, through whom last passed *Iustitia* on her way to exile (a theme from Aratus).

The surprising fact about the topic of the *laus vitae rusticae* is that, although we know it must have been a set piece amounting to a cliché when Virgil wrote, we know almost nothing of its actual history. Lucretius has a few stock lines (2.29–33), which contrast with urban wealth, but his soft grass, shady stream, and spring flowers do little more than give a sense of a prior cliché. Suddenly, in full bloom, comes Horace's *Epode* 2 (there is no saying whether before or after Virgil's lines), a lyrical catalogue of country pleasures. The trouble comes at the end of the piece, with the revelation that these are the pipe dreams of Alfius the money-lender, *iam iam futurus rusticus*, and therefore must sound hollow and tendentious, pretentious and ultimately satirical (the finally revealed narrator seems to have been a device of Archilochus). Another trouble must come from a consideration of the unusual style of the *Epode*: it is composed entirely in a succession of parallel clauses, a rambling sequence of parallel alternatives, giving a dreamlike quality to the parade of clichés. Thus, dramatic context and style must decree that this praise of country life not be taken as a sincere expression of longing for the Sabine scene. Another fully developed *laus vitae rusticae* is that in the *Culex* (58–97), long after Virgil (probably Tiberian in date), based on these lines, and obviously a satirical review of the topic in poetry.

There is no need for a discussion of parallels or poetic debts: a few simple facts are clear and allow a reasonable explanation. The few lines of Lucretius, *Epode* 2, and the *Culex* passage show obvious similarities with Virgil's *laus vitae rusticae*, to such an extent that it is reasonable to assume a topic with a set pattern of clichés which Horace drew upon for Alfius' monologue. Other instances of this assumed topic, however, are not to be found; subsequent poets generally steer clear of these clichés when writing of country life. (Tibullus is interesting here: there is a very different reality in his country in 2.1, for instance; and even the pure dream world of Messalla's visit to the country, 1.5.19–

36, makes no use of the "sweet sleep in the shade on the grassy river bank" motif.) Putting these two facts together does suggest that a popular cliché is to be assumed, perhaps not frequent in amateur poetry until after Virgil (hence the interest in it of the *Culex* poet). It must be significant that in Lucretius, Virgil, and Horace the country's simple pleasures are contrasted with the city's wealth and cares (so too, of course, in the *Culex*), suggesting a philosophical, moralizing context as the origin of the topic: this then explains why subsequent Augustan poetry, though so frequently dealing with the country in one way or another, does not often deal with it in such terms.

Here, then, is another topic of popular philosophizing, much like the topics of the two previous digressions. It is important to get an accurate sense of what Virgil is doing with these topics. Virgil is not anti-Italy, or against spring, or opposed to the simple pleasures of the country (or, for that matter, anti-Augustan just because he recognizes certain unforgettable facts of recent history). Take, for instance, one of Virgil's most beautiful and moving lines, *fluminaque antiquos subterlabentia muros* (2.157); moving in its evocation of the sad majesty of eternally ancient Italian towns and cities, so many even in Virgil's day like Ardea, *et nunc magnum manet Ardea nomen, / sed fortuna fuit* (*Aen.* 7.412–13); beautiful in some indescribable quality of the simple words. There were tears for Italian history too. Yet, at the same time, the line is set in a context that establishes a reality for Italy totally at odds with the immediate philosophical cliché of Saturnian Italy: it is a land of fortification walls and war, not a land of golden peace or eternal spring, as the cliché, or the lie, would have it.

Similarly, if we were to ask Horace whether the prospect of "wandering herds of lowing cattle in a recessed valley" (*Epode* 2.11–12) is good or bad, pleasant or annoying, we should reasonably expect only one answer, but we are not, thereby, permitted to assume that such attractions guarantee, in every case and every context, his whole-hearted, or single-minded, enthusiasm. Virgil and Horace both, I am sure, could visualize, with anticipation and delight equal to that of any modern springtime picnicker, that perfect meadow with grass so soft, smooth, and deep that a post-prandial snooze in the afternoon's warmth must surpass any posturepedic slumber. But they both also knew that no such spot exists, that the smoothest meadow on closer inspection turns out to be composed of annoyingly lumpy hummocks of prickly grass, that the droning song of the midday cicada is inevitably accompanied by the less than psithyrismatic drone of mosquito and horsefly.

This exposition of the rather obvious is necessary because it is all too often assumed that the moving and beautiful must guarantee ideal virtue, or that a love of the country must be as blind as traditional romantic love. It is possible for Virgil, the most deeply Italian of ancient poets, to recognize the geographers' lie of temperate Italy, or of Saturnian Italy, to interrupt the lie by continual suggestions of war, and at the same time to display his love not only for the Clitumnus, but for the lie itself. The beauty of the marriage of sky and earth, or of creation's Spring, is not diminished by the realization that the reality of the physical world precludes any calm between cold and heat (a peace between warring elements). The opposition between city and country, between harrassed luxury and rustic simplicity, is a trite untruth worthy of an Alfius or a Marie Antoinette in her dairy, but it is the triteness of the cliché that needed to be exposed, not the country itself.

The grand conclusion of the second book (to which we now return) ends with a series of further lies, a combination of themes from the previous digressions associated with praise of rusticity. Twenty lines (475–94), however, interrupt the *laus vitae rusticae*—the well-known contrast between scientific understanding (475–82 and 490–92) and what I would regard as imaginative understanding (or pastoral, 483–89 and 493–94). "He who knows the country gods" is then contrasted with the urban type, and the topic of the city's turbulence (495–99) opposed to the country's self-sufficiency (500–502) is neatly resumed. Virgil's method here is very similar to Horace's: the comforting succession of familiar clichés lulls us into acceptance: yes, we agree, your average country type just gathers the fruits which the branches bear, which the willing country offers of its own volition, not the least upset by iron law, or insane forum, or government bureaucracy. It is easy to pass right on, forgetting that most of the book has been spent emphasizing the struggle of wrenching a subsistence from a most uncooperative nature, and that in fact the repetitious words here (*volentia rura / sponte sua*, 500–501) not only emphasize the contradiction, but must serve as well as a reminder of the technical (Theophrastean) division of trees into the cultivated and the wild (*sua sponte* as the term of natural reproduction, 2.11 *nullis hominum cogentibus*—note the participle—and 47, where *sponte sua* are the first words of the section). No subtlety is needed to see that there is a conflict here between the didactic message of the book and this philosophical topic of country vs. city.

Following the list of urban horrors (greed and avarice, civil war and sacrilege, political ambition, fratricide and exile, 503–12), the country remains the focus until the end. Again, words and phrases so prominent previously suggest contradictions here. *Hic anni labor* (514): the repetition of the word in lines 397–419 is still ringing in our ears. *Nec requies* (516): while *labor actus in orbem* (401) allowed the farmer no rest throughout the year, here it is the earth itself that exuberantly produces all year long. *Glande sues laeti redeunt, dant arbuta silvae* (520): the acorn again, with its previous associations guaranteed by the mention of the *Cerealis mergite culmi* just above (517), and the arbute intrude a note of reality—the fruit of spontaneous production is fit only for fodder. And so on, with contradictions obvious in every line, until Bacchus (*Lenaee*, 529) and his festival.

The book closes with the sudden juxtaposition of this idyllic picture of country life (*hanc vitam*, 532) to two earlier stages, one Italian and historical, the other mythological and general: both again are conceptions easy, ready, and satisfying from a distance. First come the old Sabines, Remus and his brother, Etruria, and finally Rome made more splendid by such a life. For the Romans of Virgil's time, the *veteres Sabini* are much like the American frontiersmen or mountain men, and their descendants like the New Yorker's conception of the contemporary Vermont farmer: the historical figure exists only in romance, and the contemporary only in fancy. (For just one example, see Horace's *pudica mulier . . . Sabina qualis aut perusta solibus / pernicis uxor Apuli* of Alfius' fancy, *Epode* 2.39–42.) Remus and his unnamed brother must suggest the ultimate fratricide attending Rome's foundation: there was no escaping the association when, as Suetonius reports, the honorific *Romulus* was suggested in 27 B.C. for Octavian (*Augustus* was the far safer alternative), and no mention of the twins in Augustan verse is without suggestion of civil war. *Fortis Etruria* may include a nod to Maecenas (addressed, of course, at the beginning of the book, lines 39–41). Rome itself concludes this historical survey, *scilicet et rerum facta est pulcherrima Roma / septemque una sibi muro circumdedit arces* (534–35, to be repeated by Anchises, *Aen.* 6.783): again the wall, not only the token of war, but the cause of the original fratricide (and so associated in Anchises' mind—his repetition of the line follows his demonstration of *Mavortius Romulus*, by whose auspices, he notes, Rome will reach its peak of power, 778–83: in these lines the associations of war with Rome's founding and growth are complex). A tone of gentle irony may be introduced by *scilicet*, but an irony of fact is unmistakable.

The second point of reference is the Golden/Saturnian Age (so conflated by Virgil in his reference to *aureus Saturnus*, 538). "The sceptre of the Dictaean king" returns us to the world view of the first book, to the conception of human history in its broadest terms: the human condition that has been the subject of the book (*labor* and all its associations and implications) is now seen as the result of that historical moment described earlier in the first book (121–59), Jupiter's intervention. Further reference to Aratus (the "impious race that fed upon its slaughtered bullocks" marks the final stage in Aratus' metallic ages, *Phaen.* 132—cf. Cicero, *ND* 2.159) emphasizes the process of degeneration (as in the first book), rather than the fact. This return to a chronological, or causal, view of man's history must, however, affect what Virgil has just been saying about the *vita rustica* (if there were any question still). The farmer's carefree life of blessed abundance (so far removed from the strife and even bloodshed of the city) is subsequent to that similar existence of the old Sabines, Etruria, and Rome at its founding; and both this present and the Italian past are of course subsequent to golden Saturn's time; the result is to put this present (*hanc vitam* thrice repeated, 532, 533, 538) at a double remove from a Hesiodic-Aratean golden age, and as well to underscore the irony in the lines on the Italian past by means of the inescapable observation that it too is post-Saturnian, that the old Sabines, Romulus and Remus, Etruria and Rome are descendants of that *impia gens* which first fed upon their slaughtered bullocks, who heard the war trumpets and who forged swords.

Vituperation and Fact

The three digressions in the second book have always been recognized as laudations (*laudationes*, or simply, as Servius generally refers to them, *laus* or *laudes*), a form of oratory or rhetorical exercise. That Virgil was at the same time practicing the corresponding rhetorical category, the *vituperatio*, is an observation that appears to have been neglected since Servius. Here is another instance of the value of the ancient commentaries—awareness of technical terms and technical categories which we, in spite of scholarly reconstructions, sometimes do not recognize, for one reason or another. The *laudatio funebris*, though prominent in our view because of its extant examples and its particular importance in Roman culture (and biography), gives a wrong impression of the extent of meaning the term *laudatio* had in rhetorical theorizing: it was continually argued, for instance, whether the *laudatio* was simply a necessary component of many sorts of speeches (especially of epideictic) or whether it composed a separate genre itself. The place and nature of the *laudatio* need not concern us; we need only recognize the fact that there were two sides to this rhetorical coin, that with the *laudatio* always comes its reverse, the *vituperatio*. Cicero recognized their historical place in the *Brutus* (*quod idem fecisse Gorgiam, cum singularum rerum laudes vituperationesque conscripsisset, quod iudicaret*

hoc oratoris esse maxime proprium, rem augere posse laudando vitu-
perandoque rursus affligere, 12.47); likewise Quintilian (*Isocrates in*
omni genere inesse laudem ac vituperationem existimavit, 3.4.11),
who in this passage is discussing the nature of this entity (*lau-*
dandi ac vituperandi officium, 3.4.3; *nam et laudes ac vituperationes*
scribebantur, 3.4.5; *praeterita laudamus aut vituperamus,* 3.4.7; *est*
igitur, ut dixi, unum genus, quo laus ac vituperatio continetur, sed est
appellatum a parte meliore laudativum, 3.4.12). Seneca classes *ob-*
iurgationes et laudationes alongside *consolationes, dissuasiones,* and
adhortationes (*Ep. Mor.* 94.39), using a term equivalent to *vitu-*
peratio that is also used by Cicero (see the *Index . . . Rhetorica* of
Abbott, Oldfather, and Canter), though *vituperatio* is used most
frequently by Cicero (especially in the *de inv.*—see e.g., *laus aut*
vituperatio as constituting the *demonstrativum genus,* 1.5.7,
2.4.12) and is the term used in the *ad Herrenium* (see the discussion in 3.6–8, beginning *Nunc ad demonstrativum genus causae*
transeamus. Quoniam haec causa dividitur in laudem et vituperati-
onem, quibus ex rebus laudem constituerimus, ex contrariis rebus erit
vituperatio conparata, etc.). Even when *vituperatio* is not strictly a
rhetorical term, it nevertheless is often found in the company of
laus or *laudatio.* (A glance at representative indices will make this
clear enough: Livy, for instance, uses a formation of this word
only once, but in the phrase *laudarent vituperentne,* 27.44.2.)

We may summarize the argument thus far and indicate where
it will take us. In the three digressions of the second book Virgil
presents abstractions of a popular sort, all of which are related
at least in part to the conception of the Saturnian or Golden Age
and are thus appealing constructions of an ideal. Virgil also indicates the conflict of these ideal abstractions and the reality of
the present, in such a way that the abstractions can be seen as lies
no less than the productions of the art of grafting at the beginning of the book. The digressions, as set pieces, are presented as
laudationes (*laudibus Italiae,* 138; *res antiquae laudis et artis,* 174),
and are so taken by Servius and modern commentators. The
rhetorical laudation is not an entity in itself, but is the positive
side to which the negative *vituperatio* is complementary, and to

refer in any rhetorical context to the one is to suggest the other. (Servius, for instance, on 2.461, "ut etiam in laude fecit Italiae, non solum vitam laudat rusticam, sed etiam contrariam, id est urbanam, vituperat.")

I do not suggest that every laudation has a vituperation lurking nearby, nor will I take as compelling evidence the fact that Servius records an ancient view that (as we will see) another *vituperatio* is to be found at the conclusion of the book. We will now take a look at the rest of the book, at the didactic material rather than the digressions, at the reality rather than the ideal and abstract, at what may be the subject of vituperation rather than laudation. Our survey will confirm that the notices in Servius are an accurate assessment.

The *laudes Italiae* had been occasioned by the geographical commonplace that *nec vero terrae ferre omnes omnia possunt* (2.109). Virgil returns to his subject with a section on the character of fields (*Nunc locus arvorum ingeniis . . .* , 177–225), then with practical instruction on how to recognize their characters (*Nunc quo quamque modo possis cognoscere dicam*, 226–58). The *ingenia* are specified as *quae robora cuique, / quis color et quae sit rebus natura ferendis* (177–78). The etymology of *natura* is indicated by *rebus ferendis*—the importance of this concept should not be overlooked in what follows: again, *ingenium* is a quality fixed and unalterable, an essence common to environment and the products of that environment. The section is in fact presented in terms of four products, first the olive (179–83), then the vine (184–94), then herds and flocks (195–202), then grain (203–11)—the subjects of the second, third, and first books of the poem. The section is completed with descriptions of fields good for nothing (except for snakes, hardly good even for bees, 212–16) and good for all four previously mentioned products (217–25).

We need concern ourselves here only with the first two characters, those productive of olive and vine, the subjects of this book (and hence, perhaps, first on the list). The contrast be-

tween the two couldn't be more explicit. The olive is produced
on poor land:

> difficiles primum terrae collesque maligni,
> tenuis ubi argilla et dumosis calculus arvis,
> Palladia gaudent silva vivacis olivae:
> indicio est tractu surgens oleaster eodem
> plurimus et strati bacis silvestribus agri. (179–83)

(First, severe land and sullen hills, where there is thin clay and gravel
in thickety fields, rejoice in Pallas' grove of the long-lived olive. You
can tell by the many oleasters growing in that plot, by the fields covered with wild berries.)

Hard and begrudging is the kindest way to define its character
in the first of these lines: nasty and of evil disposition would be
another. Servius is inclined to kindness, glossing *difficiles* with
"paene steriles, parum creantes" and *maligni* with "infecundi." It
is also necessary for the olive that the land be dry (an important
contrast with vine regions—see below): Servius, at least, glosses
tenuis ubi argilla, rather inappropriately lexicographically but
most aptly for this context, with "sine umore." Gravel, of
course, assures rapid drainage. Clay and gravel in thickety
fields, but our reaction is the same: this is not the sort of land one
would farm by choice. A sign of such a field is the oleaster (wild
olive) and ground strewn with "wild berries." We noted earlier
that five of the six appearances of the adjective *silvester* in the
Georgics occur in this book, where (with one exception) it is
used to denote wild trees as opposed to cultivated. Furthermore, the cultivated olive, from the first lines of the book, is
represented by Virgil as a tree half wild, half domesticated: thus,
as we saw, the vine (*Bacche*), the *silvestria virgulta*, and the slow-
growing olive as the subjects of the book (2–3).

The vine, in sharp contrast, is produced on rich, wet lands (*at
quae pinguis humus dulcique uligine laeta*, 184), a statement that
may come as something of a surprise to oenologists. *Uligo* de-
notes a soil with permanent moisture bordering on marshiness
(Servius comments "uligo propria est naturalis terrae umor, ex

ea numquam recedens . . . uliginosus ergo ager est semper uvi-
dus"), whereas vines require good drainage and dry soil as the
grapes ripen. (Columella, when stressing that so varied are
grapes that some variety will be found to grow anywhere, says
that vines will grow even in regions *siccaque et uliginosa*, 3.1.3,
but *optimum est solum nec siccum nec uliginosum, modice tamen ros-
cidum*, 3.1.8.) Fertility, as in rich valley lands, is also a requisite
for Virgil (*quique frequens herbis et fertilis ubere campus*, 185),
though not for vine-growers (Pliny, for instance, noted, *nocet
plerumque vitibus atque oleis et nimia fertilitas, NH* 17.223). Here
again Virgil can be convicted of falsehood, and here again we
can be sure that he intended to be: the one-sided emphasis on
richness and wetness clashes with the conditions assumed in his
subsequent instructions, is obviously intended to contrast with
the requirements of the olive just before, and has a clear purpose. The section concludes:

> hic [campus] tibi praevalidas olim multoque fluentis
> sufficiet Baccho vitis, hic fertilis uvae,
> hic laticis, qualem pateris libamus et auro,
> inflavit cum pinguis ebur Tyrrhenus ad aras,
> lancibus et pandis fumantia reddimus exta.   (190–94)

> (This (field) will at some time provide very strong vines, and flowing
> with much wine, this will be fertile for the grape, fertile for its juice,
> such as we pour in libation from golden vessels when the fat Etruscan
> blows his ivory flute at the altars, and when we offer the steaming
> entrails on wide platters.)

The land and what grows upon it are identical in character: rich
and wet land, abundant wine, men of similar character. *Pinguis*
(*Tyrrhenus*) at the end of the section is identical with the *pinguis*
(*humus*) at the beginning (Etruscans were proverbial for this
quality—compare Catullus' *aut pinguis Umber aut obesus Etruscus*,
39.11). The picture of sacrifice, especially with its details of gold
and ivory, is part of a context Virgil will develop—wine and
civilization, with its wealth and strife: and animal sacrifice does
appear to be a recurrent motif in this book, from the bull, *max-*

ima victima of the military triumph in the *laudes Italiae*, to the Aratean *caesis iuvencis* of the *impia gens* at the very end.

In the next section (how to recognize each sort of land, 226–58) we may note in passing only one detail. After dense and thin soils (227–37) and salty and bitter (238–47), Virgil discusses rich (*pinguis*, 248–50) and wet (*umida*, 251–53). This is what the vine required (*pinguis*, as we just observed, was used twice there, 184 and 193, of the land and its inhabitants), and what the grass requires as well:

> at quae pinguis humus dulcique uligine laeta,
> quique frequens herbis et fertilis ubere campus
>
> . . . .
>
> hic tibi praevalidas olim multoque fluentis
> sufficiet Baccho vitis . . .   (184–85, 190–91)

(But that soil which is rich and productive with sweet moisture, and that field abundant in grass and fertile with lushness . . . this (field) will at some time provide very strong vines, and flowing with much wine . . .)

Here rich and wet lands are described in identical terms—naturally enough—but with an important addition:

> umida maiores herbas alit, ipsaque iusto
> laetior. a, nimium ne sit mihi fertilis illa,
> nec se praevalidam primis ostendat aristis!   (251–53)

(A moist land will produce excessive weeds, itself more fertile than is proper. Ah, may that field of mine not be too fertile, nor may it show itself too strong when the ears of grain begin to form.)

Herbae is again the identifying characteristic of wet land, more productive than is just. The affective *a!* (only here and at 4.526, *a miseram Eurydicen!*—never in the *Aeneid*, but nine times in the *Eclogues*, with neoteric propriety) calls attention to Virgil's wish that too fertile a land not be his (*praevalidas* occurs in all of Virgil only in these two passages). Servius aptly recalls 1.112, where, toward the end of the first grand statement of the opposition of fire and water, Virgil only mentions the practice of the farmer who controls the luxuriance of first growth (*luxuriem segetum te-*

nera depascit in herba); and *primis aristis* inevitably suggests the elaborate etymology of *arista* at the beginning of the first book, an important part of the same complex of wet and dry. The associations of rich, wet land suggest an excessive luxuriance, beyond what is proper.

Virgil turns next to planting out the vines (259–87): the focus for the rest of the book will be predominantly on the vine. The best soil is friable, achieved by allowing heat (*excoquere*, 260) and drying cold (*venti . . . gelidaeque pruinae*, 263) to work on fields plowed well in advance. Vines in the nursery are often marked so that they can be planted out facing the same direction: again, the reason for this is given in terms of heat (*calores austrinos*, 270–71) and cold (*axi*, 271)—*adeo in teneris consuescere multum est* (272). Young vines are delicate and must be grown with proper attention to a balance of conditions.

In rich soil vines may be planted more closely together (*in denso non segnior ubere Bacchus*, 275), but on hills they should be planted in the *quincunx* (spaced like the pattern of the five dots on dice), like a legion (*ut saepe ingenti bello cum longa cohortis / explicuit legio . . . / . . . necdum horrida miscent / proelia, sed dubius mediis Mars errat in armis*, 279–83). This long epic simile is the first of the outright associations of wine and war in this book: the young vines are set out like troops *before* the battle has begun.

How deep to plant? Virgil's answer would be of singularly little help to someone who really wanted to know: in one line he advises planting the vine rather shallow, but a big tree needs a bigger hole, like the oak that stretches its roots to Tartarus (eight lines, 290–97). In the *Aeneid* the oak will return in a simile (291–92 = *Aen.* 4.445–46, where Aeneas is unmoved by Dido's tears, *fletibus*, as the tree is unmoved by the winds' *flatibus*): this is *not*, however, another instance of a literary abstraction become real, since the deep-rooted oak does not seem to have been a simile before Virgil, and we must resist the urge to think of it as an image here. The contrast is between vine and oak. The young vines are shallowly rooted and (as we have just read) delicate, needing a balance between extremes. The oak is ageless, unmoved by storms (*ergo non hiemes illam, non flabra neque imbres / convellunt*, 293–94), an example of strength and endurance; in its only other appearance in the poem, the *aesculus* is the tree of Jupiter, one of the wild trees, *nemorum . . . maxima* (2.15–16).

The next section begins with four miscellaneous prohibitions about viticulture, followed abruptly by a fifth about the olive: don't graft a cultivated variety of olive onto a stock of wild olive (*neve oleae silvestris insere truncos*, 302). *Silvestris* provides immediate indication of the context for what follows: cultivated versus wild. The extraordinary vividness and length of what follows (the fire in the olive plantation, 303–14) is of a piece with the preceding miniature of the oak. Both oak and olive are subject to violent storms (the fire is described at first with verbal suggestions of a storm; a real wind storm, *tempestas* and *ventus*, arises at the end, 310–11), and are clearly intended to be contrasting or complementary *exempla*. The oak endures the storms of cold and wet (*hiemes . . . flabra . . . imbres*), the olive is destroyed by the storm of fire. Once we see what the olive actually is, the pattern is clear and consistent. The olive belongs partly to man, partly to the wild: what is destroyed here is man's part (the exemplum indicated by *num*, 303—follows from the prohibition about grafting), but the wild remains when growth returns from the roots (*infelix superat foliis oleaster amaris*, 314). This is the same *oleaster* that indicated, with its wild berries (*bacis silvestribus*, 183), land suited for the long-lived olive (*silva vivacis olivae*, 181). Thus, both oak and olive are *exempla* of the endurance and the resistance of the wild to natural catastrophe; in the case of the olive, however, Virgil's themes and motifs become more complex, for that ultimate destructive force, fire, has no effect on the *wild* olive, though it destroys the *cultivated* olive utterly.

These lines are among the finest in the poem, Horatian in size, and with that expansiveness and suggestiveness of theme and motif similar to a Horatian ode. The great storm of the first book is inevitably brought to mind, which destroyed all the results of the farmer's efforts (*et pluvia ingenti sata laeta boumque labores / diluit*, 1.325–26), and with it of course the parallel storm of civil war at the end of the book. Here, where cultivated and wild have been major themes throughout, the motif of the storm occurs again, though in miniature, acting now upon the oak and the olive/oleaster. The extraordinary power of these lines is due not to what is said (there is no message), but to what is suggested. The fire "dominates as conqueror" (*inde secutus / per ramos victor per alta cacumina regnat*, 306–7), suggesting again, momentarily, war, and through this thematic expansion connecting with other passages of storm and war. Connections are made, but no conclusions are to be drawn.

The great storm of the first book ended suddenly with the admonitions to observe the heavens and especially to revere the gods (happy advice indeed, after the total devastation we had just witnessed): then, unexpectedly, the spring festival of Ceres, *iam vere sereno*, when lambs are fattest and wine sweetest, sleep too, and the shadows heavy on the mountains. It is no coincidence that the fire that reduces the olive to its wild stock gives way to the Praise of Spring, *tanta quies . . . frigusque caloremque inter*, the *indulgentia caeli*, the second great lie of the book. We return then to further practical instruction on the growing of vines, the cultivated tree par excellence, not forgetting that among the last instructions we had was to allow the cold and the heat to work on the plowed fields, and to position the young vines carefully in respect to hot south winds and cold north winds.

Now, continuing, the emphasis is on attaining a similar balance of elements—the rain and the drying (*aestifer*) Dog Star (346–53)—until the vines begin to climb and can scorn the winds (*contemnere ventos*, 360). Likewise, there is now a suggestion of violence in Virgil's language, as force is brought to bear to create the environment necessary for the young vines (*diducere terram; presso exercere solum sub vomere*—*exercere* has had, and will shortly have again, a military connotation; *flectere luctantis iuvencos*); and it may be to the point (as we will see) that it is on the strength of uncultivated plants that the vines rely in order to overcome the elements and rise through the stories of the elms (*viribus eniti quarum et contemnere ventos*).

The theme continues in the next section (*parcendum teneris*, 363). In lines 365–66 a musical phrase recurs, suggesting toil:

ipsa acie nondum falcis temptanda, sed uncis
carpendae manibus frondes interque legendae.   (365–66)

(The young vine itself must not yet be assailed with the blade of the sickle, but the leaves must be plucked by your clawed hands and selectively gathered.)

We have noted previously the occurrence of three gerundives in two lines and shortly will sum up the effect produced (discussing lines 399–400, 418–19). Again this reminder of effort becomes a series of commands to use violence after the vines have matured, commands that include the military metaphor *exercere imperia* (*tum stringe comas, tum bracchia tonde, / . . . tum denique dura / exerce imperia et ramos compesce fluentis*, 368–70).

The next section (371–96) contains familiar themes in a recognizable sequence. Briefly, farm animals must be kept away from the vines, for they do more harm than cold or heat (note the repeated insistence on these extremes, *indignas hiemes solemque potentem*, 373, and *frigora . . . / . . . aestas*, 376–77—a line each for cold and heat). This leads to the aetiology of the goat as sacrifice to Bacchus and the description of his festival), a reminder of the Ceres festival in the first book (1.338–50) and an anticipation of the *dies festos* celebrated by the blithely happy rustic, *fususque per herbam*, at the end of this book (2.527–31)— both of which scenes are intended to appear as fanciful dream worlds at odds with reality. Bacchus' festival ends with the sacrifice of the billy goat at the altar and the feast (*pinguiaque in veribus torrebimus exta colurnis*, 396). Sacrifice is a recurrent motif in this book, as we noted in discussing another theme at the end of the book, the Aratean bronze race who first ate meat (*impia . . . caesis gens est epulata iuvencis*, 537): this is the *honorem* (end of line 393) we pay to Bacchus, *caput honestum* (end of line 392)—a verbal gloss containing, it seems to me, no little irony. This whole, rather long, section establishes these and one or two other themes to be played upon shortly.

We now come to one of the most important passages in the book, which deserves to be quoted in full:

Est etiam ille labor curandis vitibus alter,
cui numquam exhausti satis est: namque omne quotannis
terque quaterque solum scindendum glaebaque versis
aeternum frangenda bidentibus, omne levandum   (400)
fronde nemus. redit agricolis labor actus in orbem,
atque in se sua per vestigia volvitur annus.
ac iam olim, seras posuit cum vinea frondes
frigidus et silvis Aquilo decussit honorem,
iam tum acer curas venientem extendit in annum   (405)
rusticus, et curvo Saturni dente relictam
persequitur vitem attondens fingitque putando.
primus humum fodito, primus devecta cremato
sarmenta, et vallos primus sub tecta referto;
postremus metito. bis vitibus ingruit umbra,   (410)
bis segetem densis obducunt sentibus herbae;
durus uterque labor: laudato ingentia rura,
exiguum colito. nec non etiam aspera rusci
vimina per silvam et ripis fluvialis harundo
caeditur, incultique exercet cura salicti.   (415)
iam vinctae vites, iam falcem arbusta reponunt,
iam canit effectos extremus vinitor antes:
sollicitanda tamen tellus pulvisque movendus,
et iam maturis metuendus Iuppiter uvis.

(There is that other work involved in the care of vines, which is never sufficiently exhausted: three and four times every year the earth must be plowed, the clods broken with the backs of mattocks, the vineyard stripped of its leaves. The round of work returns driven back upon the farmers, and the year revolves upon itself in its own tracks. And now at length, when the vineyard has dropped its leaves and the cold north wind has struck the beauty of foliage from the woods, then the ambitious rustic extends his efforts to the coming year and pursues the abandoned vine with Saturn's curved tooth and, shearing it, shapes it by pruning. Be the first to dig the earth, the first to cart away and burn the prunings, the first to take in your supports for the winter; but be the last to harvest. Twice will the shade fall upon the grapes, twice will the weeds smother the crop with thick brambles: to fight each is hard work. Praise the large estate, but work a small farm. Then, too, rough withes of broom and reeds are cut by the stream's bank, and attention is given to the uncultivated willow. And finally the vines have been tied up, finally the vineyard is finished with the pruning hook, finally the worker sings at last over the finished rows: nevertheless, you must turn the earth again and must stir up the dust—and then your ripened grapes must fear Jupiter.)

(Following this section there are the few lines on the olive, which by contrast requires little attention (420–25); then, after a mention of fruit trees, comes an extended section on the uses of uncultivated trees (426–57), which is followed by the *laus vitae rusticae*, to end the book.)

What ought to be immediately striking is that the passage begins and ends with what we have seen as a musical motif—the recall of theme through an unmistakable pattern of sound: three gerundives in two lines occur elsewhere three times only (and never in the *Eclogues* or *Aeneid*), always to emphasize the *labor* that began with Jupiter's reign. First, as we saw, they appeared in the lines on the construction of the threshing floor (*area cum primis ingenti aequanda cylindro / et vertenda manu et creta solidanda tenaci*, 1.178–79; the sentence continues *ne subeant herbae neu pulvere victa fatiscat / tum variae inludant pestes*, resuming another musical and thereby thematic motif, *tum variae venere artes*, 1.145). They recur early in this book, where Virgil, rather extraordinarily, says that effort must be expended on all (even "uncultivated") trees (*scilicet omnibus est labor impendendus, et omnes / cogendae in sulcum ac multa mercede domandae*, 61–62). We noted just above the third appearance (*ipsa acie nondum falcis temptanda, sed uncis / carpendae manibus frondes interque legendae*, 365–66), where it added its clear suggestion of the degree of toil required by the young vines—each leaf must be picked off laboriously with hands that have become misshapen, *uncis manibus*. Here, then, on *ille labor alter, cui numquam exhausti satis est*, the motif supports the theme at the beginning and end.

The resounding emphasis on the total domination of *labor* (repeated three times in these lines) ought to be unmistakable: *every* year *all* the earth must be hewn *three* and *four* times, the clods broken *eternally*, the *whole* grove defoliated. The labor returns driven *in a circle*, the year turns *upon itself in its own tracks*. *Now finally*, when the cold season comes, the "bitter" (*acer*, with several connotations) farmer renews his worries for the *coming year* and prunes and shapes his vines. Be ye the first to dig, to burn the pruned branches, to bring in the props, but the last to harvest (a series of archaic imperatives, as if issued by Cato). *Twice* comes shade, *twice* the weeds: *each* task (defoliating and hoeing) is hard. Praise a large farm, work a small one (an old maxim, again with archaic imperatives). Even uncultivated growth requires attention and effort (for binding material and wickerwork). *Now* the vines have been tied up, *now* the last row finished: *nevertheless* the earth must be bothered, the dust stirred up, and Jupiter must *now* be feared.

I cannot see how there can be the slightest joy in this picture of the round of work required for the vine: even the vine-dresser's song among the last rows doesn't last for long. In this real world of the *acer rusticus* there is no time whatsoever for sweet sleep in soft grass: time here passes with an insistent beat, marked by tasks repeated twice or three and four times within the year, by annual cycles that have no break in the closed circle. *Hiems ignava colono* (1.299)—for the grower of grain, perhaps, but not for the keeper of a vineyard. Servius again hears Virgil's tone and sees a point that has been missed since: (on 415, *incultique exercet cura saliciti*), "quasi cum indignatione ait, causa vitium cura nos etiam sponte nascentium rerum fatigat" ("he says, as if with indignation, that for the sake of vines the care of even those things which grow voluntarily wearies us"). We have noted above that the uncultivated (the trees that grow *sua sponte*) has played a repeated part in these instructions on viticulture, being forced to contribute: the vine-grower must work even at that which requires no work. The epithet *inculti (salicti)* occurs just below in an identical function (*inculta aviaria*, 430), and (for what this fact may be worth) nowhere else in the *Georgics*; it had occurred to Virgil previously just once, in a notable context, in the Fourth Eclogue, at the birth of the child, *incultisque rubens pendebit sentibus uva* (*Ecl.* 4.29). The point is important; the olive of the next section requires no cultivation, *Contra non ulla est oleis cultura* (420): *non ulla* is emphatic for *nulla (cultura)*, and the phrase might be rewritten *incultae oleae*. In any case, should we miss the irony in the *cura inculti*, the next 35 lines will be concerned with "sponte nascentes res."

We ought now to be in a position to appreciate an extraordinary perception by Servius, one promised earlier: extraordinary, because it is so simple and obvious. Servius introduces this passage (on 397) thus: "iam paulatim tendit ad vitium vituperationem, dicens et infinitum esse earum laborem, ut 'cui numquam exhausti satis est,' et incertum fructum, ut ⟨419⟩ 'et iam maturis metuendus Iuppiter uvis,' et ipsum etiam fructum perniciosum, ut ⟨455⟩ 'Bacchus et ad culpam causas dedit' " ("Now gradually he turns to the vituperation of vines, saying that the labor involved is unending, as 'which is never sufficiently exhausted,' and that their fruit is uncertain, as [419] 'and then your ripened grapes must fear Jupiter,' and that even the fruit itself is harmful, as [455] 'Bacchus has even provided reasons for wrong' "). Someone, at some time, observed that not only are *laudes* an important feature of the book, but so too is their rhetorical counterpart, the *vituperatio*. So too at the end of the section, or rather at the beginning of the Praise of Country Life, Servius sees a smooth transition in these rhetorical terms (on 458): "non est abruptus transitus ad laudem vitae rusticae, nam ad superiora pertinet. post vituperationem enim vini ista quasi consolatio est, per quam ostenditur, quantas voluptates rusticis natura praestiterit" ("The transition to the Praise of Country Life is not abrupt, because it relates to what has preceded. For after the vituperation of wine there is a sort of consolation, through which it is shown how great are the delights which nature has bestowed on countrymen"). The vine is blamed for requiring such labor, for its fruit that may so easily be destroyed by storm, and because wine may be an evil. Servius comments further on this second point (on line 408): "hoc est, ad laborem primum te esse convenit, ultimum ad fructus legendos: vinum enim factum de uvis immaturis cito acescit. et hoc loco inest vitium vituperatio, quarum fructus aut immaturi collecti depereunt, aut si eorum fuerit expectata maturitas, ni-

hilo minus pereunt; nam dicturus est (419) 'et iam maturis metuendus Iuppiter uvis' " ("That is, you must be the first where
work is concerned, but the last when gathering the fruits: for
wine made from unripe grapes quickly turns sour. Even in this
passage there is a vituperation of vines: either their fruits are
wasted, if harvested too early, or, if you wait for their maturity,
they are lost nonetheless: for he is about to say [419] 'and then
your ripened grapes must fear Jupiter' "). To this we need only
add reminders not just of the great storm of the first book, but
of the two exemplary storms just preceding, which the oak and
oleaster survive and in which the cultivated (grafted) olive per-
ishes. At every stage, from the *pestes* that attack the threshing
floor to the rain and hail that destroy the ripened fields, man's
efforts are subject to destruction: Jupiter, to whom we owe the
very existence of *labor*, is as well the power that destroys the
products of that labor. *Ipse pater media nimborum in nocte corusca /
fulmina molitur dextra* (1.328–29, with the following lines): *et iam
maturis metuendus Iuppiter uvis* (2.419).

It is often assumed that Jupiter's purpose in causing the discovery of the arts of life was beneficent (even though Virgil does
not say so), an assumption based somehow on a sanguine reading of such passages as 1.121–23: *pater ipse colendi / haud facilem
esse viam voluit, primusque per artem / movit agros curis acuens mortalia corda*: surely, though, he would not have extended such be-
neficence to the destruction of man's efforts? I think Virgil has
made abundantly clear that there is nothing about Jupiter's *labor*,
from its inception, through its persistent inevitability, to its du-
bious and even destructive end, in which the wearied mortal can
find consolation or hope.

Virgil's purpose, though, is not theological: his concern is
with the vine, the olive, and other trees, as he announced at the
beginning of the book clearly enough that we ought to believe
him. So he continues: *Contra non ulla est oleis cultura* (420), with
emphasis on *contra*. No care is required for the olive really, just
an annual plowing, for the earth itself provides all it needs: *hoc
pinguem et placitam Paci nutritor olivam* (425). The contrast is clear
enough, if we recall the contrasting characters of the lands suit-

able for the olive (179–83: *difficiles . . . terrae collesque maligni*, clay and gravel) and vine (184–94: *pinguis humus dulcique uligine laeta, / quique frequens herbis et fertilis ubere campus*). We have seen in detail how this rich and abundantly moist land (and it should not be forgotten that this is not quite true) produces a complex of military suggestions and metaphors of violent actions (bending, cutting, forcing, breaking), of never-ending toil. We have now the briefest statement of the opposite, that the olive needs no force (*falcem rastrosque tenaces*), that the *ingenium* of its land supplies moisture enough, that its fruit is in fact rich (*pinguem*) and pleasing to Peace. The contrast has in fact resulted in a paradox: the character of a land, of its vegetation, and of its inhabitants is a single whole, but a rich and fertile soil does not produce peace (and hence Virgil's wish about a land which is *iusto laetior: a nimium ne sit mihi fertilis illa*, 251–52), nor the converse: from this can be understood the paradox, or the lie, of Italy, *Saturnia tellus, magna parens frugum, magna virum*, as well as of Media with its lemon tree, the *saporem felicis mali*, which is the antidote to (Medea's) poisons and is a general *medicina* as well.

Fruit trees and then wild trees are the subjects of the next lines, and again the point is that they require none of our effort (*ad sidera raptim / vi propria nituntur opisque haud indiga nostrae*, 427–28). Servius aptly notes, "illuc crescit vitium vituperatio, circa quas tantus impenditur labor." On this point little more need be said, as Virgil lists the benefits conferred by these trees growing in fields owing nothing to human cultivation (*arva . . . non rastris, hominum non ulli obnoxia curae*, 438–39). Yet at line 440 begins a further turn in the theme. There we see "the barren forests on the Caucasian peak," resisting the mountain winds: we may recall the character of the olive's land, especially the *colles maligni*, and the exemplum of the *aesculus* resisting winter's winds and rains, but "foliage for the flock and shade for the shepherd, protection for seedlings and food for honey" (435–36) are no longer the products of spontaneous nature. Man and Jupiter's *artes* have extended even so far, and these *steriles silvae* are forced to yield lumber for ships, cedar and cypress for building luxurious houses, wood for farmers' carts and wheels, and for ships (again). Navigation, urban development, and agriculture: three of the basic occupations or crafts that regularly and unmistakably occur in the topic of the arts of civilization. After a brief mention of the provision of wicker and fodder the list resumes (with the adversative *at*) with the myrtle good for strong spears and the cornel good for (lest we miss the point) war (*bello*) and with the yew, "twisted into bows." The linden and box "accept a shape and are hollowed by the sharp iron," submitting to the arts that have been implied throughout the book, violence and domination. Finally, the alder sails on the Po and bees build in the hollow oak, *vitiosaeque ilicis alvo* (453—*vitiosae* in what sense?).

The passage and the book's instruction close with a return to the vine:

> quid memorandum aeque Baccheia dona tulerunt?
> Bacchus et ad culpam causas dedit; ille furentis
> Centauros leto domuit, Rhoetumque Pholumque
> et magno Hylaeum Lapithis cratere minantem.   (454–57)

(What have Bacchus' gifts brought us to equal this? Bacchus has even provided reasons for wrong; he destroyed the Centaurs, after driving them to irrational violence, Rhoetus and Pholus and Hylaeus, who threatened the Lapiths with a huge mixing bowl.)

Servius again sees the essential terms (on 454): "quid similiter laudandum tulerunt dona Liberi, sicut silvae multa sponte procreantes? [Then, explaining the variant *et quae* for *aeque*,] ut hoc dicat, parum est quod vites tantum laborem requirunt, etiam munera earum causas praestant furoris" ("What have the gifts of Liber brought worth equal praise, even as the forests which produce much voluntarily? [Some accept a reading that has Virgil say that] it's not enough that vines require such labor, but even their gifts bestow the cause of irrational violence"). The Centaurs and Lapiths were for long the standard exemplum of the brute *furor* produced by wine, which comes to mind here as clearly and succinctly as a relief sculpture before the eyes, as the climax of the language of violence and force associated with the vine. Varro's etymology was probably not his own: *vitis a vino, id a vi* (" 'Vine' is derived from 'wine,' and that from 'violence'," *LL* 5.37). This return to the gifts of Bacchus does not come as a sudden departure from previous assumptions about the vine, nor as something humorous or playful, but as the natural conclusion. Bacchus too gave cause for wrong, and for blame: the phrase *ad culpam causas* comes close to a definition of *vituperatio*, as if playing with etymology. *Vitium* (the neuter singular noun) is not common in the poets (Horace's frequent uses are mainly in the *Satires* and *Epistles*): Virgil has it once in the *Eclogues* (7.57), twice in the *Georgics* (1.88 and 3.454, contexts worth some reflection), and never in the *Aeneid*. On the other hand, *culpa* is absent from the *Eclogues*; occurs in the *Georgics* only here, again associated with Bacchus in this book (2.380, *non aliam ob culpam Baccho caper . . . / caeditur*), and in the same passage and with the same meaning as *vitium* in the third book (3.468—of the ulcerating disease of the flock); and only four times in the *Aeneid* (Virgil is not a moralist). I am engaging now in pure speculation or free association, for at this point Virgil's explicit verbal connections cease. I would be willing to bet, though, that it was not Servius or an earlier commentator who first thought of this part of the poem in the precise phrase *vitium vituperatio*, and that Virgil too made the association "*vitis a vino, id a vi*," and wrote *ad culpam causas* with full awareness of its significance at the end of his *vitium vituperatio*.

Some Conclusions

It may be useful at this point to summarize where Virgil has taken us in this book, and indeed in the first half of the poem, lest our concern with certain details obscure our sense of direction.

Virgil's concern here is with the present state of the world and man's condition, rather than with historical development and causation (as in Book 1). As the grain replaced the acorn, so in the world of the present we find an opposition of the wild (*silvestria virgulta*) and the cultivated (Bacchus' vine), and, as we would expect, the cultivated will be the focus of attention throughout the book.

Like the grain, the vine is a gift of the god:

huc, pater o Lenaee, tuis hic omnia plena
muneribus, tibi pampineo gravidus autumno
floret ager, spumat plenis vindemia labris.   (2.4–6)

(Come hither, Lenaeus: here all is full of your gifts, for you the fruitful field abounds in the full foliage of autumn, the vintage foams in the flowing vats.)

What appears here to be the bounty of god's gift, freely offered and free-flowing, will by the end of the book become a reality of unending toil, of labor lost in vain, a gift of destruction both suffered and actively perpetrated. Again, at the beginning of the book, man's arts are shown to produce unnatural monstrosities—grafted mutations, for instance, never yet observed in the real world, absurd as well as impossible.

Little attention can be devoted to the uncultivated, but it is always there, nevertheless: unfruitful, but strong and vigorously growing, requiring none of the exhausting care continually demanded in an endless cycle by the vine. The olive stands midway between: it is fruitful (as the wild olive is not), long-lived and self-sufficient, the tree of peace, though subject to destruction by fire (as again the wild olive is not). The essential contrast emerges clearly: on the one side, *labor* and its products, fruitful but weak and therefore in constant need of attention, easily destroyed and potentially destructive; and on the other, the thriving growth of the wild, which cannot be permanently destroyed even by fire, offering man no sustenance, but eventually to be hewn, bent, and twisted into the implements of civilization and war.

The tenets of ethnography are assumed throughout this book too. Hence, early on, there is a full discussion of the situation, climate, and vegetation of different lands. Rich and wet soils produce a luxuriance of growth and are fit for vines (we are told to our surprise), but the poor, dry soils of barren hills are suited for the olive. But first, the East of Media and Medea had been contrasted with the West of Italy and its heroes.

Virgil juxtaposes a variety of elements from the ethnographical tradition, from popular philosophy and current mythologizing, none of which remain valid for long. The fabulous East of wicked stepmothers, poisons, and warriors sprung from the dragon's teeth becomes the land that produces the *felix malum*, whereas the Italy of the golden age is in reality a land of war. The only certainty, perhaps, is Cyrus' conclusion to Herodotus's *History*, that soft men usually grow from soft countries, that rich crops and warriors are not products of the same land (9.122). Once again, myth, dream, and hopeful concepts face a reality of science: Spring as a time of peace and balance and the Country as a place of spontaneous plenty and ease, will be subjected to the same process, not of logical refutation, but of poetic clarification, as we see these splendid lies for what they are.

Reason and knowledge, however, are no more enshrined in this book than they were in the first:

Quare agite o proprios generatim discite cultus
agricolae, fructusque feros mollite colendo,
neu segnes iaceant terrae.   (2.35–37)

We can now appreciate the depth of irony in Virgil's opening address to his farmers, and its application to East and West, its relevance to the world of the present. Just as the vine-grower is locked into his round of repeated toil, so has Virgil forced us to confront our imaginative constructions of hope and peace with scientific reason, but he has forced us at the same time back around the circle that convicts this knowledge of violence and ultimate futility.

The final movement of the book begins with Virgil's request to the Muses, dear to him beyond all things, to grant him knowledge, the understanding of science: if not, then the constructions of imagination must be his, after all. We can understand these lines now as fully as Virgil intended us to, here at the end of the first half of the poem: we will look back to them at the close of the poem, when they will have taken on far greater significance. So far, nothing has been resolved: but Virgil will now turn from the farmer's world more directly to the farmer himself, and as he does so, knowledge and understanding will become more and more his focus.

CHAPTER FOUR

BOOK III

Herds, Flocks, and Training

The third book, like the first, ends in obvious and utter disaster, the total devastation resulting from the plague. That this is a particularly bleak scene with which to end the book is generally conceded—there is no way around it after all. Comparisons with Thucydides and Lucretius serve to distract the scholarly reader from the portrayal of total desolation that Virgil clearly intended (so he began—*desertaque regna / pastorum et longe saltus lateque vacantis*, 3.476–77), but do not reach very far beyond a few not especially interesting parallels. Why such a bleak conclusion is a question which deserves fuller consideration, which will, however, reveal a darkness not just at the book's end, but pervasive.

The first two books had considered man in large contexts: in a universal setting and in a sweeping temporal development, and then as the resultant human condition that is viewed against the backdrop of the present world. The third comes closer, to man himself, as indeed its subject seems to allow. Fields and trees offer a natural background to the farmer and his activities; animals, large and small, allow accurate reflection of human conditions, without anthropomorphizing. This is accomplished, again, by that means so basic to the *Georgics*—the metaphor made real. Virgil does not say that man is like a bull or that a bull is like a man, which could be grotesque, or trivializing, or a literary abstraction (as in a Homeric simile); but because of the poem's subject, the metaphor is reality and thus avoids both the grotesque and the trivial. Another difficulty, however, is not so easily avoided, and that is that the reader may stop short of turning the reality back into the literary abstraction, or may not always have the means to do so correctly ("correctly" here means as Virgil intended, not as readers of later times have fabricated). A beginning can be made by establishing a few key terms.

The subject of the book is traditionally divided into two—large and small animals, or cattle and horses, sheep and goats. The literary abstractions behind this reality are quite clear. Horses are raised and trained only for war or—what amounts to the same thing—racing, and, as we shall see, cattle in this book share the same associations. *Arma* are never far from *armenta*. Sheep and goats, on the other hand, are not so much a complement as a contrast: the pastoral was there, a literary abstraction ready to hand. War and peace thus become the two most obvious subjects of the book, the realities of epic and pastoral, the world of the *Aeneid* and of the *Eclogues* meeting. (The *Aeneid* is anticipated, as we will see, and is in fact "referred to" in far greater detail than are the *Eclogues*.) This is only the beginning of Virgil's conception, preparation for the inversions and contradictions that are so much his own. The pastoral is, in fact, only a setting for its one concern, love—a cool setting for reflection upon the heat of passion. War is fire itself, the prime destructiveness, represented in epic by Achilles becoming fire in his battle with the Scamander. The conclusions to each half of the third book are obviously complementary, but it should be noted that sexual frenzy and disease are still the realities of the subject: the abstractions that Virgil points to throughout are love and fire (the *sacer ignis* of the book's final line), precisely the forces properly belonging to the opposite literary world. One element dominates the book, but will appear in each half, and in each world, in ways sometimes unexpected: the fire of love and the fire of disease can be appreciated only through an awareness of the metaphor behind the reality.

To begin with, cattle and horses come to the same thing:

Seu quis Olympiacae miratus praemia palmae
pascit equos, seu quis fortis ad aratra iuvencos,
corpora praecipue matrum legat.   (3.49–51)

(Whether one raises horses, marveling at the prize of the Olympic
palm, or strong bullocks for the plow, let him choose with particular
care the mothers' bodies.)

Servius (on line 49) notes the obvious division of the book ("dicturus est de armentis et gregibus . . . armenta sunt equorum et
boum, quod haec animalia apta sunt armis"), giving the usual
etymology of *armenta* ("apta sunt armis"), but in so doing seeming to involve himself in an absurdity (cattle as martial animals?), from which he barely escapes ("ut scutis boum coria,
equi proelio"). But if we think about this, the absurdity is not
Servius', but rather Virgil's, for whom cattle elsewhere in the
poem (as we have noted more than once) have all the pacific
characteristics (the plowman's friend, slaughtered first in the
Age of Bronze, etc.) which the real world attributes to them as
a matter of course. Virgil is once again taking extraordinary lib-
erties with both fact and convention.

The transformation of the cow into a creature of equine valor
begins with this well-known description of the mother (*optima
torvae / forma bovis cui turpe caput*, 51–52), large and intentionally
ugly, in fact more like a bull (*et faciem tauro propior*, 58), and not
unlike the traditional Sabine women in the contemporary
cliché, that embodiment of the old virtues in combat boots. No
formosa iuvenca this. Youth is the time for breeding (*dum laeta
iuventas*, 63), but sexual passion is no more than controlled procreation (*mitte in Venerem pecuaria primus*, 64). Suddenly, however, there is an interruption of moving intensity:

optima quaeque dies miseris mortalibus aevi
prima fugit: subeunt morbi tristisque senectus
et labor, et durae rapit inclementia mortis.   (3.66–68)

(Each best day of life for wretched mortals is the first to fly off: then
come diseases and bitter old age, and toil, and the rough hand of hard
death reaches out.)

We may observe first, though rather analytically, how these lines suddenly make it plain that Virgil sees his animals as human without anthropomorphizing in the least: these lines come as a shock simply because they suddenly remind us that the (animal) reality we had been accepting is in fact a (human) metaphor. With the intrusion of the metaphor comes the vision of the central truth: youth is brief, then come disease, age, effort, and death. The theme is epic; hence the *miseris mortalibus* (the Homeric δειλοῖσι βροτοῖσιν—*mortales* began its career in Latin poetry as an Ennian epicism for *homines*, but Virgil could not have known, alas, that βροτοῖσιν and *mortalibus* are cognates). In the underworld *Morbi, tristisque Senectus, Letumque Labosque* are among the figures sitting before the vestibule of Orcus (*Aen.* 6.275–77): here youth, *optima quaeque dies*, is the one brief period of life free from these evils, a period of bright and glorious activity that makes Achilles' choice so eminently heroic. Virgil, no doubt, was aware as well that Hesiod's Golden Age was characterized by the absence of pain, age, work, and hard death (*WD* 112–15). These three lines are but the final touch to the marvelous incongruity of the entire passage.

That the horse, especially the young male, of the next passage has all the qualities of the heroic is only to be expected: fire is his proper element (*collectumque premens volvit sub naribus ignem*, 85). He is like Cyllarus, the horse of Spartan Pollux, or the horses of Mars and of Achilles, and like Saturn turned into a horse on Mt. Pelion, at the unexpected arrival of his wife (as related by Apollonius, *Argon.* 2.1231–41). These last two references are connected, for the tryst interrupted by Ops was with Philyra, who as a result bore Chiron, half man, half horse, and the teacher of Achilles (*Phillyrides Chiron* re-enters the book at line 550). That Chiron ought to be remembered here is indicated not only by the preceding mention of Achilles, but by Apollonius (Χείρωνα πελώριον ἄλλα μὲν ἵππῳ / ἄλλα θεῷ ἀτάλαντον 1240–41). The associations are all martial and point to Troy.

The rather strange reference to Saturn and Philyra is perhaps to be understood from the context immediately following:

Hunc quoque, ubi aut morbo gravis aut iam segnior annis
deficit, abde domo, nec turpi ignosce senectae.
frigidus in Venerem senior, frustraque laborem
ingratum trahit, et, si quando ad proelia ventum est,
ut quondam in stipulis magnus sine viribus ignis,
incassum furit.   (95–100)

(But this one too, when he slows down weighted with sickness or
now sluggish with age, shut him away inside, and don't forgive vile
age. An old horse is cold in sex, and all in vain does he draw an un-
congenial load, and, should it ever come to war, he rages to no purpose, like a great fire, once upon a time, in a field of stubble, without
strength.)

The antecedent of *hunc quoque* was left some lines back, before
the epic comparisons: "this one as well" at first would seem to
suggest Saturn ("the latter too"). However, the subject of this
next section is the sick or old horse. We are back to lines 66–68,
the brief glory of youth soon to yield to disease, age, effort (*labor*), and death. Here, the theme of fire is for the first time in the
book associated with both war and sexual passion in the same
context: the old horse is *frigidus in Venerem* and burns purpose-
lessly like a fire in the stubble when it comes to war. (Servius
notes the mixing of metaphors for love and war.) If *hunc quoque*
might at first suggest Saturn, then it becomes clearer why the
last and longest of the comparisions is his: fire as war (through
Chiron and Achilles) and as passion are both implied (as "the
Greek poets recounted") through his figure.

Not only is the identity of martial valor and sexual vigor
being established, but the sphere and definition of the latter are
growing and changing. Venus first, just a few lines before, had
stood for practical animal husbandry (*mitte in Venerem pecuaria
primus*, 64), similar to this present context (*frigidus in Venerem
senior*, 97). Saturn's meeting with the nymph Philyra was a very
different matter, and still different is the suggestion that comes
with the mention of the Lapiths at line 115. Lapiths and Centaurs may be intentionally conflated in the reference (and *Pele-
thronii* points to the cave on Mt. Pelion where Chiron taught
Achilles—cf. above Saturn on Mt. Pelion, far from Apollonius'

island home of the Oceanid Philyra), but must bring to mind in any case that great exemplum of animal passion, mentioned by Virgil toward the end of the previous book (*Bacchus et ad culpam causas dedit; ille furentis / Centauros leto domuit, Rhoetumque Pholumque / et magno Hylaeum Lapithis cratere minantem*, 2.455–57). At one end of the scale, the farmer controls his livestock for breeding purposes in an (as yet) impersonal, practical way; at the other, sexual passion is an impulse that drives even gods (Saturn) to unrestrained violence (the Lapiths and Centaurs), and hence both war and sex find expression in these equine figures.

A new movement begins at 123 (*His animadversis*), dealing with three stages in breeding, rearing, and training:

123–37: before mating
138–56: care during pregnancy
157–78: care and training of the young.

The first and third sections are similar in content and tone; the second is very different.

Before mating, the males are to be fattened, in order to meet the demands of this *blandus labor*, and that their offspring not be thin and weak. This is the only time we meet such an animal, overweight with "thick fat" (*denso pingui*). The females, on the other hand, are to be exhausted with exercise and denied both food and drink, during the heat of early summer. There was precedent for this advice (it is given by Vaccius in Varro, *RR* 2.5.12), but it has a familiar ring—the exhaustion, the dry heat, *nimio ne luxu obtunsior usus / sit genitali arvo* (135–36). We have seen before that *luxuries segetum* (1.112) is to be controlled, that a field too rich is to be avoided (*a, nimium ne sit mihi fertilis illa*, 2.252), that this is a traditional precept (important in Herodotus' geographical-ethnographical philosophy) well-established in the poem. The breeder is to control the basic conditions for procreation, just as the farmer does for his fields, and these conditions are similar. (Servius has an interesting note on 135, observing that Virgil avoids Lucretian bluntness in his description of copulation, using instead agricultural metaphors: "et bene rem turpem aperte a Lucretio tractatam vitavit translationibus, quas omnes ab agricultura traxit, ut 'luxu' propter luxuriam segetum." The metaphors, of course, make the connections.)

Passing on to the third section (157–78), the care and training of the young bulls: we are given instruction in terms that have become familiar in many contexts, as in the preparation of fields or in the training and care of vines. The young are to be branded immediately (*notas et nomina inurunt*, 158), marked for stud, for sacrifice, for work.

> tu quos ad studium atque usum formabis agrestem
> iam vitulos hortare viamque insiste domandi,
> dum faciles animi iuvenum, dum mobilis aetas.   (163–65)

(Those which you will mold for practical duties on the farm, urge them on while they are still young and take steps to subdue them, while their young spirits are flexible, their age pliable.)

The emphasis is on shaping by subduing, while age allows; through violence, submission to actual slavery is achieved:

> ac primum laxos tenui de vimine circlos
> cervici subnecte; dehinc, ubi libera colla
> servitio adsuerint, ipsis e torquibus aptos
> iunge pares, et coge gradum conferre iuvencos;   (166–69)

(First, hang on their necks loose hoops of light withes; then, when their necks have freely grown used to slavery, yoke the bullocks in pairs joined by those very ropes and compel them to march in step.)

The rest of the passage is similar, and in tone is much like the preparation of the mothers for conception, except that the young bullocks are to be well fed.

Very different from the total control by violent methods exercised by the breeder and trainer is the scene of calm and ease in the middle section (138–56), obviously an intended contrast. In more than one sense the scene is pastoral. The pregnant mothers are kept specifically from work and from running (140–42) and instead are to be kept in a setting where we might expect to hear some Tityrus piping on an oaten reed:

saltibus in vacuis pascunt et plena secundum
flumina, muscus ubi et viridissima gramine ripa,
speluncaeque tegant et saxea procubet umbra.   (143–45)

(They pasture in lonely glades and along full streams, where moss
grows and the banks are lush with grass, and caves offer cover and
the rock's shadow stretches forth.)

We are miles from Epirus, or "brave Mycenae" (just above,
121), but the setting is specified—the groves around the river Silarus, the mountain Alburnus, the river Tanager, all in Lucania,
the haunts of the dreaded gadfly which drives herds to madness
in the midday heat of high summer. This one impediment to
perfect pecorine contentment will concern us shortly.

The next section (179–208) is in fact a continuation of the preceding section on the training of bullocks, but concerns horses
and therefore (primarily) war: *Sin ad bella magis studium tur-
masque ferocis*, it begins. Racing (*aut Alphea rotis praelabi flumina
Pisae*, it continues) is but a form of war, or the other side of the
same coin. High spirits are required, but again youth is to be
shaped and formed, and again the process is one of subduing
through violence and coercion, just as in the case of bulls:

tum demum crassa magnum farragine corpus
crescere iam domitis sinito: namque ante domandum
ingentis tollent animos, prensique negabunt
verbera lenta pati et duris parere lupatis.   (205–8)

(Then finally, when they have been subdued, allow their bodies to
grow great on thick mash: for before they are conquered they will
vaunt their lordly spirits and when bridled will refuse to endure the
supple lash and to obey the hard bit.)

The trainer can break the "huge spirits" (*ingentis animos*—
again *ingens* is suggestive of *ingenium*) of his horses, presumably,
but whether he can "turn away Venus and the goads of
blind(-ing) love" is another matter (*Sed non ulla magis viris industria firmat / quam Venerem et caeci stimulos avertere amoris*, 209–10).
Some idea of the magnitude of this task is conveyed by the notice that some herdsmen therefore pasture their bulls on the op-

posite side of a mountain or across wide rivers, or keep them
within their stall: for a woman saps strength, and kindles a fire,
just by being seen, and drives her lovers to battle, allowing them
no thought for glade or pasture (215–18). Suddenly we are back
in Lucania: *pascitur in magna Sila formosa iuvenca* (219). Sila, as
Servius noted, is a mountain in Lucania, heavily forested and
known for its pitch. (The manuscripts conspire to read *silva*—
except for a correction in the Medicean.) There is an intimate
and far-reaching connection between the mountain Sila here and
the river Silarus in the passage beginning at line 146, which will
lead on into the *Aeneid*. (This connection, and similarity of the
names, may have led to the notice in Servius that Silarus is as
well a mountain in Lucania: Virgil was undoubtedly relying on
the similarity of the names, which are not metrically equivalent.)

The ASILUS *and the Fire of Love*

First, the *asilus*:

est lucos Silari circa ilicibusque virentem
plurimus Alburnum volitans, cui nomen asilo
Romanum est, oestrum Grai vertere vocantes,
asper, acerba sonans, quo tota exterrita silvis
diffugiunt armenta, furit mugitibus aether
concussus silvaeque et sicci ripa Tanagri.
hoc quondam monstro horribilis exercuit iras
Inachiae Iuno pestem meditata iuvencae.
hunc quoque (nam mediis fervoribus acrior instat)
arcebis gravido pecori, armentaque pasces
sole recens orto aut noctem ducentibus astris.   (146–56)

(There is a fly that swarms around the groves of the river Silarus and
verdant Mt. Alburnus, called by the Romans the *asilus*, but by the
Greeks the *oestrus*—fierce, sharply buzzing, frightened by which
whole herds scatter in the woods, and the high sky resounds with
their enraged bellowing, and the banks of the dry Tanager too.
Through this very monster once upon a time Juno took out her fear-
some anger on Inachus' daughter Io, hatching this plague for her,

now a cow. You, too, will ward off this fly from your pregnant herd
(for it comes on more fiercely at the midday heat), and you will pasture your herds when the sun has newly risen or when the stars bring
on night.)

The initial ecphrastic *est*, the etymological aetion in *cui nomen
asilo*, the reference to the Io story (*Inachiae . . . iuvencae*—she is
not named), and the mention of the *Grai* are all indications of the
stylized and learned nature of the lines and thus call for special
attention. Much of what lies behind this passage we need not repeat: Aeschylus, Callimachus, and Apollonius referred to the
two names (μύωψ and οἶστρος) of this insect, the latter two concerned to point out that μύωψ was the herdsmen's name. To these
poets, then, Virgil refers with his *oestrum Grai vertere vocantes*
(and the taxonomy may have been the subject of a ζήτημα, as
Thomas suggests), but he mentions only the Greek *oestrus*, perhaps because "it is the gadfly set on Io by Juno" (so Thomas),
perhaps also because this term had acquired in Greek the general
meaning "madness."

It is Apollonius, however, whom Virgil had particularly in
mind: twice in the *Argonautica* he had used the gadfly in similes,
in the first book when Heracles, having lost Hylas, is compared
to a bull stung to madness by a gadfly (ὡς δ᾽ ὅτε τίς τε μύωπι
τετυμμένος ἔσσυτο ταῦρος . . . ἵησιν μύκημα, κακῷ βεβολημένος
οἶστρῳ, 1.1265, 1269), and in the third when Eros himself is
compared to an οἶστρος . . . ὅν τε μύωπα βοῶν κλείουσι νομῆες
(3.276–77). One unanswered question arising from these lines
and from Callimachus' ⟨οἶστρον⟩ βουσόον ὅν τε μύωπα βοῶν κα-
λέουσιν ἀμορβοί (*Hec.* fr. 301 Pf.) is why these two poets make
it a point to note that μύωψ was the term used by herdsmen. Etymology supplies a possible answer: in Apollonius' first simile,
in the first and last lines (cited just above), the μύωψ produces the
μύκημα (a pun at least, but suggesting the novel etymology for
the insect named "moo-face"), and hence the passing reference
in the third book to the μύωψ as the herdsmen's word. (This answer almost necessarily argues for Apollonius' priority, by the
way, since 1.1265–69 supplies the context for the play on, and
interest in, the word.)

Furit mugitibus aether: Virgil is playing with a recognizable gadfly, etymologized particularly by Apollonius, notably in two similes dealing with the madness of love. (Here again is a previous literary abstraction that has become a reality in Virgil's poem.) Yet this gadfly had in a former incarnation been the same which drove Io halfway around the world (Aeschylus, *Suppl.* 306–8, *Prom.* 566, etc.)—eminently suited, then, as the token of bovine frenzy and passion. The real gadfly of the *Georgics* is a creature of heat (*nam mediis fervoribus acrior instat,* 154) and summer in the reality of southern Italy, in Lucania. It is the river Silarus which gives the *a-silus* its name (just as the *a-mellus* takes its name from the river Mella, 4.271–78), an etymology that appears to be Virgil's own.

All of this might seem totally gratuitous, learned simply for the sake of learning, but the light comes some seventy lines later, when Virgil advises the herdsman "to turn away Venus and the goads of blind(-ing) love." *Pascitur in magna Sila formosa iuvenca*: there follows the story (heroic, hyperbolic, and strangely anthropomorphic) of the defeated bull, his exile and return (219–41), a story of empire regained even more than of love avenged (*multa gemens ignominium plagasque superbi / victoris, tum quos amisit inultus amores,* 226–27). The passage is a remarkable achievement: Virgil has managed somehow to stay just this side of the comic. Beginning right off with the *formosa iuvenca*, there are phrases and turns that are of almost Ovidian wit; in fact, anyone reading the passage with an eye or ear ready for its comic possibilities must wonder whether Virgil has managed to keep this side of the comic. Burlesque is the obvious danger, the mock-heroic attitude that puts great themes in incongruously small and unheroic settings; another danger is the superficiality of the anthropomorphic, amusing but insignificant. How does Virgil manage to avoid these dangers?

He avoids them not only here: Mt. Sila and these same bulls return, of course, at the climax of the struggle of Aeneas and Turnus, in the well-known simile (12.715–22), *ac velut ingenti Sila summove Taburno . . .* (prepared for earlier in the book by another simile with direct repetition of the *Georgics* passage,

12.103–6). Again, the comic is dangerously close to the sur-face—compare for instance the mumblings of the consternated cows (*mussantque iuvencae / quis nemori imperitet, quem tota armenta sequantur*, 718–19) with Latinus just a few lines earlier (*mussat rex ipse Latinus / quos generos vocet et quae sese ad foedera flectat*, 657–58). The simile has no dignifying Homeric precedent (Apollo-nius has a one-and-a-half-line version, too brief to have "influ-enced" Virgil, *Argon.* 2.88–89): as the direct similarities of lan-guage show clearly enough, the precedent is Virgil's own version in the *Georgics*, with all its own inherent dangers. Why?

> dat gemitum tellus; tum crebros ensibus ictus
> congeminant, fors et virtus miscetur in unum.
> ac velut ingenti Sila summove Taburno . . .   (*Aen.* 12.713–15)

(The earth groans; then they redouble the quickened clashes of swords, and chance and courage meet together. Just as when, on huge Sila or Taburnus' heights . . .)

The mention of "great Sila" takes us back to the reality of *Georgics* 3.219, *pascitur in magna Sila*, and in turn to the *asilus / Silarus* aetion just before. Mt. Taburnus (which occurs in Virgil only here and in the unrelated mention at *Georgics* 2.38) is, I sus-pect, a further clue to the *asilus* aetion: the common Latin word for "gadfly" was *tabanus*. The important connection, though, with the *Aeneid* simile and the *asilus/Silarus* aetion was ready to hand, though hardly fortuitously: Virgil had concluded his ae-tiology with the great exemplum of the gadfly's frenzy, Io the daughter of Inachus—*hoc quondam monstro horribilis exercuit iras / Inachiae Iuno pestem meditata iuvencae* (3.152–53). It may be that Calvus' Io stands more closely behind these lines than we are in a position to appreciate, but it was not just coincidence that Io's frenzy occurred to Virgil more than once as he contemplated the actions of Turnus and Juno in the *Aeneid*, a frenzy summing up through suggestion the great themes of passion and its inevita-ble madness, conflict, historical causation, divine vengeance and anger (Juno's).

Briefly, we need only remember that when Juno, the *saeva Io-vis coniunx*, enters the story of Book VII, for no reason then ap-

parent she comes from Inachian Argos (*Inachiis . . . ab Argis,*
7.286–87); that when Amata tries to convince Latinus to accept
Turnus, she concludes by referring to his Argive descent (*"et
Turno, si prima domus repetatur origo, / Inachus Acrisiusque patres
mediaeque Mycenae,"* 7.371–72); and that in the catalogue of the
same book, when Turnus is introduced, very little is actually
said about him (only two lines, 783–84), but a great deal about
his armor, especially his shield:

> at levem clipeum sublatis cornibus Io
> auro insignibat, iam saetis obsita, iam bos,
> argumentum ingens, et custos virginis Argus,
> caelataque amnem fundens pater Inachus urna.   (7.789–92)

> (But his polished shield was distinguished by Io, of gold, with raised
> horns, now covered with bristles, now a cow (the significant story of
> his house), and by Argus, her guard, and by her father Inachus, in-
> laid, pouring water from an urn.)

One should never forget that it is Io's story, *argumentum ingens,*
that Turnus carries before him through the rest of the epic. (Virgil's interest in the root meaning of *ingens* may allow us to read
it here as "in-born," characteristic of his family's *ingenium.*)
Likewise, in the poem's final scene, one should not forget that
Pallas' belt has on it a related scene (it is to this scene that the
words *saevi monumenta doloris,* 12.945, must refer); Turnus had
stripped the belt from Pallas' lifeless body,

>   rapiens immania pondera baltei
> impressumque nefas: una sub nocte iugali
> caesa manus iuvenum foede thalamique cruenti,
> quae Clonus Eurytides multo caelaverat auro.   (10.496–99)

> (. . . seizing the monstrous weight of the belt, and the engraved
> scene of crime: the band of young men foully slain in one night, and
> the bloody marriage chambers, inlaid with much gold by Clonus
> Eurytus' son.)

Impressumque nefas: the fifty daughters of Danaus, another *argumentum ingens,* a legend of the *ingenium* of Inachus and Io.

When we come to consider again, in the light of all this, our original question—how Virgil manages to avoid the frivolous or comic in the battle of the bulls in the *Georgics*, and why he returns to it at the climax of the *Aeneid*—the answer lies in the richness of the literary associations and how they are combined and reworked. We know almost nothing of Calvus' *Io*, but it must have been of prime importance for Virgil, and it must have been a poem of a more serious character than our sensibilities can allow, clouded over with animal passion, with divinity, vengeance, madness, and final release and revelation—of all of which we hear only the echo *a virgo infelix, quae te dementia cepit* (*Ecl.* 6.47) of an even fainter original, *a virgo infelix, herbis pasceris amaris*. The Io of Aeschylus happened to have recurred to the Alexandrians, but in a characteristic way involving etymological inventiveness, which led Virgil, in turn, to his *asilus/Silarus/ Sila* complex: quiet humor is there (though no mock heroics or Ovidian reductions to the absurd), but the final result was the grand pattern of passion, frenzy, and conflict which recurred to Virgil at the end of his epic, again with a whole new set of associations, an *argumentum ingens*. From the beginning, then, we must adjust our sensibilities to see not the hyperbolic but the tragic and heroic:

> furit mugitibus aether
> concussus silvaeque et sicci ripa Tanagri.   (*Geo.* 3.150–51)

> vasto
> cum gemitu, reboant silvaeque et longus Olympus. (*Geo.* 3.222–23)

> mugitus veluti cum prima in proelia taurus
> terrificos ciet   (*Aen.* 12.103–4)

> gemitu nemus omne remugit.   (*Aen.* 12.722)

All of which eventually looks back to Apollonius' bull and the herdsmen's μύωψ:

> ἵησιν μύκημα, κακῷ βεβολημένος οἴστρῳ·   (*Argon.* 1.1269)

Finally, let us note again that source of the peculiar power of the poem: Virgil has taken Aeschylus' Io, the etymologizing of the Alexandrians, the similes of Apollonius, Calvus' epyllion (with perhaps more), but he has removed from his extraordinary synthesis that curtain of literary abstraction that almost necessarily had to intercede, with the result that a stark reality is left, with all traces of the anthropomorphic, or even the symbolic, effectively eliminated.

★

Virgil's pastoral world is an extraordinarily complex creation, involving oppositions and the balance of opposites of different sorts: to simplify it is to distort it, and to paraphrase in an attempt to give it "meaning" is a greater distortion. Of the little that will be said about it right now, then, let the reader beware.

The pure pastoral may be represented by Tityrus with his pipe beneath the spreading beech, teaching the woods to echo "Amaryllis." Love is the subject of his song, and his ease and contentment (*lentus in umbra, Ecl.* 1.4) suggests that he is having it all his own way. The first and most obvious opposition is the real world—Meliboeus leaving his country for exile, uprooted by a foreign soldier (*Ecl.* 1.70–71). War can come no closer to the pastoral world than this, but reality finds expression in terms of *amor*. If "Amaryllis" is the ideal, then Corydon is its exponent and practitioner: he will prune his vine and find another Alexis (*Ecl.* 2.69–73). Real love, however, comes again and again into this idyllic setting, just as does the real world, in various forms and dimensions, until, at the end, the final pastoral figure and poet, Gallus himself, must yield to Love ("*omnia vincit Amor: et nos cedamus Amori,*" 10.69), and the singers rise to go, finding the shade now harmful (*surgamus: solet esse gravis cantantibus umbra,* 10.75). There comes a time when Tityrus or Corydon can no longer transform reality.

So it is that in the section dealing with the care of mothers, a pastoral world—a cool retreat—is created: no work, no training and denial, but empty pastures, river banks rich with grass, grottoes and shady caves (*saxea umbra, Geo.* 3.145). Frenzy enters, however, with the gadfly, Io's torment—the intrusion of *furor* and its consequence. *Omnia vincit Amor,* and hence the sub-

sequent instruction to keep off "Venus and the goads of love."
Again a pastoral setting is suggested; the female does not allow
the bulls to think of groves and grass (*nemorum . . . nec herbae,*
216), and the exemplum begins with the verb *pascitur* (*in magna
Sila formosa iuvenca,* 219). The result of the intrusion of love this
time is war of epic dimensions, kingdoms lost and regained,
reges et proelia, and appropriately the passage ends with an Homeric simile (237–41: at *Iliad* 4.422–26 the ranks of the Danaans
go to battle like a wave cresting and breaking on the shore).

So vivid and intriguing are these panels that we may forget
for the moment that the subject of the first half of this book has
been, for the most part, the training of horses for war and of
bullocks for heavy work, training that requires violent domination. The final section of the first half (242–83) shows even
this world totally subject to the domination of passion. The intrusion of love into the pastoral was the central concern of the
Eclogues, where love became in fact (in *Ecl.* 10) the intrusion of
reality, and reality was the real world of the *impius miles.* Here
love is an expression for a madness that dominates even that
reality.

> Omne adeo genus in terris hominumque ferarumque
> et genus aequoreum, pecudes pictaeque volucres,
> in furias ignemque ruunt: amor omnibus idem.   (3.242–44)

> (Every sort of man and beast on earth, and the creatures of the sea,
> and flocks and bright birds, rush headlong into madness and fire:
> love is the same for all.)

"Love is the same for all"—a headlong rush into madness and
fire. Fire is the key element of this book and thus at the beginning of this final section of the first half it is said to dominate all
creatures, of the earth (*in terris*), of water (*genus aequoreum*), and
of air (*pictaeque volucres*). Earth and water are no barriers (*non
scopuli . . . atque obiecta retardant / flumina . . . ,* 253–54). Lean-
der is driven through earth, water, and air (*quem super ingens /
porta tonat caeli, et scopulis inlisa reclamant / aequora,* 260–62).
Mountains and rivers are no obstacles to mares in heat (*superant
montis et flumina tranant,* 270), though the herdsman was in-

structed earlier to separate the bulls in just this way (*post montem oppositum et trans flumina lata*, 213).

"Love is the same for all. *At no other time* is the lioness more savage" (*tempore non alio*, 245: followed by *tum . . . tum . . . tum*, 248–49). When is there such savagery and slaughter (*funera volgo / tam multa . . . stragemque . . . / per silvas*, etc., 246–48)? Virgil doesn't say, until, almost as an afterthought some twenty-five lines later, he notes that the flame in the marrow occurs in the spring (*vere magis, quia vere calor redit ossibus*, 272), a physical explanation based on the obvious return of heat in the annual cycle of the seasons. The repetition *vere . . . vere* takes us back to the Praise of Spring in the preceding book (*ver adeo frondi nemorum, ver utile silvis, / vere tument terrae et genitalia semina poscunt*, 2.323–24). Virgil's emphasis on spring here as the time for natural savagery seems to be another pointed contradiction of the unreal Praise of Spring (we have noted others), again one based on the physical elements that have reappeared in this passage.

Finally, the passage concludes with another aetiology, beginning at line 266, *scilicet ante omnis furor est insignis equarum*. The *furor* of the mares is the *subdita flamma medullis*, which drives them toward the north and the cooling, wet north winds (*in Borean Caurumque, aut unde nigerrimus auster / nascitur et pluvio contristat frigore caelum*, 278–79). Behind this is the ancient belief that mares did conceive through impregnation by wind (so the mythical horses born of Zephyrus or Boreas, and so the serious accounts of Aristotle and Varro, to which Virgil alludes), but Virgil's contribution is precisely the opposition of the hot (drying) fire within the mares and the cold moist winds they seek. (Servius has the point, but mistakenly attributes to Varro what is Virgil's own: "hoc etiam Varro dicit, . . . equas, nimio ardore commotas, contra frigidiores ventos ora [!] patefacere ad sedandum calorem.") However, our understanding of these lines must remain incomplete: the mythological exemplum of Glaucus and his mares, though we have several variations of the story, doesn't quite make satisfactory sense, and lines 276–78 (with the spondaic ending *depressas convallis*, the apostrophe *non, Eure, tuos*, and the list of proper names) sound very much as if they had a poetic (and probably Alexandrian) origin, of which we are ignorant. Glaucus and his mares presumably served the same purpose here as did Medea in the aetiology of the lemon tree and Io in that of the *asilus*, and a particular poet in some specific poetic context probably gave further point, just as Apollonius (especially) did in the μύωψ/μύκημα complex.

The actual etymological aetion, however, is clear enough: *hippomanes* (*vero quod nomine dicunt / pastores*, 280–81) is the *furor equarum* (266), the ἵππου μανία (as Servius noted). A resounding anticlimax? Not when it is recognized that Virgil has conflated several sources here, as well as several *hippomanes*. First, and perhaps best known to readers of Virgil, is the love-charm used by Dido: *quaeritur et nascentis equi de fronte revulsus / et matri praereptus amor* (*Aen.* 4.515–16). This unlovely globule (black, the size of a fig, according to Pliny, *NH* 8.165) had to be taken from the forehead of a new-born colt before its mother could consume it—a potent love-charm, according to many, but clearly not what Virgil had in mind here—except insofar as Dido is anticipated through Medea, who is here brought into the context by the *novercae* repeated from the lemon aetion (2.128, and 2.129 = 3.283). The *hippomanes* Virgil refers to most clearly is the distillation from pregnant (and sometimes specifically wind-impregnated) mares—*lentum destillat ab inguine virus*. However, the name *hippomanes*, as Virgil remarks, was used by shepherds. We are undoubtedly invited to think again of Apollonius' gadfly (ὅν τε μύωπα βοῶν κλείουσι νομῆες, *Argon.* 3.277), but there were shepherds, or one particular *pastor* at least, who had an interest in a third *hippomanes*, a plant in Arcadia, sought by a later Medea figure, Theocritus' Simaetha (she refers herself to Medea, line 16): ἱππομανὲς φυτόν ἐστι παρ᾽ Ἀρκάσι, τῷ δ᾽ ἔπι πᾶσαι / καὶ πῶλοι μαίνονται ἀν᾽ ὤρεα καὶ θοαὶ ἵπποι (2.48–49). The result of Virgil's conflation is that the "madness of mares" becomes a poison, used in witchcraft to produce further madness, a distillation that is the very essence of passion and frenzy.

In Book 1 the first movement ended with the picture of the oarsman rowing continually against the current to keep from being swept back downstream (*sic omnia fatis / in peius ruere ac*

retro sublapsa referri, 1.199–200), and the book itself concluded
with the charioteer out of control, carried away by his horses.
Both images, in the context of the book, apply to the course of
degeneration in the broadest outline of human history. The focus in the third book has been more specific, on the nature of the
individual (caution is necessary here—there is no allegory involved): if anything, the conclusion is bleaker, and certainly
more terrifying. The charioteer (Glaucus—whatever else Virgil
may have had in his model) is actually devoured by his horses,
and the savagery and slaughter wrought by other animals is a
backdrop for the entire passage. *Et mentem Venus ipsa dedit*
(3.267): not only is all this the work of Venus herself, but it is
also the result of spring. (Virgil is not thinking of Lucretius
here, but to read over the Lucretian proem, with this passage
fresh in mind, is to realize just how extraordinarily intense Virgil's lines are.) The stereotype of vernal regeneration, of Venus
and the Graces, has been inverted and taken to the extreme. In
physical terms, fire is supreme over the other elements. In the
terms of the subject of the book, the fire of love has destroyed
not only the peace of the pastoral shade, just as it had ultimately
in the *Eclogues*, but it has also come to dominate the horses
themselves that are the actual embodiment of fire. The trainer,
who must dominate through violence and subjugation, is ultimately destroyed in the figure of Glaucus, by his own mares:
scilicet ante omnis furor est insignis equarum.

The Pastoral Idea

"Time passes not to be regained: the subject of love has fasci-
nated us long enough. So much for herds (*hoc satis armentis*—
again with its etymological significance): flocks are now our
concern." This transition (284–94) leaves behind love, war, and
epic concerns and passes on to small animals and what is properly pastoral. That the transition includes a rather original variation on the *recusatio* need neither surprise nor detain us: the entire book thus far (including of course the introduction 1–48)
has dealt with the great (war, fire, and epic concerns), with oc-

casional suggestions of a literally pastoral peace. Now the small is to be Virgil's subject (*angustis rebus*, 290). The invocation of *veneranda Pales* points (again, as in the first line of the book, *magna Pales*) directly and etymologically to the pastoral, but with a difference: *magno nunc ore sonandum* is a call to a higher level of poetic purpose.

Ice, snow, and cold northern winds are unimaginable in the pastoral landscape; only in the Tenth Eclogue (and there for good reason, lines 46–49, 65–66) are wintry conditions even contemplated. The conditions and requirements of the pastoral can't be met without the heat of summer and the long midday, for reasons too obvious to need attention here. (The seasonal activities of Daphnis and Chloe are in this regard worth a moment's reflection.) When Virgil begins his instruction with a few words on the importance of the care and feeding of sheep and goats during the cold of winter, while anticipating with expressive longing the return of summer pasturing (*dum mox frondosa reducitur aestas*, 296), he is accurately reflecting the shepherd's real concerns. When, however, he points to the Tenth Eclogue (*glacies ne frigida laedat / molle pecus*, 298–99 = *a, te ne frigora laedant! / a, tibi ne teneras glacies secet aspera plantas!*, Ecl. 10.48–49), he is setting his instruction as well in the poetic pastoral, where the cold and snow that here concern Gallus are the reality beyond the borders of a very unreal Arcadia. Virgil keeps his shepherd right at the border of these two countries, for the most part attending to business on some Italian hillside, occasionally crossing to what appear (at first at least) the greener grasses of an entirely poetic pasture, and sometimes even standing with one foot on each side of the line.

So it is in this first passage that the shepherd must protect the sheep against likely infections (*scabiem . . . turpisque podagras*, 299) that a Tityrus would hardly even notice, whereas the goatherd who is next instructed (300–304) to provide "the leafy arbute," fresh water (in the highly poetic phrase *fluvios recentis*), and a yard turned from the winds to face the winter sun at midday, is employed on tasks that have at least a reasonably Arcadian ring. Goats, in any case, are not to be despised (305–21),

and certainly the goats Virgil describes here are curious creatures (though not quite as remarkable as the flocks in the Fourth
Eclogue which come pre-dyed, 4.43–45). Goats are as sound an
economic venture as sheep, though dyed Milesian wool is
bringing a high price on the commodities market these days (*nec
minor usus erit, quamvis Milesia magno / vellera mutentur Tyrios in-
cocta rubores*, 306–7): the market value of Tyrian purple is not a
subject on which Corydon and Thyrsis would speculate. And
yet, when Virgil wants to point out that in addition goats require little care, he does so in a way that has definite overtones
of poetic pastoral and suggestions, too, of an age tinged with
gold:

> pascuntur vero silvas et summa Lycaei,
> horrentisque rubos et amantis ardua dumos.
> atque ipsae memores redeunt in tecta, suosque
> ducunt, et gravido superant vix ubere limen. (314–17)

(Indeed, they graze in the woods and on the top of Lycaeus, on bristling brambles and thickets which love the heights. Too, they return
home conscientiously themselves, bringing back their own, and
scarcely do their full udders manage to clear the doorstep.)

Lycaeus is the Arcadian mountain, and *silvae* is almost the technical term, of course, for the landscape of the *Eclogues* (as, for
instance, at *Ecl.* 4.3 and 10.8); the behavior of these goats is
strangely like those quasi-Saturnian animals in the Fourth Eclogue which will require no attention whatsoever—*ipsae lacte
domum referent distenta capellae / ubera* (4.21–22). Again, these
goats are Libyan (*Cinyphii hirci*, 312—from the Libyan mountain), which makes them exemplary (as we will see) rather than
Italian. However, just as in the reference to Tyrian purple (suggesting Roman political activity as well as extravagance), so in
the other mention here of economic utility there is an obviously
jarring note: goat hair is useful for army tents and for sails for
wretched sailors (*usum in castrorum et miseris velamina nautis*, 313).
Warfare and navigation/sea trade are markedly post-Saturnian
and anti-pastoral.

At the very end of this opening section there occurs a sudden and intrusive change in tone and scale much like the lines similarly placed at the opening of the first half (66–68, *optima quaeque dies miseris mortalibus aevi / prima fugit; subeunt morbi . . . senectus / et labor et . . . inclementia mortis*):

ergo omni studio glaciem ventosque nivalis,
quo minor est illis curae mortalis egestas,
avertes, victumque feres et virgea laetus
pabula, nec tota claudes faenalia bruma.   (318–21)

(Therefore, to the extent that they require less of man's attention, [by so much the more] will you keep from them with all zealousness the ice and winds of winter, and gladly bring them fodder and brush to eat, nor will you close your haylofts all winter.) Or (Therefore, inasmuch as Want, man's condition, concerns them less, you will keep from them . . .)

The question is just what line 319 means. Generally, modern editors and translators take these lines as I have first translated them—to paraphrase, "just because they don't seem to require much care, don't assume that in winter you needn't be concerned for them." This sense is acceptable, though rather bland, but in order to achieve this apparently simple message, violence has been done to Virgil's language. *Egestas* means "poverty" (*paupertas*) or "want, lack of," where the want or lack is real or compelling, a need of something that cannot be done without. In the sentence, "I have no need of your help, thanks just the same," *egestas* could not be used in Latin for "need"; and conversely, *mihi auxilii tui egestas est* means "I need your help (without which, I will die)." If Virgil meant "to the extent that goats require less of man's care," then *egestas* was the wrong word. *Curae mortalis* is also a very awkward periphrasis for "man's care, attention," just as "mortal care" would be in English. Servius took *curae* as a dative, and *mortalis egestas* as "necessitas mortalitatis" (though a second explanation follows, that of modern commentators, which, though introduced by *nam*, is totally at odds with what Servius has just said); and Servius Auctus paraphrases with "mortifera egestas." Therefore, I take Virgil's sense to be, "To the extent that Want, dire Need, which is the lot of wretched mortals, is less of a concern to them, you will (still, all the more) keep the icy winds of winter from them." *Egestas* is to be allowed the context that Virgil has already developed for it. *Improbus labor* and *egestas* (*duris urgens in rebus*) are (as we saw in detail) almost one and the same in Jupiter's new order in the first book (1.145–46); Virgil (it is fair to anticipate) puts them together again at the entrance to the underworld (*Aen.* 6.275–77), along with Disease, Age, and other abstractions; and *optima quaeque dies* (again we turn to those remarkable lines, 66–68 of this book) gives way to disease, age, effort, and death—a succession of evils lacking only Want (*egestas*) to complete the Virgilian company.

The import of these lines, then, is that goats, being able to fend for themselves for the most part very well, are little concerned with man's want and need (*mortalis egestas*) that are part of his post-Saturnian condition; goats are therefore creatures of some golden age (and are still able therefore to live on brambles and thickets, or on the arbute, that antithesis to Ceres' grain), which has some affinity with pastoral conditions; and therefore the real danger to goats, from which they must be protected with every effort, are ice and snowy winds (*ergo omni studio glaciem ventosque nivalis*, 318). There is one note of Virgilian discord in all this: goats do come home, unattended, to provide freely an abundance of milk, but they are also valuable for providing material for military tents and for sails.

This first section deals with winter care; the next moves on to summer pasturing (*At vero Zephyris cum laeta vocantibus aestas / in saltus utrumque gregem atque in pascua mittet*, 322–23). The seasonal qualities are worth attention here. The wet and cold of winter (as in the *glaciem ventosque nivalis*, 318) are opposed by the hot and dry of summer. The heat of midday that is the essence of the pastoral world (the gadfly is the fiercest *mediis fervoribus*, 154) must be guarded against by the shepherd (just as he guards against the extremes of winter), and thus he will pasture his flocks in the dewy cool of morning or evening (*frigida rura . . . ros gratissimus*, 324–26; *frigidus Vesper . . . roscida luna*, 336–37: cf. also at the end of the gadfly aetion, *armentaque pasces / sole recens orto aut noctem ducentibus astris,* 155–56). The section closes with the sounds of evening, *litoraque alcyonen resonant, acalanthida dumi* (338), which, as its two Greek nouns suggest, may well have an original in (I would guess) Hellenistic pastoral. In between dawn and dusk, cool shade and springs are to be sought (327–34): what is interesting here, however, is the insistence upon oak (*ilignis,* 330; *quercus,* 332; *ilicibus,* 334), the sacred shade of the oak grove (334), and specifically Jupiter's oak (*magna Iovis antiquo robore quercus,* 332—Servius notes "quia omnis quercus Iovi est consecrata": and in any case we are well familiar with Jupiter's acorn). The emphasis on Jupiter again sounds a discordant note, just as had the reference to war and navigation in the passage just preceding: Pan and Pales have been displaced.

This short section, then, has established a pastoral setting that lies across our border: on the one side, a real shepherd with his flocks, following common sense and established practice by seeking out the cool of a grove at midday, a grove that happens to be Jupiter's; his pasture extends unbroken across a border until a change in terrain does become noticeable, where the song of the cicada at midday is more intense (*et cantu querulae rumpent arbusta cicadae,* 328: cf. *sole sub ardenti resonant arbusta cicadis, Ecl.* 2.13), and of the kingfisher and finch at evening (338). These first two sections, as well, have established the opposition between winter and summer, in familiar elemental terms and have established too the importance of the seasons for the pastoral climate. The next two sections follow inevitably.

> Quid tibi pastores Libyae, quid pascua versu
> prosequar et raris habitata mapalia tectis?
> saepe diem noctemque et totum ex ordine mensem
> pascitur itque pecus longa in deserta sine ullis
> hospitiis: tantum campi iacet. omnia secum
> armentarius Afer agit, tectumque laremque
> armaque Amyclaeumque canem Cressamque pharetram;
> non secus ac patriis acer Romanus in armis
> iniusto sub fasce viam cum carpit, et hosti
> ante exspectatum positis stat in agmine castris.   (339–48)

(Why should I discuss with you in my verse the shepherds of Libya, their pastures and camps with but few tents? Often they graze both day and night, for a whole month together, and the herd goes off into the deserted wastes—no welcome there: the plain stretches endlessly. The African herdsman carries everything with him, home and hearth and equipment and Amyclaean dog and Cretan quiver; no different than the keen Roman soldier in his country's arms when he is on the march with his cruel rucksack, and, before the enemy is aware, has pitched his camp and stands in battle order.)

For Virgil, the pastoral climate and pastoral people *par excellence* had been the Libyans of northern Africa, since southern heat and dryness there reached its extreme (the Theocritean precedent, *Id.* 7.111–14, was just a beginning for Virgil). Gallus, at the end of the Tenth Eclogue, yielding finally to the power of love and admitting the inadequacy of poetry ultimately to cure love's wound (*tamquam haec sit nostri medicina furoris / . . . iam neque Hamadryades rursus nec carmina nobis / ipsa placent; ipsae rursus concedite silvae, Ecl.* 10.60, 62–63), then goes on to take pastoral song to its extreme, finding it of no help "even if we pasture Ethiopian flocks under the summer constellation of the Crab, when even the bark withers from drought on the lofty elm" (*nec si, cum moriens alta liber aret in ulmo, / Aethiopum versemus ovis sub sidere Cancri*, 67–68).

All the conditions of the pastoral landscape have been magnified—an empty waste, almost uninhabited, with a continual wandering over a land that has no end. This is the landscape of a nightmare, rather than of a Theocritean dream, but it is the direct result of extending the pastoral midday heat to its logical conclusion. The solitary shepherd, too, finds his prototype there in the *armentarius Afer*, totally self-sufficient, carrying with him everything he needs. In this he is like the Roman soldier on a forced march—an extraordinary simile. The point of comparison is established verbally again, with the etymological play *armentarius (Afer) . . . armaque . . . Romanus in armis* (344–46). Servius notes that Virgil is writing about flocks, not herds ("ARMENTARIUS AFER abusive: nam de gregibus loquitur"), a comment useful as a reminder that Virgil has gone out of his logical way to make this connection. Beyond the verbal play, however, is the real comparison that is obvious as soon as the dominating element of the book is recalled: the fire of war (of Achilles, of the horse) and the fire of love (*furor*, beginning with the gadfly's appearance in the pastoral peace *mediis fervoribus*) are both assumed in this reduction of the pastoral condition to the final extreme of continual dry heat. The fire of the shepherd and the fire of the soldier are ultimately one and the same, just as in the first half of the book war and love were ultimately reduced to the same terms. The logic that makes these connections is that of the poet, the verbal magician, not of the philosopher. We see the shepherd at summer's noon, then the African herdsman in an even more intense and endless heat and solitude, who is, with a blinding flash of fire, transformed into a soldier whom previously we would have considered his antithesis: we ought not to ask how the trick was done.

A further transformation follows. In geographical and ethnographical terms the logical opposite of Libya is Scythia, established even before Herodotus and the *Airs, Waters, Places* where we have already seen it. Virgil had noted these conventional extremes in the first book (*mundus, ut ad Scythiam Riphaeasque arduus arces / consurgit, premitur Libyae devexus in Austros*, 240–41). The southern hot and dry is opposed by the cold and wet of the north, each unending and unrelenting, but as North Africa showed the pastoral world carried to its limits, Scythia and Mt. Rhodope should be its antithesis. What sort of opposite is it, and why is so much space devoted to it (fifty lines, as opposed to ten devoted to Libya)?

First of all, as would be expected, there is no pasturing whatsoever. In winter, the Italian shepherd keeps his flocks in pens and folds, protected from the effects of ice and snowy winds; there, in the land of perpetual winter, flocks (actually, *armenta* again) can never graze: *illic clausa tenent stabulis armenta, neque ullae / aut herbae campo apparent aut arbore frondes* (352–53). Ten feet of snow, and always winter, always cold winds (*semper hiems, semper spirantes frigora Cauri*, 356—the Caurus, we may note in passing, was one of the northern winds sought by the mares in heat, 3.278). It is, however, a land that presents us with an inversion of reality:

concrescunt subitae currenti in flumine crustae,
undaque iam tergo ferratos sustinet orbis,
puppibus illa prius, patulis nunc hospita plaustris;
aeraque dissiliunt volgo, vestesque rigescunt
indutae, caeduntque securibus umida vina,
et totae solidam in glaciem vertere lacunae,
stiriaque impexis induruit horrida barbis.   (360–66)

(Ice forms suddenly even as the river flows and the wave now bears on its back the ironclad wheel: that which before had received boats, now welcomes wide carts. Bronze commonly shatters, the clothes on your back freeze stiff, they chop the liquid wine with axes, whole lakes turn to solid ice, and bristling icicles stiffen on unkempt beards.)

Rivers stand still, water supports the iron-bound wheel, carts go where ships went before. This sounds very much like the conventional *adynaton* with the deer and the dolphin exchanging habitats: earth and water change functions. Furthermore, bronze cracks, garments grow stiff, wine is cut with axes. Again, the inversion of nature is implied—wine, for instance, was by nature hot (we have seen this ancient commonplace before), as Servius notes here ("etiam vinum naturaliter calidum illic gelatur").

We then find flocks frozen to death in a blizzard (somehow, contrary to line 352, there has been some "pasturing" going on), along with oxen and deer huddled together antler-deep. Hunting is one of the minor delights of the pastoral condition, which here is transformed by a sort of inversion and taken again to an inevitable conclusion. No dogs or nets are required here, since the deer (normally swift in flight) are all but immobile, "pushing in vain against an opposed mountain," allowing the hunter to slaughter them hand-to-hand (*comminus*, a military metaphor

again) and joyfully carry them off home. It is their home life,
though, that is particularly intriguing:

> ipsi in defossis specubus secura sub alta
> otia agunt terra, congestaque robora totasque
> advolvere focis ulmos ignique dedere.
> hic noctem ludo ducunt, et pocula laeti
> fermento atque acidis imitantur vitea sorbis.   (376–80)

(They themselves, in dugout caverns, live a life of carefree ease deep
in the earth, and they pile heaped oaks and whole elms on their
hearths and feed them to the fire. Here they spend their nights in
revel, and happily produce an ersatz wine from an acidic fermenta-
tion of service berries.)

Inversion of pastoral convention is observable at every point.
They live below ground, rather than in shaded groves or cool
grottoes (though *defossis specubus* may be seen as the extreme extension of the "cave"—*antrum* usually—which is often the scene
of pastoral song or revelation). Lacking of course the midday
heat, they make up for it by burning oaks and whole elms on
their hearths. Instead of the day (pastoral song ends with evening when the flocks return home—see the final lines of *Eclogues*
1, 6, and 10, for instance), these northerners play all night, happily (*laeti*, 379, as again just above, 375) drinking an imitation
wine. Above all, it is a life of carefree ease (*secura otia agunt*), with
every want seemingly supplied, sport and song in settled
homes. As a contrast to the endless wandering of the unsettled
armentarius Afer, nothing could be plainer, and just as the no-
madic existence was comparable to that of the Roman soldier,
so this scene of peace, ease, and delight is a vivid contrast. Inversion has turned the hot, dry south into the wet, cold north,
and, by way of the impossible, has found there the essence of
pastoral ease, even in a land where the flocks themselves perish
from the cold. Virgil concludes:

> talis Hyperboreo Septem subiecta trioni
> gens effrena virum Riphaeo tunditur Euro
> et pecudum fulvis velatur corpora saetis.   (381–83)

(Such is the wild race of men, lying under the Hyperborean Great Bear, beaten by the Riphaean east wind, their bodies draped in tawny animal skins.)

Here again is the received cliché of the northern savage, *gens effrena virum*, clothed in the skins of his flocks, inhabiting mountains named from the wintry blasts (on 382 Servius gives the aetiology, "Riphaei autem montes sunt Scythiae . . . a perpetuo ventorum flatu nominati: nam ῥιφὴ graece impetus et ὁρμὴ dicitur ἀπὸ τοῦ ῥίπτειν"). The cliché had been summoned up again in *armenta* (352) and especially *comminus obtruncant* (374), but is belied in the details of the inversion itself, especially those of the *secura otia* enjoyed by these strangely civilized wild men.

The SACER IGNIS

The instructional tone is resumed immediately, as is usual: the next sections cover briefly wool (384–93), milk and cheese (394–403), and dogs (404–13). If they are pregnant with meaning and suggestion, I don't know what the point may be. The first of these minor movements closes with an allusion to Pan's seduction of Luna by the gift of white wool, which is strange because this was Endymion's act, transferred to Pan by an invention of Nicander (according to Servius and Macrobius, 5.22.9): here this source might have afforded a clue. Otherwise, though there are points of interest, we can pass right on to the lengthier passage on snakes (414–39).

The snake, like the *asilus* earlier in the book (*asper, acerba sonans*, 149; *pestem*, 153), is a bitter plague to cattle (*pestis acerba boum*, 419); it is as well a clear forerunner of the disease to come shortly. The passage opens with 11 lines (414–24) of animated advice to the *pastor* to clear his sheds and folds of snakes, the first named being the *chelydrus*. The name is important, as is its literary precedent. Servius noted, "chelydri dicti quasi chersydri, qui et in aquis et in terris morantur: nam χέρσον dicimus terram, aquam vero ὕδωρ"; and the *chelydrus* is described at length by Nicander (*Theriaca*, 411–37). Virgil then devotes fifteen lines to a description of a particular though unnamed snake, which lives in swamps in Calabria, feeding on fish and frogs until the parching heat of summer drives it forth, maddened. The initial *est* (*est etiam ille malus Calabris in saltibus anguis*, 425) indicates a formal ecphrasis, like that of the gadfly (*est lucos Silari circa . . .* , 3.146–53) and of the *amellus* in the next book (*est etiam flos in pratis cui nomen amello*, 4.271). Geography and etymology are again mutually suggestive: this unnamed snake is a Calabrian (*Calaber*), which I suspect is an intentional play on *coluber* in the same metrical position seven lines earlier, though more important is the fact that the setting, like that of the *asilus*, is southern Italy. The real etymology involved, however, has been already mentioned, for this generic snake (*ille malus anguis*) is Nicander's *chersydrus* (described in lines 359–71), whose name includes both earth and water.

Nicander's snake feeds on "molurides" (which may be beetles or other small snakes) and frogs, as Virgil's on fish and "loquacious frogs," during its life as a marsh creature. The occasion of its going forth onto dry land, however, is specified as the "expectation of the Gadfly's distasteful onslaught" (σπέρχεται ἐκ μύωπος ἀήθεα δέγμενος ὁρμήν, 417—so runs the Gow and Scholfield translation, though ἀήθεα ὁρμήν might better refer to the *chelydrus* itself, "receiving an unwonted impulse from the gadfly"). This connection with the gadfly, as fortunate as fortuitous, was enough to catch Virgil's attention, but more germane was the madness Virgil conceived as driving this creature from his accustomed haunts and habits to the land:

> postquam exusta palus, terraeque ardore dehiscunt,
> exsilit in siccum, et flammantia lumina torquens
> saevit agris asperque siti atque exterritus aestu.   (432–34)

(After the swamp has been parched dry and the earth cracks open in the heat, it springs forth onto the dry land and, rolling its flaming eyes, rages in the fields, fierce from thirst and terrified at the heat.)

We are reminded again of the gadfly, *nam mediis fervoribus acrior instat* (154); again, both creatures are invaders of pastoral tranquility (*ne mihi tum mollis sub divo carpere somnos / neu dorso ne-*

moris libeat iacuisse per herbas, 435–36) and represent the extremity of the dry heat of the pastoral landscape, an inversion of its qualities through extension (by now, a familiar technique in this book). The savagery of this snake of water and land, lulled or dormant in the wet, cool spring (*vere . . . udo . . . ac pluvialibus Austris*, 429), is excited by the summer's sun, which drives it forth to plague the shepherd's midday sleep.

The book concludes with diseases (440–77) and the great plague (478–566). *Morborum quoque te causas et signa docebo* (440): Servius noted the categories of technical instruction, "tria dicit, signa morborum, causas, remedias," but (though remedies are detailed in what follows immediately) he did not note that Virgil promises no remedies here, any more than he had when introducing the weather signs (*certis signis*, 1.351—*certis signis* occurs again at 1.394, and *certissima signa* at 1.439). The *quoque*, "also," is to be appreciated: we have just had the causes and indications of snakes, presumably, to which the origins and symptoms of diseases will be parallel or similar. So it is: the *turpis scabies* first attacks when the cold rain of winter (*frigidus imber* etc.) pierces to the quick. Virgil's terms are familiar, but an adjustment must be made at this point. The reader is fresh from the inversions of Libya-Scythia and the snake (not to go back further to the *furor* of passion at the end of the first half of the book, where, through extension to the logical extremes, the heat of the pastoral midday had become a destructive fire): here, suddenly, we are back to the real world of instruction (*docebo*, says Virgil), to the practical shepherd who must be concerned with the effects of winter (as we learned at the very beginning, *Incipiens . . . edico . . .* , 3.295–321) while awaiting the return of summer pasturing (*At vero Zephyris cum laeta vocantibus aestas / in saltus utrumque gregem atque in pascua mittet*, 322–38).

Frigidus imber returns us to the reality of the dangers of winter, but not for long: summer's parching fire is too well-established an element in the book to be long absent at this point, and the snake has been fixed as the precedent of disease. The disease lies hidden (*alitur vitium vivitque tegendo*, 454), like the snake in the earth (*vipera delituit . . . fovit humum* etc., 414–20) or swamps (*stagna colit*, 430), so long as the shepherd does nothing but pray; it glides (*lapsus*, 457—a key verb, for instance, in the snake imagery in *Aeneid* 2) deep into the bones and turns into a parching fire, a *furor* (*cum furit atque artus depascitur arida febris, / profuit incensos aestus avertere*, 458–59). The disease, a *vitium* just before (454) is now a *culpa* to be checked with a knife (468—Servius saw that the terms are inappropriate, "atqui habere morbum culpa non est"), before the dire contagion can "slither" through the herd (*serpant*, 469). At this point the two sections begin to be mutually illuminating. The shepherd must operate, must in fact strike deeply and cleanly with the knife (452–60, summed up here with the words *continuo culpam ferro compesce*), to open the hiding place of the ulcer, just as violent action was called for to destroy the snake (*cape saxa manu, cape robora, pastor*, 420) before it could return to its hiding place in the earth. The clear, and indeed striking, designation of this disease as a "moral wrong" in turn suggests that the heat-induced madness of the snake is similarly something lying and waiting within, to be brought forth when conditions are suitable: the seasonal raging of the serpent is, after all, no different from the destructive madness of other wild life in the spring's heat (3.242–49, 265–66, of which madness the *furor equarum* is the most significant, *insignis*).

Further connections will suggest themselves, but two more are clearly present at the close of this passage. One is made by a return to an earlier, well-established musical motif: *non tam creber agens hiemem ruit aequore turbo / quam multae pecudum pestes* (470–71). Previously in Book I rhyme and rhythm, as well as proximity and context, connected the *artes* and the *pestes* of Jupiter's new order:

tum variae venere artes   (1.145)

tum variae inludunt pestes   (1.181)

Sound and meaning unite the *pestes* here with that first view of man's historical evolution: his evolving world came to include arts and the forces of destruction or degeneration with equal inevitability. Here, where individual character is central, the *pestes* (disease proper) are suggested through this musical motif as being similar to those larger historical *pestes* that were the main concern of the first book, that led to degeneration and caused the *furor* of civil war at the close of the book. War is, in fact, the second connection Virgil makes there: the sickness does not strike individuals, but rather entire "summer camps" (*sed tota aestiva*, 472—the military term for "summer quarters"), and the specific example of a plague is the *Norica castella*, as a result now empty of shepherds (*desertaque regna / pastorum et longe saltus lateque vacantis*, 476–77). Shepherds and soldiers are oddly associated, though understandably after the identification of Libyan shepherd and Roman soldier earlier (3.339–48).

The plague that follows (478–566) is the great exemplum of fire's destructiveness. It is as clear as it is moving. The "storm" (*tempestas*, 479—we need not dwell on the fact that this passage and the preceding passage on love are parallel to the "storm" of civil war and the great storm sequences in the first book) arose in the autumn, a time of seasonal imbalance we have remarked upon often enough. Servius' note (on 479, *totoque autumni incanduit aestu*) gives a general, common view of the instability and resulting danger of autumn in particular: "exarsit prima autumni parte, quae semper gravem efficit pestilentiam. ut autem autumnus abundet morbis, facit hoc confine frigoris et caloris: quod licet etiam vernum tempus habeat, caret morbo, quia tunc corpora praecedenti durata sunt frigore, quae autumnus corrumpit, laxiora inveniens post aestatis calorem" ("It flares forth in the first part of autumn, which always produces serious illness. Autumn, because it borders both cold and heat, thereby abounds with diseases: though spring too is bordering, it lacks disease, because then constitutions have been strengthened by the preceding cold, but autumn corrupts constitutions which it finds weakened after the summer's heat"). The plague is thus introduced as the result of, as well as the essence of, heat: its first symptom is an *ignea sitis*, which contracts the limbs, and such terms (the reality of medicine, after all) are to be found throughout and need not detain us. It is clear enough that the plague is, again, an extension of pastoral warmth to its extreme.

Just as in the excursus on Libya and Scythia, extension to the extreme produces inversion. The plague has destroyed the pastoral order: the horse is *immemor herbae* (498: so, as Servius notes, with the effect of love, 215–17), the pastoral landscape with its shade, soft meadows, and clear stream (520–22) has no power to move the sick spirit, and the cliché of the simple life (now, at last) is revealed as an empty dream (526–30). But beyond this denial of any effectiveness is Virgil's inversion which produces, not a blank, but a sharp negative image. Men must perform the work of animals, scratching the earth with rakes instead of plowing, digging in plants with their own fingernails, dragging their carts with their own necks (534–36). Things have gone further than this, however. Wolves no longer prowl about the sheep folds at night, and deer and dogs wander around the yards together: here is an obvious topic, the impossible become fact; and, as well, conditions are established that are those of a golden age, arrived at not by an envisioned return to a lost harmony and innocence, but by the enforced inversion of the natural order. So it is in every element: creatures of the sea turn to land (541–43), the snakes of the earth (actually both vipers and "water snakes," *hydri*) die nonetheless (*frustra defensa latebris*, 544–45), and birds fall from a now inhospitable sky (*aer non aequus*, 546–47). Human knowledge in any form is helpless: *cessere magistri, / Phyllyrides Chiron Amythaoniusque Melampus* (549–50). Chiron returns from the very beginning of the book where, in a short list of the exemplary horses and trainers *quorum Grai meminere poetae*, he had characteristically not been named (90–94); son of Saturn turned into a horse, he was, as Apollonius saw him (*Argon.* 2.1240–41), "a monster like to both horse and god." Servius noted that Chiron represents the power of medicine, Melampus of religion, and in a general way he was right. It might be more to Virgil's point, however, to see Chiron as knowledge of a scientific sort, and Melampus as magic, a power derived from some unseen source (hence divine) which can change the world in ways beyond comprehension. But in any case, neither master can prevail. Pale Tisiphone comes from Stygian shadows into light (here may be a further inversion of pastoral shade) driving before her Diseases and Fear (*Morbos . . .*

Metumque, 552), and again we must anticipate the figures in the Stygian vestibule in *Aeneid* 6, as we again recall the beginning of this book,

> optima quaeque dies miseris mortalibus aevi
> prima fugit: subeunt morbi tristisque senectus
> et labor, et durae rapit inclementia mortis. (3.66–68)

These are indeed the forces beyond man's control, just as the plague is beyond his medicine. Fire again is the dominating element, the *sacer ignis* of the final line.

A Review

This is a pastoral book—not georgic. Servius draws this distinction clearly in his comment on the first line: "Sane non est mirandum, usum esse eum prooemio, sicut est usus in primo: nam aliud quodammodo inchoaturus est carmen, pastorale scilicet, post completum georgicum" ("It's not strange that Virgil uses a proemium here just as he did in the first book, for he begins, in a sense, another poem, a pastoral poem clearly, after the end of the georgic poem"). This is a distinction more marked for Servius, and for Virgil, than for us, and therefore one that we ought to pay some attention to.

What was the pastoral? For Virgil, we may be sure, there were two very different pastoral worlds. One was the imaginary landscape of his shepherds and herdsmen that he had just left behind, a land of continual summer, of singing in the sleepy quiet of the shade of midday, of a return home as the evening's shadows lengthen on the hills. In such a land there are no cares or pain: unhappiness in love yields to song, and another lover, just as good, can always be found; no winter ever comes and no sudden storms ever intrude. The other pastoral world is that of the ranchers and sheepmen for whom Virgil's instruction (ostensibly, of course) is intended. This is the real world where breeding records are kept, of innoculations and dipping, of shearing and marketing.

Book II presents us with a basic reality of natural growth and cultivated groves and vineyards, against which three major digressions show us idealized conceptions—the grand dreams, or lies, of Italy, of Spring, of Country Life. Book III, conversely, assumes as its basis the idealized land of the pastoral poet, which is interrupted continually by intrusions from the real world of commercial husbandry: this is not quite true, to be sure, because, for one thing, Virgil is writing (ostensibly, again) a didactic poem, not a pastoral, and therefore has no choice other than to offer practical instruction, and, for another, the first half of the book, devoted to larger animals, is very much based in the real world. However, the very fact of the *Eclogues* meant that, even in the first half of this book, the pastoral land of idealized peace could never be very far removed from Virgil's didactic poem: thus, even while we are being given practical instruction on cattle breeding, we often feel that we are in a poetic Arcadia, not on a Lucanian ranch. I think that it is fair to say that Book III is primarily concerned with an important Ideal, just as Book II was concerned with a present Reality, and that this was what Virgil had in mind; furthermore, just as scientific knowledge and physical reality are the focus of the first half of the poem, so the pastoral imagination, which creates the idealized landscape free from care and pain, will be Virgil's ultimate concern in Book III.

The book's proemium sets the real world of Caesar's future and triumphal games against the pastoral ideal of the present. Some day Virgil will sing Octavian's exploits—the battle of Actium, victories in Asia and Egypt, the Trojan beginnings of family and people; but for the present his subject will be the *Dryadum silvas saltusque . . . intactos.* This, of course, is a variation on the standard *recusatio*, with its long history and development, but this refusal to sing of kings and battles is no mere formality of thinly disguised homage. One Virgilian theme is predominant—that of the bullocks to be slaughtered at the triumphal celebration:

> iam nunc sollemnis ducere pompas
> ad delubra iuvat caesosque videre iuvencos.   (22–23)

(Then it will be our pleasure to lead the solemn procession to the temples and to see the slaughter of the bullocks.)

This theme takes us back immediately to the end of the book just preceding, where praise of country life, its ease and peace, concluded abruptly with Remus and his brother, with Rome's walls, when, before Jupiter's reign, war trumpets and swords were as yet unknown and "the impious folk had not yet fed upon the slaughtered bullocks" (*et ante / impia quam caesis gens est epulata iuvencis*, 2.536–37). We are taken back to the praise of Italy, that review of military might with its triumphal processions and sacrificial victims:

> hinc albi, Clitumne, greges et maxima taurus
> victima, saepe tuo perfusi flumine sacro,
> Romanos ad templa deum duxere triumphos.   (2.146–48)

(Hence, Clitumnus, your gleaming flocks and the bull, the greatest victim, often bathed in your sacred stream, have led Roman processions to the temples of the gods.)

Kings, battles, triumphs, and the slaughter of bullocks have been linked, and, as well, Rome's past and that of Aratus' *impia gens*, the bronze race who first fed upon their slaughtered bullocks (*Phaen.* 129–32), have been associated, but we have reached again a point where the poetic elements of Virgil's reflections are too intricate for discourse: we can only point to the opposition of the pastoral and the worldly in the book's proemium—the opposition of ideal peace and Roman wars, of grazing flocks and horses trained for racing and warfare, of the Dryads' groves and Caesar's *templum*.

The book is divided into two parallel halves. The first deals with herds of larger animals (*armenta*), animals raised for war, subject to the fire of physical passion, represented by the gadfly and the warring bulls; the second half is concerned with the flocks of smaller animals, raised in a protected environment of sufficiency and peace, but subject to the devastating fire of disease, represented by the lands of the Libyans and Scythians.

Fire is the book's key element. First, the fire actually blown from the nostrils of the horse fit by nature for war (85), the feeble fire of age (99), the heat of youth (119), innate martial passion controlled by the breeder with *remedia ex contrariis* (123–37), just as the farmer effects elemental balances in the first part of Book I. Next, the gadfly's fire, fiercer at the heat of midday, then the passion of the warring bulls and the fire of sexual frenzy: *in furias ignemque ruunt: amor omnibus idem* (244).

The fire of the second half begins with the perpetual warmth of the land of the pastoral ideal, though the spring of the real world still rings in our ears, *avidis ubi subdita flamma medullis / (vere magis, quia vere calor redit ossibus)* (271–72), and though flocks must be protected from winter's icy winds. No lines in the entire poem have a more seductive loveliness than 322–38, describing the summer pasturing, didactic instruction, yes, but bound to a summer's day of exquisite fragility: morning, noon, and resonant evening such as exist only in memory. What happens if an ideal of such delicacy is subjected to the laws of the physical universe, if one carries the warmth of the pastoral midday to its extreme, to the point where heat and cold become the same? The Libyan shepherd and the Roman soldier are identical, Scythia becomes the pastoral world inverted, fire becomes ice. Fire is now the all-consuming *sacer ignis*, turning the shepherds' realm into a barren waste.

Why has the idealized pastoral landscape been so devastated? I am reminded of Corydon's beeches in *Eclogue* 2, in whose shade he used to come to sing and cure his pain (*tantum inter densas, umbrosa cacumina, fagos / assidue veniebat, Ecl.* 2.3–4), and which, in the shattered world of *Eclogue* 9, represent the lost ideal (*veteres, iam fracta cacumina, fagos, Ecl.* 9.9). The plague has not been sent by a god, nor is it a matter of blind chance. The *sacer ignis* is the heat of the pastoral world, intensified and extended, and represents the inherent failure of pastoral understanding.

In the first two books scientific knowledge was subjected to Virgil's poetic scrutiny, as we saw, and, at the end of the second book, reached a culmination in Bacchus' vine, requiring unending toil, producing uncertain and potentially destructive fruit (as

Servius summarized). The alternative to science is the pastoral, as Virgil proposed at the end of the second book (2.475–94), but the pastoral itself is subject to the gadfly's *furor* and to the burning fever of disease. Passion and madness will inevitably destroy the imagination's ability to create a world of comforting fiction: the power of pastoral song must yield to love, and the heat of midday become the final fire.

CHAPTER FIVE

BOOK IV

The fourth book of the *Georgics* seems to stand apart from the first three: field crops, trees and vines, and animals form three basic divisions of agriculture which can be found in the ethnographical tradition, and though we have no agricultural work that clearly follows these divisions, it is not unlikely that such a work had existed. We can say, though, that Virgil knew what he was doing when he appropriated these divisions for his poem. The subject of the fourth book, however, is incongruous: bees simply do not compare in importance with crops, trees, and animals. Virgil might just as well have written on poultry, or farm dogs, or fishponds, for bees, as an agricultural topic, are of no greater importance. Virgil himself, except at the very beginning of his poem, always summarizes its content by reference to the first three books alone, as he does at the end, *Haec super arvorum cultu pecorumque canebam / et super arboribus* (4.559–60: cf. Aristaeus' *silvae . . . stabulis . . . messis*, 4.329–30; or the old man's abandoned land not good for *iuvencis . . . nec pecori . . . nec Baccho*, 4.127–29; or 1.54–56, 4.128–29).

The book is strange, too, in that its last half is taken up with the stories of Aristaeus and Orpheus. Even in antiquity an explanation had to be found for this oddity: the story was invented that all or part of this half had originally contained the *laudes Galli*, which Virgil was forced to suppress, substituting (it is to be supposed) some epyllion he had had lying around, unpublished, with his *juvenalia*. (I will say no more about this absurdity, preserved by Servius, in which the only truth is the notice that Gallus in some way figured at the end of the poem: Virgil's Orpheus can be shown to have developed from an Orpheus of Gallus.) Modern literati explain the incongruity of this last half in a variety of ways, none of which would be necessary if it were at all clear what Virgil intended, and why these stories follow on the death of the bees. What the bees are intended to represent is anything but clear as well. The problem, then, is to understand why this book is appended to the three properly agricultural books, what the bees signify, who are Aristaeus and Orpheus, and what relation there is between the two halves. These large questions are only the beginning: any number of details pose questions that beg to be answered, but without satisfactory resolution of the larger issues, no solutions to difficulties of detail will be generally acceptable. Nothing Virgil wrote presents the reader with greater uncertainties on every level than this book.

The Bees and Primitive Society

Studies of Virgil's bees have produced two conclusions which can be assumed here at the start: that the bees in some way stand for men, if not Man, and that the form of Virgil's description is in some way related to ethnography. If it is clear that the first three books of the poem are more than a technical treatise on the three main divisions of agriculture, then it ought to be assumed that the first half of the fourth book was not simply intended to offer instruction to the beekeeper. Yet, if the bees do represent a human society, what sort of society is it? Here there is no consensus whatsoever. Did Virgil describe a model to be followed? Or is this an ideal which human societies cannot be expected to attain? Was Virgil thinking of Rome, and if so, to what extent? Are Antony and Octavian to be seen behind the two king bees, for instance? The difficulty, quite simply, is that no coherent and consistent explication has yet been offered, that after most of the pieces have been put into place, a few remain that seem to have no place at all. For instance, if we assume that the description is an ideal that we should contemplate but cannot hope to emulate, then why are there still wars in this ideal society, and why is it

ultimately so fragile, and why is it consistently so frigidly in-
human—arguably devoid of individual love and of beauty? If we
are to view these bees as a model, how can we be expected to do
so (usefully at any rate) when the bees are not troubled by what
in Virgil's mind was most characteristic of man—*furor*, mani-
fested as *amor* or as any all-consuming passion? In either case,
why is the insignificance of these creatures sometimes so pointedly suggested: why can their wars be settled "with a handful of
dust," or why was it necessary for Virgil to point out that all it
takes to keep a colony from leaving is to pull the wings off its
king (*nec magnus prohibere labor*, 4.106)? Furthermore, who is
this great beekeeper, especially if we are to see his swarm as a
paradigm for Rome, which Virgil's language seems to invite us
to do? Such are the sorts of questions and difficulties that confront any interpretation (and that keep alive, and alluring, the
notion that perhaps Virgil was writing, after all, simply about
bees).

Related to the assumption that the bee society must in some
way reflect human society is the view that Virgil's description
often uses specific terms of ethnography and approaches the
form of ethnographical writing. Here again, though, there are
extra pieces that don't quite fit: the form, though suggested, is
not reproduced precisely. We have observed Virgil previously
playing with the forms and topics of ethnography (as in the
laudes Italiae in Book II, or in the descriptions of Scythia and
Libya in Book III), where an awareness of ethnography was
helpful, or necessary, in seeing what special purposes Virgil
had, and where those special purposes in fact meant that the ethnographical forms and topics were not (and could not) be reproduced precisely. Where ethnography is suggested, it ought to be
allowed to offer the sort of help it has before.

There are other assumptions to be made. We ought to be
aware of terms and ideas that have been of importance earlier in
the poem: this book does not continue with the subjects of instruction (crops, trees, and animals), but seems to stand outside
the agricultural "matter" of Virgil's poem, and so it seems fair
to assume that it must summarize, or deal synthetically with,

what has preceded, and that consequently we should be ready to react to suggestions of ideas, themes, topics, motifs, or whatever, that were important previously. Finally, I will assume something not previously (I think) explored, that Virgil was not writing a static description of a society or culture (such as an anthropologist or ethnographer would write), describing the bees as they existed at a certain time; but we may assume (as a hypothesis) that he wrote rather as an historian, describing the bees as they developed at successive times or stages in their past, that the description is a progression. Certainly Virgil's announced topic (*duces totiusque ordine gentis / mores et studia et populos et proelia dicam*, 4–5) sounds like the topics of *res gestae*, and *ordine* may be an invitation to see a progression in the events recorded. This assumption might explain certain of those inevitable contradictions: what was true of, or important about, the bees at a certain stage of their development might not be true at a later stage.

> Principio sedes apibus statioque petenda,
> quo neque sit ventis aditus . . .
>
> at liquidi fontes et stagna virentia musco
> adsint . . .
>
> haec circum casiae virides et olentia late
> serpylla et graviter spirantis copia thymbrae
> floreat, inriguumque bibant violaria fontem.   (8–9, 18–19, 30–32)

(First, a residence and locale must be found for your bees, where there is no access for the winds . . . But let there be clear springs and pools green with moss . . . And around let the green marjoram flower and the far-fragrant thyme and an abundance of strong-scented savory, and let the violet beds drink the waters of a spring.)

Quite clearly, here at the beginning, Virgil suggests the essential opening topics of an ethnography, a description of the land (*situs*) in terms of its air (here *ventis*, 9—note that it is repeated at the end of the line, *nam pabula venti*) and water (with lines 25–29). Seasons as well are prominent (*vere suo . . . calori*, 22–23; *hiems . . . calor*, 36). The types of hives and their construction (in

the second half of the passage, 33–46) can also be seen as standard topics in a description of the *situs*. Such an ethnographical
beginning would be in no way foreign to the writings of historians from Herodotus on, and at Rome in fact had been given
fresh life and interest by Posidonius, as we have previously seen
reflected in the *Georgics*. There is nothing inconsistent with the
notion that through his bees Virgil is describing the origins of a
people.

In this setting we may now draw attention to certain unmistakable Virgilian ideas, some of which are inherent in the ethnographical topics, some foreign and seemingly intrusive. First,
set forth in the rhetorical opposition of *absint et* (13) and *adsint et*
(19), comes a list of the bees' enemies—sheep, kids, the heifer,
which harm the bees' pastures (as they had harmed the young
vines, 2.371–75); then lizards "with painted, scaly backs," and
the bee-eater and other birds, and Procne "marked on her breast
with bloody hands," all of which "lay waste" (*vastant*) everything and carry off the bees themselves (*dulcem escam*) to feed
their own young. This second group of enemies seems particularly monstrous, not unlike the *monstra* (also called *pestes*) that
attack the threshing floor (1.181–86), or in fact the unnatural
creatures of Eastern lands (2.140–42), and it is perhaps to
heighten the contrast that it seems to interrupt the ethnographical airs and waters topic, for the "waters" (*at liquidi fontes . . .
adsint et . . .*, 18–19) is a setting of perfectly naturalistic serenity,
much like the commonplace of the *locus amoenus*.

By the side of these clear springs and mossy pools, and on this
grassy bank is the "entrance hall" (*vestibulum*) shaded by palm
and "native oleaster" (*ingens oleaster*, 20). Again the epithet *ingens* carries Virgilian suggestions, "native" and "natural" (that
is, untampered with by man), that we have seen before (for instance, ironically of the grafted tree at 2.80, and of Media's native lemon, 2.131), and that must be remembered simply because the oleaster is hardly "huge." The oleaster itself is, in fact,
the wild olive, unproductive but vigorous enough to survive
even fire (*infelix*, 2.314). The suggestiveness of *ingens oleaster*

should be kept in mind as we come to see other implications of this original *situs* of the bees.

The clearest ethnographical topic in this section is that of climate and season: situation affords a tempered climate *par excellence*; not only is there protection from winds, but there is shade and the stream's bank as a retreat from the heat of summer (20–23), and the hive itself provides a temperate environment (35–36); the might of cold and heat are equally to be feared (*utraque vis apibus pariter metuenda*, 37). The necessity of a tempered climate for young things has been a commonplace: we need remember only the shepherd's first task (guarding his flock against winter's cold and summer's heat (3.295–338), or the farmer's first efforts to create a balance between hot and wet (1.71–117), or the vine-grower's concern to achieve these same balances for his young vines (2.346–53, 373–77), or the herdsman's treatment from opposites (3.123–37), among many other similar passages. Of most obvious relevance, though, is the Praise of Spring (2.315–45), which concludes with the spring of the world's creation, a balance necessary for the beginning of life itself:

> nec res hunc tenerae possent perferre laborem,
> si non tanta quies iret frigusque caloremque
> inter, et exciperet caeli indulgentia terras.　　　　(2.343–45)

(Nor would delicate creatures be able to endure this struggle, were there not such a period of calm between cold and heat, and did heaven not embrace the earth with gentleness.)

Virgil does have in mind the emergence of the young bees and their need particularly for a tempered environment:

> ut, cum prima novi ducent examina reges
> vere suo, ludentque favis emissa iuventus,
> vicina invitet decedere ripa calori.　　　　(4.21–23)

(. . . in order that, when the new kings will first lead forth their swarms in their springtime and the youth will play, just emerged from the combs, the neighboring bank may invite them to shelter from the heat.)

Vere suo might seem odd (attempts have been made to change
suo to *novo*, in conformity with the *vere novo* of 1.43), but it is
precisely the bees' first spring, the time of their creation, the
precarious beginning of their society, that Virgil is attempting
to stress by beginning the line *vere suo*, in much the same way
that *Principio* (8) now seems to point to more than the first step
in Virgil's instructions. We must remember, however, that creation's spring is part of the Praise of Spring, one of the three
grand lies of the second book; that such a balance is typical of
the Golden Age ideal (the *ver aeternum*), and as such was granted
to Italy in the *laudes Italiae (hic ver adsiduum,* 2.149); that in the
real, physical world, spring on the contrary is the time of conflict, the meeting of opposing elements—suggestions of which
Virgil has in fact dropped throughout this passage in his references to the *utraque vis metuenda* of heat and cold.

The emergence of the bees (to sum up) occurs in a somewhat
idealized spring, affording the tempered balance necessary for
all young and tender things: always in the background, however, are not only the opposing elements, but the bees' enemies,
a sinister presence in this scene of extraordinary tranquility.
Their temperate climate ("their own spring") demands no special effort from the bees, beyond the lining of their rather primitive hives: here is a detail, toward the end of the first section,
that carries us on a new path leading into the next section. The
bees do no building. It is not just a matter of the demands of the
didactic manner that requires Virgil to have the beekeeper provide hives for the colony at this point: building will be part of
the bees' (anthropomorphic) activity soon, as if no beekeeper
existed; and in any case the hives provided are a most primitive
sort of shelter, of sewn bark or woven wicker (33–34). Just a few
lines later we find other sorts of homes, information of no use
to the beekeeper whatsoever, and offered by Virgil with some
hesitation as mere hearsay:

> saepe etiam effossis, si vera est fama, latebris
> sub terra fovere larem, penitusque repertae
> pumicibusque cavis exesaeque arboris antro.   (42–44)

(If the report is true, they often made a home even in dugout holes under the earth, and have been found deep within the hollows of porous rock and in the cavern of a hollowed tree.)

"If the report is true," these first bees lived underground, or in caves, or in hollow trees: it seems indeed to be Virgil's purpose to stress that this primitive society lived an entirely natural existence, with no building whatsoever, not unlike the anthropological view of primitive man, living in caves or rude shelters, that we find, for instance, in Lucretius (5.955–57) or Juvenal (6.1–13). The origin of these bees, then, is no simple conception—neither, on the one hand, idealized as the *ver adsiduum* of a Golden Age, nor, on the other, as a time of purely naturalistic primitivism of scientific anthropology. Virgil's picture is eclectic and unifying—as always.

(I must call attention to the last four lines of this section, 47–50. The injunction against planting the yew near the hive is understandable, for the yew is a malignant tree that loves the cold [cf. 2.113, 257, and especially *Ecl.* 9.30], and stagnant swamps seem *prima facie* unsuitable. But when, and where, and why were crabs ever burned on ancient hearths? This remains perhaps the most intriguing minor puzzle of the poem. The *vocis imago*, at the very end, seems as well to conceal something of importance.)

The next section (51–66) reveals a further stage in the development of this primitive society—building, though on a small scale. The time is still spring (*ubi pulsam hiemem sol aureus egit / sub terras caelumque aestiva luce reclusit*, 51–52), but purposeful activity is to be observed, exploration, gathering flowers and water, raising the young, building honeycombs and making the honey itself, done with "art" (*hinc arte recentis / excudunt ceras*, 56–57, where *arte* is almost modified by *recentis*). Spring swarming (an important "fact" of apiculture) is Virgil's next subject: the swarm seeks fresh water and leafy homes (58–62); the beekeeper can attract the swarm with significant foliage ("honeyleaf" and "wax-flower"), or—in spite of bees' well-known aversion to loud noises, which Virgil has just cautioned against (49–

50)—by clashing the cymbals of the Magna Mater (*tinnitusque cie et Matris quate cymbala circum*, 64).

The Magna Mater takes us necessarily to Phrygia and Mt. Ida, with a stop at the (frequently conflated) Mt. Ida on Crete, where the Curetes, who themselves had connections with the Magna Mater and Phrygia (see for instance Lucretius, 2.629–39), hid the infant Jupiter's cries from Saturn by clashing their cymbals, in return for which service the bees received from Jupiter their subsequent nature (according to Virgil a bit later, 149–52—Virgil seems, purposely of course, to conflate this service of the Curetes with the bees who sometimes feed the infant Jupiter). This web of associations must lead to the Troad, and is itself only one signpost of several we have neglected so far. Just previously the bees were lining their hives with propolis "stickier than the pitch of Phrygian Ida" (*et Phrygiae servant pice lentius Idae*, 41): Ida was known for its pine forests, but there would seem to be no real reason for this precise reference here. There may have been another suggestion of the Troad preceding this: Servius, at least, preserves a connection between the *thymbrae* of 31 (*et graviter spirantis copia thymbrae*) and Phrygia, "herbae genus est abundantis in Phrygia": there is good reason for crediting Virgil with this association, because the temple of Apollo at Thymbra (a district or mountain in the Troad) was visited by Aeneas:

> Templa dei saxo venerabar structa vetusto:
> "da propriam, Thymbraee, domum; da moenia fessis
> et genus et mansuram urbem; serva altera Troiae
> Pergama, reliquias Danaum atque immitis Achilli."   (*Aen.* 3.84–87)
>
> (I prayed at this temple of the god, built from ancient rock: "Give us our own home, Thymbraean Apollo; grant walls for the weary, and a future line, and a lasting city; protect another Trojan citadel and these survivors of the Greeks and savage Achilles.")

Another figure associated with *Thymbraeus Apollo* is Aristaeus, his son (*Geo.* 4.323), who, in the beginning (at least) of his entreaty to his mother, is cast in the pattern of Achilles calling upon his mother Thetis on the shore at Troy (*Iliad* 1.348–58).

The pattern of suggestions here is similar to that early in the first book, where military language and the references to Mysia and Gargara (at first sight gratuitous) led to the simile of irrigation from the *Iliad*, when Achilles confronted the Scamander, fire opposing water. Troy seems even more persistently suggested here, by geographical references again seemingly gratuitous but with an even more intricate weaving of associations. What was the point? The Trojan origin of the Roman people was an ancient tradition, recently exploited for political purposes by the Julian *gens*. It seems that Virgil was adding a further dimension to his already extremely eclectic description of the origins of this society. I do not want to suggest that the bees are solely, or simply, a paradigm for the Roman people, or that their development will trace in any allegorical manner the history of Rome, but I do think that Virgil did intend (what else?) to leave with his reader these fleeting impressions of Phrygia and Troy clearly associated with his emerging swarm, itself already partly idealized in a golden spring, partly rationalized according to the theories of the anthropologists.

At this point it will be helpful to take our bearings in the course of Virgil's presentation. Next comes a section on wars (67–87), then one on the two types of kings and of peoples (88–102), then a brief section on the prevention of migration (103–15). At this point there is the major digression on the old man of Tarentum, as enigmatic as it is striking and of obvious importance (116–48). Then the account of the bees resumes, with the character given to them by Jupiter, another hundred lines (149–250) which seems to cover much of the same material surveyed in the (roughly) first hundred (8–115), until the introduction of the subject of diseases begins the movement into the second half of the book. Discussions of the bees generally make no distinction between the first hundred lines (preceding the old man) and the second, developing their arguments and drawing their illustrations from both parts simultaneously: indeed, much of what Virgil presents seems the same from one part to the other— kingship, communal building and society, the gathering of honey, wars, and inevitably many other details. Since we are proceeding here, however, with the working assumption that there may be a progression, we need to make sure of our place on Virgil's map, realizing that we are approaching what seems to be a major divide between two areas approximately equal in size, and that west of the divide the land may be entirely different than it was on the east.

Sin autem ad pugnam exierint (67): the battle which follows is epic in scale as well as in style—up to a point. The description is complete, from the first *discordia* between two kings, to preparations, to the actual engagement with the victor in pursuit of the defeated. The time is again spring and the weather is fine (*ergo ubi ver nactae sudum*, 77): there is something not quite real about this whole conflict, as if it was staged for the spectacle alone, a stylized affair directed solely by the kings for their own pleasure and display, a pageant in which there is no suggestion of real suffering or death. This ceremony (*imitata* may be literal, 72) of war will be ended, in fact, by casting a bit of dust:

> hi motus animorum atque haec certamina tanta
> pulveris exigui iactu compressa quiescent.   (86–87)

(These impassioned commotions and these struggles, great as they are, will be calmed, suppressed by throwing a little dust.)

If we have been led to think of a Trojan site just before, then we may be allowed to do so again in this epic presentation of regal combat, a war removed inevitably from present reality, a scene from intangible history long since settled into dust. Though the nobility of the participants is not to be denied (*ingentis animos angusto in pectore versant*, 83), the view of the event which we must take is that of remote objectivity.

The next passage (88–102) is similar: when you have recalled both kings from battle (as if it had indeed been a fine day's outing), kill the lesser one: there are two sorts of kings, two sorts of peoples. This passage, as all else, is founded in apiary lore (see Varro, *RR* 3.16.18–19), which enables us to see what is Virgil's own point. Virgil begins with the instruction to allow the better to rule alone in the palace (*melior vacua sine regnet in aula*, 90), and ends with the purpose of this choice, sweet honey (*haec potior suboles, hinc caeli tempore certo / dulcia mella premes*, 100–101): the "better" (*melior*, 90 and 92) produces better honey (*mel*), a pun straight from Varro (*qui ita melior, ut expediat mellario*—see context, 3.16.18) appreciated by Virgil but, for good reason, played down. Varro's types are the black and the reddish (*ruber*—with a third possible, *varius*), but Virgil's better king, and his people, are brilliant with gold and red-gold (*auro . . . ardens*, 91; *rutilis clarus squamis*, 93; *elucent aliae et fulgore coruscant / ardentes auro*, 98–99), and their bodies are like drops (*et paribus lita corpora guttis*, 99—presumably suggesting drops of honey). Contrarily, the poorer sort appear dry and dusty, like a dust-covered traveller (*ceu pulvere ab alto / cum venit et sicco terram spuit ore viator / aridus*, 96–98), a detail Virgil has in fact transferred from Varro's signs of sickness (*ut pulverulentae*, 3.16.20). Dryness and richness form a familiar polarity, but the richness here has become that of royal gold, a necessary attribute of the producer of honey.

Then a third, parallel vignette: to prevent the migration of a swarm, just pull the wings off the king, which, as Virgil stresses, requires no great effort (*instabilis animos ludo prohibebis inani. / nec magnus prohibere labor*, 103–106): again we feel a remoteness from the royal splendor we have just observed. There is a second way, though, to keep the bees, providing gardens presided over by the guardianship of Priapus of the Hellespont:

> invitent croceis halantes floribus horti
> et custos furum atque avium cum falce saligna
> Hellespontiaci servet tutela Priapi.   (109–11)

(Let gardens, fragrant with saffron flowers, entice them, and let the guardianship of Priapus of the Hellespont protect them, the watchman against thieves and birds with his willow sickle.)

Here is a detail that doesn't receive much attention. Priapus' native city was by tradition Lampsacus, on the Hellespont (Catullus, fr. 1, *Lampsaci . . . ora Hellespontia*): again we are directed to the Troad, and, in fact, *every* geographical reference or suggestion thus far in the book has directed us to the Troad. Just as in the description of the battle, the feeling of remoteness (much like that of viewing through the wrong end of a telescope) inevitably aligns itself with the references to Troy to produce the impression that the bees, with their kings and battles and gold, existed in a distant past, somehow a part of us, but somehow too separated to have the substance of real flesh and blood.

One potential difficulty with this part of the poem has been resolved without special effort, the question of the identity of the great beekeeper who towers above kings and battles, settling the latter by a casting of dust, pulling the wings blithely off the former. He is, it would seem, Virgil's reader, who receives and carries out the instruction presented for him, who stands superior to and removed from his bees. He is, too, a contemporary Roman reader, who is superior to and removed from the origins of this society, from the idealized spring that allowed and fostered its emergence, from its naturalistic and primitive beginnings, and remote as well from the nobility, the magnanimity of heroic battle, and the golden glory of its Trojan past. To this Roman reader nothing remains but the contemplation of the swarm of tiny creatures, none of them individuals, in the spring air (58–61): the scale of time has reduced the events correspondingly. In these lines, directed to the great beekeeper, there is no Virgilian sympathy, no *lacrimae rerum*: it is worthwhile to establish this absence clearly (Virgil has insisted upon it), and to reflect why. The Roman reader is looking to a past blurred in a variety of ways by inevitable distortions, among which idealization is the most distorting. But even so, "with this harsh effort let him blister his hands, let him plant cuttings that will bear fruit, let him bring the friendly rains," all to keep the swarm:

ipse labore manum duro terat, ipse feracis
figat humo plantas et amicos inriget imbris.   (114–15)

The Old Man and Primitivism

The call to provide gardens leads directly to the excursus on the old man of Tarentum, the master gardener, but whose identity and function in the poem are anything but clear. Is he a model and paradigm? Hardly: Virgil is not preaching, nor would the simple life be his message, an unreal retreat from the complexities he has presented thus far, nor is any "answer" likely to have been outlined so elusively in such a brief space, and with so much darkness to follow in the book. If we are not to pattern our own lives after this model, then, what is he the representative of? Is he the human equivalent of the bee society in some way and for some reason? Whatever he is, we ought to be able to count on Virgil providing the answer in terms previously established.

The most striking thing about this old character is that he is totally unrealistic, to the extent that one can wonder whether his solitary existence hasn't addled his brains. If we meet him without romantic bias or interpretative preconceptions, we can see, I think, that his world is not our world. We don't meet him until late at night (he puts in an inordinately long day, for someone who so often is made to represent the ease of the sane rustic existence), when he comes home to load his table with "a feast not bought" (130–33), but the delights of his self-sufficiency are not entirely digestible: his board groans with the odd vegetable, true (*hic rarum tamen in dumis olus*, 130 — even this he has had to burrow out of the brambles), but also with lilies, verbena, and poppies, thus "equaling the wealth of kings with his spirit." His is the first rose to bloom in spring, his the first fruits in autumn (134), but what he does next is as impossible as the evening meal we have just seen: it is cold enough to split rocks, and streams are frozen (note that this is no idealized landscape of the pastoral sort), but somehow, without the benefit of a hot house or even a cold frame, he has hyacinths in full bloom (135–38). He raises bees, therefore, and for them he plants flowers and flowering trees which bear him fruit (139–43); but again Virgil has injected a false note, for he *even* sets out rows of mature (?) elms (*ille etiam seras in versum distulit ulmos*, 144) along with pears and wild plums (?), and the totally unproductive, but shady, plane trees (*iamque ministrantem platanum potantibus umbras*, 146). These last lines raise a number of questions that ought to be faced. Why elms? The only horticultural purpose of the elm is to support grape vines (the leaves stripped to provide sun were used for pig fodder), which *in versum* ("in rows") must suggest, but we know that this is no extensive vineyard (*nec commoda Baccho*, 129). Why has he transplanted "mature" elms (*seras* cannot mean anything else—so Servius Auctus, " 'seras' hic vetulas et magnas"), and mature plums and plane trees as well (as *iam . . . iam* must suggest, 145–46)? (*Distulit* can mean "he has transplants grown to maturity," but Virgil's language is odd, to say the least, and the first impression necessarily is that the old man has accomplished the impossible—transplanting fully grown trees.) Then, why plane trees to give shade to drinkers, if this old man grows no grapes for himself, and buys no wine for his table? Any one of these questions, inconsistencies, or contradictions would be a quibble not worth bothering a poet with, but there are so many here that it seems reasonable that Virgil planted them intentionally, suggesting that this old man is not part of any real world—he has summer, after all, when everyone else is deep in winter. We have seen before that the impossible, when clearly recognized as such, often provided the key to Virgil's purpose.

One such passage concerned trees "wild" and "cultivated" at the beginning of the second book, in which Virgil blurred the previously established distinction between wild and cultivated (in lines 47–68), until finally the wild were grafted (impossibly) with the cultivated (69–72—the plane with apple, beech with chestnut, ash with pear, and finally even elm with oak). So the old man here has lindens and "wild bay trees" (*tinus* is a difficult tree to identify, and the reading here in any case might be *pinus*, as above in line 112 where the same variants occur), which are certainly unfruitful (as Servius felt compelled to note, " 'illi uberrima' scilicet: nam per naturam et tiliae et pinus steriles esse dicuntur"), but which Virgil seems to present *precisely as the source* of the old man's autumn fruit:

> illi tiliae atque uberrima tinus,
> quotque in flore novo pomis se fertilis arbos
> induerat totidem autumno matura tenebat.   (141–43)

(He had lindens and the succulent viburnum [? or "pine"?], and his tree in the ripeness of autumn retained fruits as many as the flowers it had first dressed itself in.)

We then find that he has pears (though what the epithet *eduram* suggested we don't know), and what appear to be wild plums, and then, again the unfruitful elms and planes (all of which, remember, Virgil has implied were transplanted not only in large numbers—as "in rows" must suggest—but when fully matured). This is nonsense compounded: if Virgil meant only to say that the old man was a marvelous orchardist, he would have had him growing apples, figs, pomegranates and the like.

Bees produce honey from the wild: from flowers and grass (11–12), in the shade (at least) of the palm and "natural" (*ingens*) oleaster (20), using willows as bridges (26), from various aromatic plants like thyme (*casia, serpyllum, thymbra*, 30–31), from "honey-leaf" and "wax-flower" (63), from thyme and *tinus* (or *pinus*, 112), from the narcissus, acanthus, ivies, and myrtles (123–24) and others in the present passage. Man's use of the wild produced the fantastic monstrosities of his grafting (all, as Virgil knew, unreal—and hence literally fantastic: "ingens fantasia," as Servius noted at 2.82) or wrenched from them the uses of civilization to create, among other things, luxurious homes, wheels, ships, and the spears and bows of war: see especially 2.434–57, a passage ending with bees who inhabit the hollow of a "corrupt" oak, *vitiosae ilicis alvo*, and with the *ad culpam causas* of Bacchus, with the complex of suggestions conveyed by the Varronian gloss "*vitis a vino: id est a vi*," at the end of Virgil's *vituperatio vini*. (We may properly draw attention to the inclusion of this important complex as a minor theme here in the fourth book, where the passage on the two sorts of kings and peoples ends with honey sweet and clear *et duram Bacchi domitura saporem*, 102.)

One further observation on these gardens, and then we will be in a position to offer a conclusion about the old man. His garden, as we have seen, is totally unreal, an observation worth repeating simply because it is not common: its seasons are its own,

what is planted is unimaginable in several ways, what is produced (the *rarum olus*, and *poma* of *tilia* and *tinus*) is of doubtful
substance. It occupies abandoned land good for no georgic purpose (*nec fertilis illa iuvencis / nec pecori opportuna seges nec commoda
Baccho*, 128–29: we have here again the three main divisions of
agriculture and of the first three books). These two facts of its
nature—its unreality and its uselessness—set it beyond any real
time and place, almost as if it were a conception such as the
Golden Age: indeed, the *biferi rosaria Paesti* suggest that unreal
mark of the never-never land, twice-bearing trees or animals
(roses, though, *do* have two annual periods of heavy bloom).
Why then, or how, does Virgil claim to have seen this particular
garden (*memini me . . . vidisse senem*, 125–27)?

This is the unreality of the poet, but one different from the
Golden Age, or the Isles of the Blessed, or the dream of country
peace and sufficiency, or any of the other dreams that have occupied so much of Virgil's attention thus far, different in that it
was neither inherited nor shared but was a conception all Virgil's own. "I remember that I saw . . ."; not just *memini* or *vidi*,
but a double remoteness, a personal vision of what *once* existed
in a fusion of imagination and remembrance. The *senex* himself
is a man of two worlds and belonging to neither, living now in
the southern extremity of Italy, as far removed from Rome as
was possible, *sub Oebaliae turribus arcis* (Tarentum, that is, if we
translate the designation), but originally from Corycus in Cilicia. Because Virgil was, apparently, so specific here, readers
have always assumed a certain reality behind this figure, and
have made the most of what began with Servius, the "history"
of Pompey's Cilician pirates, or the fact that the Cilicians were
gardeners of note. But Servius began his note with a neglected
comment quite different, and of interest precisely because of its
apparent irrelevance: "Corycos enim civitas est Ciliciae, in qua
antrum illud famosum est, paene ab omnibus celebratum." This
Corycian cave, though, is not in Cilicia (with the exception of
this conflated notice), but on Mt. Parnassus, and was indeed
well known (τὸ Κωρύκιον ἄντρον, mentioned by Herodotus,
8.36, for instance; for a description see Pausanias, 10.32.7—it

was very large, and sacred to Pan and the nymphs, and associated later, naturally enough, with the Apollo of Delphi). The ancient scholarly tradition thus associated the Corycian cave above Delphi with the *Corycius senex*, as preserved in Servius' somewhat garbled note, and I expect that Virgil made the association too—not, of course, explicitly, and perhaps not even primarily: but he chose his Corycian, I would think, just because the suggestion of that well-known cave ("illud famosum") would add dimension and a certain mysteriousness of association to his old man. What would seem to be specific in the identification of the *senex* is actually quite otherwise—he is Italian, but not quite, Cilician in origin, but more remotely from a cave on Parnassus: to be fixed clearly, as it turns out, in no land we have ever known.

Only Virgil (to resume) knew this man or had imagined his locale. He is closely connected with the bees and is like them in many ways—ultimately in that he is able to live off the unfruitful plants which are nature's, not man's concern. He is not, however, representative of them, or their equivalent in human terms, because he himself gathers their honey and must be their keeper, and because he himself is far from "human" but is drawn with a few bold, purposely unrealistic strokes. In the progression of the book he is presented in the transitional panel between the origins and early development of the bee society and that same society after it received the (present) nature of its character from Jupiter. What is unrealistic about the old man is very much like what is idealized in the primitivism of the original bees. Both are representations, I would conclude, of the same image: the old man does not reflect these bees, or vice versa, but both are reflections of a highly eclectic and (therefore) original conception of the origins of man and of his early society—the origins, in fact, of the Roman people. The unreal primitivism of the old man is clearly parallel to that of the bees; he too exists in an unreal condition of benevolent spring, where nature (even nature's flowers) seems to provide for this table, in conditions that are like those of the Golden Age (this is *not* the Golden Age, just as it is not pure primitivism, either for the bees or the man, because in both cases Virgil is shaping his own representation of the beginning); he does work, and for long hours, but it is work that is in happy co-operation with nature—the only such representation in the poem, I must add; and finally, he is not simply Italian, and indeed not Italian at all, but rather from the east (Cilicia, or Asia Minor), from a town that would seem to have been chosen by Virgil solely because it was homonymous with a well-known cave on Parnassus, a settler in an Italian town whose Greek origin is suggested by the only name Virgil gives it, and all this again parallel to those brief but illuminating suggestions of Trojan geography in the account of the early bees. (I might add here, parenthetically but for the sake of completeness, what I think is, in the light of what is to follow, another possible parallel: the innate disposition of the early bee society toward war, which thus far has been shown as both rather harmless and certainly insignificant, may have been intended as the equivalent to the suggestions of drinking (Bacchus) we have observed in the context of the old man; both may represent latent destruction.)

We have, then, two different representations of man's origins, one as seen in terms of the most social of insects, one drawn as an individual man, but both extraordinarily original and imaginative, employing images and ideas from a variety of other conceptions. They are complementary, often tangent, and together form a purely Virgilian vision of what has frequently been seen earlier in the poem in traditional terms. In both descriptions there is much that is, intentionally, unreal, because the nature of our (real) world had not yet been given to the bees by Jupiter.

The Bees and the Mature Society

Nunc age, naturas apibus quas Iuppiter ipse
addidit expediam, pro qua mercede canoros
Curetum sonitus crepitantiaque aera secutae
Dictaeo caeli regem pavere sub antro.   (149–52)

(Now then, I will relate what character Jupiter himself gave to the bees, as a reward for their feeding him, the king of heaven, in the Dictaean cave, when they followed the tuneful sounds of the Curetes and the rattling of bronze.)

The present character of the bees will occupy Virgil now. There can be no question about this reference to Jupiter: we must remember his new order, presented by Virgil most fully early in the first book in the lengthy description of the enforced discovery of the arts of civilization (1.118–59). Indeed, the bees have reached an entirely different stage in their development, with the large-scale building of a city: they had previously occupied the rather primitive structures provided for them (33–34), or had even, *si vera est fama,* lived underground, in rocky caves, or in hollow trees (42–44). Furthermore, they are governed by "great laws," a sure sign of the new age. Gone is their perpetual spring (*venturaeque hiemis memores aestate laborem / experiuntur,* 156–57): the process is very much like that described in the first book, where Jupiter affected conditions so that labor became necessary, bringing with it the arts, discovered gradually by *usus. Experiuntur* here may be a reflection of *apibus quanta experientia parcis* in the proem (1.4)—this rather awkward as well as specialized noun is used by Virgil elsewhere only at *Geo.* 4.316, with *extudit artem* ending the preceding line (cf. *varias usus . . . extunderet artis,* 1.133), where Virgil asks the Muses who discovered the art of *bugonia.* In the next lines, in fact, the arts mentioned closely parallel those mentioned in the first book (136–44): the bees have agriculture (158–59), they build for the future (159–64), have an army (165) and astronomy (or at least a weather bureau, 166). The simile of the Cyclopes as iron-workers concludes with *ferrum* (170–75), putting us very much in an age of iron (how else could Virgil have made this point?), just as (*non aliter*) the bees are pressed by the inborn love of possession (*Cecropias innatus apes amor urget habendi / munere quamque suo,* 177–78). Finally (191–96), there is a suggestion of sailing, though here the expeditions, when rain impends, are brief trials; in the beginning of the book, when Virgil advised the beekeeper to provide "bridges" for his bees (25–29), he may have been pointing to the absence of "navigation" at that early stage.

The communal life of the bee society may be worth notice. They have children in common (153), and mindful of winter they have common stores (157). This aspect of their city life is illustrated further in lines 184–90: all work is done in unison, all rest is taken together (*omnibus una quies operum, labor omnibus unus*, 184). *In medium quaesita reponunt* (157) would appear to be another suggestion of the first book (*in medium quaerebant*, 1.127), but there this communal living was due to the abundance of provision *before* Jupiter put an end to it, whereas here it is Jupiter's gift. There is no inconsistency or contradiction: Virgil's description of the development of the bee society is his own, employing terms or ideas eclectically, refashioning a variety of sources at once. The bees' communal living should not suggest a pre-Jupiter, "Golden Age," but rather a prominent characteristic of Roman society at an early stage in its development, as the next section makes clear.

The bees do not indulge in sexual intercourse, but their race remains immortal: so begins and ends this brief paragraph, an ethnographical wonder (*mirabere*, 197–209). The import of the passage, however, is somewhat different. The bees quite suddenly are called *Quirites* (201), which is something quite different from the sort of metaphorical anthropomorphizing resulting from their having the artifacts or institutions of human society, even such specifically Roman artifacts as *lares* and *penates*. *Quirites* would have been striking, and must suggest the Roman citizen body boldly and unmistakably. A further detail reinforces this equation: the bees give their lives gladly *sub fasce*, still bearing their burdens (204); the phrase occurred previously in the Libyan passage in the third book, when the wandering of the Libyan shepherd was compared, paradoxically, to the toil of the Roman soldier, *iniusto sub fasce* (3.347). The bees labor gladly and die gladly for the love of flowers and the glory (*gloria*, 205—it is easy to overlook the Roman import of this word) of producing honey. Even without the bold suggestions of Rome the context here must suggest the early history of the Republic (and the regal period as well), a time of unusual devotion to *patria*, which contrasted so vividly with the subsequent stages of decline, in the minds of later historians. (Sallust alone will produce abundant "parallels," if such commonplaces are needed—see *Cat.* 6–9: Griffin has a brief collection of passages illustrating the characteristic *concordia*—Polybius' ὁμόνοια—of this period.) Little more need be said here, but it is perhaps worth pointing out again that the rather clear implications of this passage are consistent with the rest of Virgil's account if we view that account *as a progression*: difficulty comes only when other details in what has preceded, and in what will follow, are distorted to form a single description of a static whole.

That wonder of the bee society is followed by an even briefer section on their love for their king, greater even than that of eastern peoples. This has seemed strange, if the bees are to be Romans of some sort, because the Romans were of course antagonistic to even the word *rex*, and because if Octavian (for instance) could be assumed to have been in Virgil's mind here, he would not have appreciated this comparison to eastern potentates. There is no need to make Virgil, in either instance, so specific. The fact (which Virgil had to work with throughout) is that bees have kings—*reges*, not consuls, not *principes*, or anything else. Why, though, insist upon their devotion to their king, to the extent of nine lines on the theme? Their love is in fact that of soldiers for their general:

> ille operum custos, illum admirantur et omnes
> circumstant fremitu denso stipantque frequentes,
> et saepe attollunt umeris et corpora bello
> obiectant pulchramque petunt per vulnera mortem.   (215–18)

> (He is the guardian of their operations, him they all stand in awe of and surround with a compact droning and accompany in numbers, and often they carry him on their shoulders and in battle protect him with their own bodies and seek a beautiful death through wounds.)

The Roman soldiers' obedience and devotion to their leader constituted a great deal of their early history (think of any catalogue of Republican heroes), and of course became the most im-

portant reality of the last century of that history: the allusion to
this panorama, with such brevity, is characteristically Virgilian.

Immediately, though, Virgil pulls back from historical suggestion to a very different abstraction—the *pars divinae mentis*
that pervades all creatures, not just bees but "flocks and herds,
men, and every sort of beast" (219–27). The passage is too brief,
and the ideas presented are too general, to allow us to prescribe
any particular philosophic purpose to Virgil. (The immortality
of the great Roman statesmen, as revealed by Cicero in the *Som-
nium Scipionis* at the end of his *Republic*, may have been one of
the suggestions in Virgil's mind in the last lines of the section,
sed viva volare / sideris in numerum atque alto succedere caelo, 226–
27.) But I think Virgil wanted to convey only a general impression, not of Pythagorean or Stoic philosophy, but of the unity
of all living things, their common mortality. From this point on
he focuses more and more narrowly on that last traditional period of Rome's past, the degeneration that involved the end of
the harmonious balance in their order, a process viewed by their
historians as having the inevitability of a disease. Virgil, however, never makes such a bold equation, and we should not
either, thereby sparing ourselves any further review of Roman
political theorizing.

Since the digression on the old man of Tarentum, Virgil has
been descriptive: he now becomes once again the didact, ad-
dressing the reader directly with instruction on how and when
to take honey from the hives (228–50). The perspective changes
abruptly. Again the bees are viewed as the tiny creatures they
are, objectively, needing protection against the coming of winter (*duram hiemem*, 239) and against their enemies. The bees
grow angry at their shattered realm (*res fractas*, 240), and will
sting the invader and die. They have other enemies too, lizards,
beetles(?), the idle drones, hornets, a fierce sort of moth(?), and
spiders. Here is another list of *pestes*, similar to those which attack the threshing floor (1.181–86), agents of Jupiter's new order like (again) the goose, the Strymonian cranes, weeds, and
shade (1.118–21), like the birds, weeds, and shade that consti-
tute the *labor* "added" (*additus*) to crops (1.150–57). *Pestes* are

part of Jupiter's world, and the bees are subject to them, part of the nature Jupiter gave them (*addidit*, 4.150), and these enemies are powerful enough to bring about the "ruin of their fallen race" (*generis lapsi . . . ruinas*, 249), which the bees must strive to repair.

The ruin and the *pestes* become more specific in the next section—actual disease:

> Si vero, quoniam casus apibus quoque nostros
> vita tulit, tristi languebunt corpora morbo—
> quod iam non dubiis poteris cognoscere signis.   (251–53)

(If indeed their bodies grow sick with bitter disease, since life has brought to bees our misfortunes as well—but you will be able to recognize this by signs perfectly clear.)

Again, destruction and disease may be anticipated, but they cannot be averted. Virgil's final symptom (the low buzzing to be heard) is universal:

> tum sonus auditur gravior, tractimque susurrant,
> frigidus ut quondam silvis immurmurat Auster,
> ut mare sollicitum stridit refluentibus undis,
> aestuat ut clausis rapidus fornacibus ignis.   (260–63)

(Then there is heard a low sound, an increasingly perceptible murmur, as when once the cold south wind murmurs in the forest, or when the sea, aroused, roars with its breakers, or when a raging fire seethes in the enclosing forge.)

Behind these lines, as Servius recognized, are three successive similes of two lines each in the *Iliad*, comparing the shouting of Greeks and Trojans rushing upon each other to the roar of a wave breaking on the beach, then to the sound of a fire in a mountain ravine, then to a wind in lofty oaks (*Iliad* 14.394–99). Virgil thus sees the onset of disease as the beginning of battle, but finds in Homer as well the elemental oppositions (air, water, and fire) that serve his purpose so well. The remedies listed in the next lines seem for the most part to have reference to the elements or the qualities (as if according to the precepts of treatment *ex contrariis*), until the final cure, the *amellus*:

est etiam flos in pratis cui nomen amello
fecere agricolae, facilis quaerentibus herba;
namque uno ingentem tollit de caespite silvam
aureus ipse, sed in foliis, quae plurima circum
funduntur, violae sublucet purpura nigrae;
saepe deum nexis ornatae torquibus arae;
asper in ore sapor; tonsis in vallibus illum
pastores et curva legunt prope flumina Mellae.   (271–78)

(There is indeed a meadow flower which farmers call the 'amellus,' a
plant easy enough to find if you look; for it grows as thickly as a huge
wood on one plot, itself golden, but in its leaves—which it has in
abundance—there is the sheen of dark purple-violet. Often are the
altars of the gods decked with wreathed garlands of it; it has a bitter
taste in the mouth; shepherds gather it in mown valleys and around
the meanderings of the river Mella.)

The *amellus* is the subject of one of the four major, related aetiologies we discussed earlier, and as such is of significance both
in its own context and in its relation to the other three. This was
not a literary flower: the entire description seems to be Virgil's
own, and therefore all its details ought to be significant. It is presented as a riddle not difficult to solve (*facilis quaerentibus herba*)
and indeed, especially after the *asilus/Sila/Silarus* complex, it is
easy: the endings of the first and last lines give the etymology
(see Servius on 278), *cui nomen amello* and *prope flumina Mellae*
(i.e., *flumin-amellae*, as in *pascitur in magn-asila*, which connects
Sila at 3.219 with the preceding *Silarus/asilus*, 3.146–51). A
gloss on the name has been noted: *asper in ore sapor* seems to suggest *a-mellus* as "honey-less," taking the initial *a-* of the name as
a privative. That may be so, but otherwise the connection with
honey is clearly indicated. The flower itself is golden, sur-
rounded by a mass of purple leaves, suggesting royal wealth,
and recalling the description earlier of the better bee king and his
people, in which the prominent, repeated characteristic was the
gleaming of reddish gold. The adjective *ingens* occurs again (and
again where vast size is clearly inappropriate), and again must
suggest "native," a notion confirmed by the north Italian Mella
(which flows by Brescia into the Oglio—Virgil's own Mantua is

not far off). Finally, it is a flower named by farmers, gathered by shepherds.

Servius, as we noted earlier, connected this description with that of the *felix malum* of Media (2.127) and noted that it follows the botanical form ("dicit ubi creetur, qualis sit, quid possit"), and a glance back at our table will show some of the formal connections with the three other major aetiologies. First, the *amellus* is Italian, not exotic like the lemon, and, furthermore, is from Virgil's native northern Italy. It is a beneficial plant, curative like the lemon, which was an antidote to the poisons and spells of *novercae*. It is "gathered" (*legunt*) by shepherds, not (like the *hippomanes*) by *novercae* (*legere*, 3.282). (The *amellus* was named by farmers, the *hippomanes* by *pastores*, the μύωψ by herdsmen in Callimachus and Apollonius as "footnoted" by Virgil in the *asilus* account: I mention these connections, though I do not find them particularly significant otherwise.) The *amellus* is used to adorn the altars of gods (a line sometimes suspected of being an intrusion, because apparently vague or inappropriate): the gadfly had, unhappily, divine associations (set by Juno upon Io), and the *hippomanes* and lemon are associated with rites of black magic. Thus the *amellus* alone emerges as natural, native, and beneficial, in habitat, characteristics, and use, and as such it ought to be a powerful medicine against our diseases (*nostros casus*, 251).

Virgil's progression, however, is complete. In lines 228–50 the *pestes* were listed, attacking *res fractas* (240), though the bees themselves seemed capable of restoring "the ruins of their fallen race" (*generis lapsi . . . ruinas*, 249). Disease, though, required outside help and drugs, including the *amellus* (251–80). Now, suddenly and in spite of such help, the entire race (*proles omnis, genus*, 281–82) has died. (The native *amellus* ultimately was of no benefit: again the contrast with the foreign *felix malum* is implicit, which drives deadly poisons (*atra venena*) from the body, and hence, being the *medica malus*, is the true *medicina*.) The death of the bees, which immediately leads to the account of the *bugonia*, brings to a sudden close the didactic half of the book. We have learned of their origins, we have seen their character and observed their society, and we have witnessed the dissolution, sickness, and final (and apparently inevitable) death of the entire people: there is not much left, it would seem, for Virgil to relate.

Aristaeus and Orpheus

The difficulty with the second half of the book may be simply stated. The stories of Aristaeus and Orpheus are about loss: Orpheus loses Eurydice and eventually dies violently himself, and Aristaeus loses his bees, which represent his entire achievement. Aristaeus, however, through some sort of expiation, is able to regain his lost swarm, and so, following his instruction, the modern beekeeper is able to produce a new swarm after the death of a former swarm. The question, obviously, is what all this meant for Virgil: is death final, or is there in some sense a restoration of life?

Modern scholarship and interpretation has been directed primarily (I would say) at this obvious question: the phrase "in some sense" explains the diversity of interpretation offered, since opinions about the particular restoration of life that Virgil had in mind have differed widely, from restoration of political and social order, to moral order, to intellectual or poetic order. It is generally felt that there must be a useful message here for mankind, even if its utility is not especially practical. If bees are restored to Aristaeus, then something ought to be restored to the reader, and loss and death, consequently, are not as final as might appear.

All of this, however, supposes that we have got the question right, that Virgil really was concerned with the finality of death and with the possibility of a restoration. It is clear that the facts of the matter all point in this direction (it is this, after all, that makes the question seem obvious): Eurydice dies, is almost restored, but is lost a second time and forever; Aristaeus' swarm is lost, and (another) is restored after certain steps have been taken; the beekeeper can (re-)gain a swarm (once lost). But it is possible, too, that within these stories there are other questions that concern Virgil more, that the facts are simply a structural framework supporting other concerns. That so many different answers and messages have been found may suggest that there is no answer given (and as well that our questions may have been improperly posed), and that the poet may not in fact have a message. What does Virgil actually say? (That is, what can we be sure are *his* interests and concerns, as previously established?) What is the sequence of events as he relates them? (That is, we ought to allow again the possibility that there is a progression or development in this part of the book, just as there was in the first half: it may be misleading to consider sections out of order, or to try to establish a coherent interpretation by relating ideas that Virgil separated.)

A useful, and proper, view of the *bugonia* itself has recently been offered by R. F. Thomas. He notes that "the *Georgics*, to the extent that they define the realities of an agricultural dilemma, end with the death of the hive, in mid-sentence, at 4.282," that what follows is introduced as "a colorful ethnographical notice," "an Eastern *thaumasion*, pure and simple," whose main function is "to provide a transition to the epyllion on Orpheus." The implications of this view should be considered. The insight that the *bugonia* is presented as an ethnographical *thaumasion* is novel and valid, and comes from an awareness of the special literary form that Virgil had been working with frequently in the *Georgics*: the extended description of Egypt (287–94) thus has a purpose. Since we are to read this account as a *thaumasion*, we are not necessarily to believe it, at any level. Several levels of belief might seem possible, after all, and since Virgil has related such a diversity of beliefs throughout, we ought to try to see just what we have here. First of all, neither Virgil nor anyone else had ever acquired a swarm of bees from this procedure: the idea of the *bugonia* grew from the species of fly (genus *syrphus*), strikingly resembling bees, that breeds in rotting animal carcasses, but these flies will of course neither swarm nor produce honey. In practical terms, then, no one (and Virgil especially) would have had any practical experience with the procedure, just as no one had ever produced, or seen produced, apples by grafting an oak. What is more, at another level, no one would ever have thought of trying—it was never difficult to acquire a new swarm, and two-year-old calves are of far greater value than a swarm of bees in any case. All this should warn against crediting Virgil, or any Roman, with credence in the *bugonia*. But is it not possible to see that Virgil intended "belief" at an altogether different level, a belief in an intellectual abstraction? This possibility, it seems to me, is what has been denied by the demonstration that the passage is an ethnographical *thaumasion*: I doubt that anyone was supposed really to believe in flying snakes, or, for that matter, in fire-breathing bulls and armed men sprung from the dragon's teeth.

Wonder and belief are not the same: a *thaumasion* is worthy of wonder, but is not intended to be believed. Virgil himself calls the *bugonia* a *famam* (286), which should be a clear indication of where he stood, and *insincerus* (*cruor*) immediately preceding may be another indication (it is a word both rare and odd in its context here). This *fama* is not practical science: we are already in a world of fiction just as unreal as that of Aristaeus and Orpheus. The point needs stressing, for the simple reason that more often than not the bugonia is made to represent (at least) a reality—that is, to stand symbolically for an abstract truth (regeneration, the restoration of life). We ought to remember, though, how often in the poem we have been presented with delusion, and we ought to be ready, at least, for the possibility that this may be another wonderful delusion, as *fama* could well imply.

In this light it is interesting to observe how Virgil seems to have rationalized the *bugonia*. Two oddities stand out: the origin of the practice is set in Egypt, which has no connections with Aristaeus; and when Aristaeus finally sacrifices to appease Orpheus, he does so in a way totally unlike the extraordinary procedure detailed here. We have seen that one function of the Egyptian setting is to present the *bugonia* as an ethnographical *thaumasion*, and the references to Persia and India as well seem to reinforce the unreality of the foreign (and eastern). Egypt, too, is the Nile (287–94), which annually overflows to produce rich life from the deposit of dark silt: *et viridem Aegyptum nigra fecundat harena* (291). Sand is sterile, of course (as Virgil seems to have had in mind previously as a minor theme: *sterilem harenam*, 1.70; *male pinguis harenae*, 1.105; and compare the unexpected East, *turiferis Panchaia pinguis harenis*, 2.139, and context); *niger* (and *ater*) almost always suggests "death" in Latin; and *viridem* is not so much "green" as "full of life and new growth": thus, the Nile produces new life from its black sand—precisely what the *bugonia* creates—and it may properly be said, then, that this whole region finds its sure salvation in this practice, *omnis in hac certam regio iacit arte salutem*, 294. The most memorable account of the production of life from the warm ooze of the Nile's flooding is Ovid's in the *Metamorphoses*, where the spontaneous production of life after Deucalion's flood (from water and fire, *postquam vetus umor ab igne / percaluit solis, Met.* 1.417–18) is like the Nile's annual production of spontaneous life, rationalized by Ovid playing the scientist in these extraordinary lines:

> quippe ubi temperiem sumpsere umorque calorque,
> concipiunt, et ab his oriuntur cuncta duobus,
> cumque sit ignis aquae pugnax, vapor umidus omnes
> res creat, et discors concordia fetibus apta est.　　　(*Met.* 1.430–33)

(Plainly, when moisture and heat have achieved a balanced mixture, they conceive, and all things arise from these two, and although fire is inimical to water, moist heat begets all creatures, and this discordant harmony is suited for procreation.)

Here, as elsewhere earlier in the poem, Ovid as scientist writing on the creation is making good use of Virgil's scientific poem. Virgil's *bugonia* must take place at the very beginning of spring (305–7), to allow the increasing heat to work upon the moisture in the carcass (*interea teneris tepefactus in ossibus umor / aestuat*, 308–9), until the bees burst forth like a summer rain (*donec ut aestivis effusus nubibus imber / erupere*, 312–13). The process is thus given a rational basis by Virgil (so too the four windows directed toward the four winds, 297–98, suggesting balance), all the details of which we have of course seen before—spring as the time of creation (hence creation's Spring, one of the great lies), the *temperies* of the opposites (the farmer's first concern at the very beginning of the poem).

In all this, it seems to me, lies Virgil's reason for introducing Egypt, totally foreign though it is to Aristaeus, and for introducing details in the process which concern Aristaeus' rite not at all. The *bugonia* is thus something of a paradox, or even a contradiction, because (as we have just stressed at greater length than was necessary) it is a *fama* totally without any practical basis in scientific agriculture, a story beyond belief; and yet it is given an explanation by Virgil that uses the terms of science, an explanation so clearly intended to be rationalizing, even in the choice of the locale. We must let this contradiction stand for a bit, even as Virgil does, because the *bugonia* serves yet another purpose: it is clearly the means of transition from the bees to Aristaeus.

*

Quis deus hanc, Musae, quis nobis extudit artem?
unde nova ingressus hominum experientia cepit?   (315–16)

(Who, o Muses, what god hammered out for us this art? From whence did man's new learning by trial and error take its beginnings?)

We have noted above that *experientia* returns here from the fourth line of the poem, just as *extudit artem* returns from the first explication of Jupiter's new order (*ut varias usus meditando extunderet artis / paulatim*, 1.133–34). But before we continue, there is one extraordinary piece left to put in place. We noted one simile, that the bees burst forth from the carcass "like a rain from summer clouds," but we neglected to continue with a second, longer simile, with which indeed the whole passage ends:

. . . aut ut nervo pulsante sagittae
prima leves ineunt si quando proelia Parthi.   (313–14)

(. . . or as arrows from the resounding string, when the light-armed Parthians first begin the battle.)

The Parthians are suitable as another people neighboring Egypt and were notable archers (to say the least), but the real point of the simile comes only after this address to the Muses, which completes the metamorphosis of the *bugonia* from a *fama* to an *ars*. The violence that must be used to kill the bullock (suffocation of the animal *multa reluctanti*, then beating) has often been noted as extraordinary, but violence in fact and in language has so frequently been a part of the arts of agriculture in the first three books. War, too, and military language, has been associated with the new arts, from the farmer effecting a balance of hot and wet, irrigating as if he were the farmer in the simile at *Iliad* 21.256–64 come to life, as Achilles (fire) battles the Scamander (water). The violent *bugonia* concludes with the simile of war (the Parthian archer), immediately after which the poet asks the Muses what god discovered this new art, this *experientia*: the distance between violence and the arts of Jupiter's order is never great.

The figure of Aristaeus is defined by Virgil in this first section: he is the inventor of all the arts of agriculture; he is a *pastor*; his father is the Trojan Apollo; his mother is Cyrene, a water nymph. Each of these details represents a significant aspect of his function in the poem.

Aristaeus, of course, is the answer to Virgil's question to the Muses: he is responsible for this particular *ars* (the *bugonia*) and the source of this *nova experientia*. His sphere of activity, though, is remarkably increased in his final complaint, when he refers to his achievements as his *honor* and *laus*, won, again, by him "hammering out everything by trial," and he taunts his mother to destroy what in fact stands as all knowledge represented in the first three books of Virgil's poem:

en etiam hunc ipsum vitae mortalis honorem,
quem mihi vix frugum et pecorum custodia sollers
omnia temptanti extuderat, te matre relinquo.
quin age et ipsa manu felicis erue silvas,
fer stabulis inimicum ignem atque interfice messis,
ure sata et validam in vitis molire bipennem,
tanta meae si te ceperunt taedia laudis.   (326–32)

(Look—though you are my mother I abandon even this, the very crown of human life, which conscientious attendance to fields and

flocks scarcely hammered out for me as I experimented with everything. Come on, then, with your own hand destroy my fruitful
groves, bring hostile fire upon my folds and pens and wipe out the
harvests, burn my plants and hew down my vines with a strong
axe—if my renown has now become so wearisome to you.)

Aristaeus, clearly, is a figure representing the discovery of all
human knowledge, all the *artes*.

He is introduced, however, as a *pastor* (*pastor Aristaeus fugiens
Peneia Tempe*, 317), and was so employed in his only previous
appearance in the poem, *cultor nemorum, cui pinguia Ceae / ter centum nivei tondent dumeta iuvenci* (1.14–15), where Servius notes
that Hesiod had called him "the pastoral Apollo" ("quem He-
siodus dicit Apollinem pastoralem": P. Oxy. 2489 may have
Ἀρι]σταῖον in its first line, with ἐπίσκοπος ἠδὲ νομήων in its
third line, Hesiod, fr. 217 Merkelbach and West. So Pindar,
Pyth. 9.65, has Apollo, "watcher of flocks," called Agreus,
Nomios, and Aristaeus; and Apollonius, *Argon.* 2.506–7, has
Aristaeus—whose mother was a shepherdess when Apollo took
her—called also Agreus and Nomios, "hunter and shepherd").
In Apollonius, too, we find Aristaeus made the shepherd of the
Muses' sheep, after they had given him healing and prophecy
(*Argon.* 2.509–15). There was thus good precedent for Aristaeus
the *pastor*, but it is not in fact a role he ever plays in the *Georgics*,
after these two first appearances. I would suggest that Aristaeus,
as the counterpart to Orpheus, is designated a shepherd because
that was indeed the function fulfilled by Linus, the counterpart
to Orpheus in the *Eclogues*: but this will wait until we consider
Orpheus.

Aristaeus rebukes his mother, even questioning whether
Thymbraeus Apollo could in fact have been his father (323). When
we took note of the *graviter spirantis . . . thymbrae* earlier (31), we
were directed by Servius and by Virgil himself (*Aen.* 3.84–87) to
Troy. The herb *thymbra* was part of a pattern of specific and exclusive references to Phrygia, the Troad, and Troy occurring
throughout the discussion of the origins and early development
of the bees, and it would be hard not to let this (otherwise point-

less and gratuitous) mention of the Thymbrean Apollo suggest that pattern and become part of it: Aristaeus has Troy in his family history, though this is no more than a fleeting suggestion. There is a more apparent purpose to this reference, which is of course the reinforcement of the general (and well-recognized) literary parallel between Aristaeus, calling upon his mother Cyrene, and Achilles, on the shore of Troy calling similarly upon his mother Thetis. For Virgil, though, I think this antecedent (which of course was his own creation) had further associations, of which we can be sure simply because they fit familiar patterns of association and suggestion.

Cyrene is a water nymph, the daughter of the river Peneus. The next 50 lines (333–85) catalogue her sister nymphs and describe Aristaeus' entrance through "the wave curved in the shape of a mountain" and under the stream, his wonder at his mother's *umida regna* and at all the rivers of the world, and his reception—a passage both very long and of extraordinary baroque beauty. This is the source of all water and the home of the *numina* of all waters (*"Oceano libemus" ait. simul ipsa precatur / Oceanumque patrem rerum Nymphasque sorores,* 381–82). In his final taunt to his mother Aristaeus had called upon her to destroy his work, to set fire to his stockyards and to burn his crops (*fer stabulis inimicum ignem atque interfice messis, / ure sata,* 330–31): "hostile" fire is as bitterly ironic and as mocking as anything in his complaint. It is now clear why Virgil suggested Achilles; again Virgil returns to the ultimate elemental conflict of fire and water, and again we are inevitably taken back to Virgil's first instruction in the first book with its suggestions of Troy and then of Achilles' battle with the Scamander, fire and water. We must go back even before that, though, if we are to hear all that Virgil intends us to hear. Aristaeus was not named in the list of agricultural *numina* in the proem: *et cultor nemorum, cui pinguia Ceae / ter centum nivei tondent dumeta iuvenci* (1.14–15). His name was to be supplied from *pinguia* and the previous play on *pingui arista* (8), which, as we noted, was established by Virgil to be the very token of the essence of agriculture (Ceres' gift), the art of effecting a productive balance between fire and water: the *pinguis arista* is the token of the entire poem. Aristaeus is his mother's son, and just as fire can be the ultimate destroyer (whether it be Achilles' fire, or the fire of the *furor* of passion, or the *sacer ignis* of disease), so water can be the ultimate nurturing element. A more elaborate review of such associations would take us again through the entire poem.

This, then, is the Aristaeus I think Virgil intended. He represents the arts of civilization, both as the discoverer of knowledge (science), and as the son of Cyrene, whose *umida regna* hold all waters that give life. He enters his mother's realm, though, to seek aid in his present crisis, the loss of his bees through sickness and hunger (*morboque fameque*, 318), precisely what his arts ought to prevent, or cure. It is a failure of knowledge.

The Proteus episode can be seen not only as the next event in the story of Aristaeus, but as a further stage in the progression of Virgil's ideas. Proteus is the source of knowledge, and *how* Aristaeus learns from him seems to concern Virgil even more than what he learns. We have just seen the failure of knowledge: we now see how knowledge is acquired, which, in the progression, ought to be related to its failure.

Cyrene introduces Proteus as the great seer, revered by all the nymphs and by Nereus himself, because he knows all things:

> hunc et Nymphae veneramur et ipse
> grandaevus Nereus: novit namque omnia vates
> quae sint, quae fuerint, quae mox ventura trahantur.   (391–93)

(We Nymphs hold him in awe, as does aged Nereus himself: for he is the seer who knows all things that are, or were, or that afterwards will be brought to pass.)

Proteus is indeed the source of all knowledge: in the story, therefore, Aristaeus must learn from him the cause of his bees' death (*ut omnem / expediat morbi causam*, 396–97), but we are to observe something more. Virgil returns here to an unmistakable theme important at the beginning of the poem and recurring throughout—the *praecepta* (which are of course the discoveries of *usus/experientia*) won by means of force and violence:

nam sine vi non ulla dabit praecepta, neque illum
orando flectes; vim duram et vincula capto
tende; doli circum haec demum frangentur inanes.   (398–400)

(For without force he will give none of his teachings, nor will you
sway him by prayer; put forth harsh force and chain him once taken;
finally, in chains, his deceptive trickery will be broken, useless.)

Again Virgil is drawing on an old idea—the ritual binding of the
seer, who must be forced into revealing his knowledge: this
Proteus is after all the same figure with whom Menelaus wres-
tled (or will wrestle) in the *Odyssey* (4.351–570), and similar figures occur down to Virgil's Silenus in Eclogue 6, who is ritually
bound with his own garlands (18–26) before he sings his song.
Proteus' binding here, however, and the "hard force" (repeated—*sine vi* and *vim duram*) necessary to achieve it, have special relevance to the *praecepta* of the first book of the *Georgics*.
Again, a survey of all the associations of knowledge and force
would take us line by line through that book and on through the
rest of the poem. We need only recall the lines on Jupiter's new
order, realizing that *labor* and its ramifications are a part of the
unending force that must be exerted to carry out the newly won
praecepta, force which is central in the next section on the *duris
agrestibus arma* (1.160–75), and which of course is explicit
throughout the following section of the *veterum praecepta*
(1.176–203). It is at the end of the *veterum praecepta* that the image of the rower occurs, striving continually lest he be swept
back downstream (*sic omnia fatis / in peius ruere ac retro sublapsa
referri*, 1.199–200); and so must the farmer select every seed by
hand, because degeneration is inevitable *ni vis humana quotannis
/ maxima quaeque manu legeret* (1.198–99), on which Servius
noted, "tamen verius est, ut 'vis' quasi violentia sit in rebus,
quae contra naturam vertuntur in melius: sic enim Donatus sensit, dicens: nisi violentia fiat naturae, omnia in deterius cadunt";
to which Servius Auctus has in addition, "et hoc est, quod ait,
'labor omnia vicit improbus'." *Nam sine vi non ulla dabit praecepta*: this is a specific invitation to consider all this, and more;

human knowledge only comes from force applied against the natural course of things, and the *praecepta* so won can only be carried out in the same way. Water flows downstream, but the rower must go against the current and must never cease his effort.

There is another, certain indication that Virgil intended us to remember the contexts of the *praecepta* and *labor* in the first book: Cyrene tells Aristaeus that when he does take hold of Proteus, *tum variae eludent species* (4.406). The musical motif heard previously recurs unmistakably: from the passage on Jupiter's new order (immediately preceding *labor improbus*): *tum variae venere artes* (1.145); from the *veterum praecepta* section itself (when the threshing floor has been made, by hand and with three gerundives): *tum variae inludunt pestes* (1.181); and from the onset of disease in the third book: *quam multae pecudum pestes* (3.471), which would seem to be correlative with (or, in any case, structurally balancing) the universal war of the first book (*tot bella per orbem*): *tam multae scelerum facies* (1.506—wars that leave the fields as empty as does the plague in the fourth book). Again the associations of ideas and themes are far more potent than they can be when listed by the interpreter: the coming of the *artes* (1.145) is ultimately joined with Aristaeus' wrestling with Proteus for knowledge, a struggle over the deceptions of appearance (*eludent species*), like the appearances of the crimes of war (*scelerum facies*, 1.506), like the mocking deceptions of the pests that attack the threshing floor (*inludunt pestes*, 1.181), which are as many as the diseases that attack flocks (3.471). There is no end to Virgil's circle of knowledge, violence, and toil, war and disease.

We can be certain, then, that the Proteus episode concerns the discovery of knowledge and its consequences, whatever else it may do and however it forwards the story. There is a further aspect of the winning of knowledge which we ought to observe, and which will be more important shortly. Virgil insists (again at greater length than would seem at first sight necessary) that

Aristaeus' struggle must take place in the dry heat of midday.
Cyrene first tells Aristaeus,

> ipsa ego te, medios cum sol accenderit aestus,
> cum sitiunt herbae et pecori iam gratior umbra est,
> in secreta senis ducam.   (401–3)

(I myself will lead you to the retreats of the old man, when the sun
has kindled the midday heat, when grass thirsts and the shade is now
more welcome to the flock.)

Then, after she has hidden him, Proteus comes in the midday
heat, like a shepherd driving his flock to the cool of a grove:

> iam rapidus torrens sitientis Sirius Indos
> ardebat caelo et medium sol igneus orbem
> hauserat, arebant herbae et cava flumina siccis
> faucibus ad limum radii tepefacta coquebant,
> cum Proteus consueta petens e fluctibus antra
> ibat.   (425–30)

(Now the seething Dog Star, parching the thirsting Indians, was
flaming in heaven, and the fiery sun had exhausted its midcourse; the
grass was drying, and the sun's rays were cooking the deep rivers
heated even to the mud, dry-jawed: then did Proteus seek his cus-
tomary caves, leaving the waves.)

The prophecy of the seer must come from a cave (which is as
necessary as the ritual binding), but it is all the more notable
therefore how the scene set by Virgil is not the coolness of the
cave but rather the searing heat of midday in midsummer. The
associations of intellect and heat are as complex as those of
knowledge and violence, but can best be reviewed when we
consider Orpheus. There is a limited contrast that ought to be
pointed out here, however, and that is the opposition between
the *umida regna* of Cyrene and the heat and parching dryness of
this scene of struggle: Cyrene offers a mother's comfort and
love and receives Aristaeus in the depths of the nurturing element itself, the life-giving *umor*, but she cannot give the knowledge he seeks; that can only come when the Dog Star burns the

earth and the sun's rays heat the deep rivers, their throats dry, to their depths (425–28), and only as the result of violence.

★

If the *bugonia* can be seen mainly as a transition to the story of Aristaeus, so that in turn can be seen as a transition to the story of Orpheus. We must not forget that it was Virgil who made the connection between Aristaeus and Orpheus, and that he did so by making Aristaeus guilty of Eurydice's death: the connecting link may thus serve no more than a purely functional purpose, and indeed the lines that make the connection are few and rather bare (453–59), so bare, in fact, of detail other than narrative that to see in them any other purpose requires that meaning be imported. Virgil, for instance, attributes no *furor* of passion to Aristaeus, as he might easily have, had this been his point; and the matter of Aristaeus' guilt (how and why, for instance?) is strangely obscure. That Aristaeus caused Eurydice's death is a fact of the narrative, invented by Virgil to serve an obviously structural purpose: to assume that it does more may not be either safe or productive, and it will be best not to try to make the fact of Aristaeus' guilt yield significance it may not have.

Virgil, after these few transitional lines, seems concerned only with Orpheus, who in turn is concerned with Aristaeus and his guilt not in the least. (And it is not clear even at the end of his story that Orpheus wasted much thought on Aristaeus, for Cyrene, summing up for Aristaeus, tells him that the *Nymphs*—she makes no mention of Orpheus until line 545—destroyed his bees, that *they* will give up their anger if supplicated (532–36)—*irasque remittent* ought to identify the source of the anger mentioned in Proteus' first words, 453, *Non te nullius exercent numinis irae*). If the two stories are not related by cause and effect, then we may look again at a possible progression of ideas from one panel to the next. Orpheus was already established, for Virgil, as a significant figure, representing "scientific poetry," which is to say intellectual understanding of the world. The *Georgics* concludes with his ultimate failure to bring Eurydice back from death: again we see the failure of knowledge, but this time we see it played out. The progression of ideas will be more clear after we have considered Orpheus.

Our discussion of Orpheus can be relatively brief: I have previously set forth my reasons for seeing him as the exemplary poet of science, and have explained what this (modern) term is intended to suggest. A brief review may be helpful, however. In the *Eclogues* Orpheus and Linus appeared together at the end of *Eclogue* 4 (55-7), where Calliope was named as Orpheus' mother, Apollo as Linus' father, thus establishing those two semi-divine singers as counterparts, children of Apollo and a particularly significant Muse. In the Third Eclogue two sets of cups were wagered, one set engraved with representations of Conon and Aratus (40–42), the other with Orpheus "leading the trees" (*Orpheaque in medio . . . silvasque sequentis*, 46): Orpheus thus balances the Alexandrian astronomer and versifier. Orpheus is mentioned, *in silvis*, at *Ecl.* 8.55, but is particularly significant in *Eclogue* 6, where he is named, with Apollo, just before Silenus begins his song, which song begins with a cosmogony clearly patterned to suggest Orpheus' cosmogony at Apollonius' *Argonautica* 1.496–502. Finally, I still feel confident that later in the Sixth Eclogue *ille* must refer to Orpheus (*calamos . . . quibus ille solebat / cantando rigidas deducere montibus ornos*, 6.69–71), establishing a succession from the Muses and Apollo, to Orpheus and Linus (67–69), to Hesiod and finally through the Alexandrians to Gallus, *errantem Permessi ad flumina* (64).

In the *Eclogues* Linus was the counterpart to Orpheus, and as Orpheus was the poet of scientific understanding, so Linus was the poet of pastoral imagination. Orpheus' power was also his magic, his ability to charm the natural world, and thus ultimately can be said to represent for Virgil control of nature through intellectual understanding; the pastoral imagination, on the other hand, controls nature by re-creating it, by establishing its own patterns of truth through which those who remain in the pastoral shade can find solace in an ever benevolent landscape. In the final lines of the Tenth Eclogue, Gallus finds both these ways inadequate and must yield to the reality of *Amor*

(64–69), and Virgil himself concludes by leaving the pastoral shade (*surgamus: solet esse gravis cantantibus umbra,* 75).

This is the proper occasion to review the well-known passage (475–94) from the end of the second book, *Me vero primum dulces ante omnia Musae / . . . accipiant caelique vias et sidera monstrent . . .* (2.475–77). Virgil interrupts his Praise of Rustic Life (which will continue, 495, without a break) and, following a clear reference to Aratus (*Iustitia,* 473–74 = Dike, *Phaen.* 127–28), asks the Muses to receive him and teach him science (475–82); but "if the blood stands cold around the heart" (483–84), then he would like to inhabit what seems to be a pastoral environment. Blessed is he who knows the causes of things and can overcome fear and fate and death (490–92), and blessed too he who knows the rustic gods, Pan, Silvanus, and the Nymphs (493–94). The contrast, repeated for emphasis, is between science (clearly enough) and what, in the light of the *Eclogues,* can be called pastoral (so especially the shade in the summary prayer, *et ingenti ramorum protegat umbra,* 489) but is also simply the *rura* of the *Georgics.* There may be, however, an impediment to scientific understanding: *sin has ne possim naturae accedere partis / frigidus obstiterit circum praecordia sanguis* (483–84). Servius has a relevant comment here, which sums up a medical commonplace, "secundum physicos, qui dicunt stultos esse homines frigidioris sanguinis, prudentes calidi. unde et senes, in quibus iam friget, et pueri, in quibus necdum calet, minus sapiunt" ("So according to medical men, who say that the stupid are men of colder blood, and the smart are men of warm blood. And thus old men (in whom the blood is now cold) and boys (in whom it is not yet warm) are less intelligent"). The commonplace goes back (at least) to Empedocles, for whom thought was the blood around the heart (fr. 105 DK, αἷμα γὰρ ἀνθρώποις περικάρδιόν ἐστι νόημα—cf. Virgil's *circum praecordia*); blood, universally, is the warm and moist humor, and so failure of intellect is seen as cold blood around the heart. (Horace took this Empedoclean concept to its extreme at the end of the *Ars Poetica,* where Empedocles, wishing to become immortal as a thinker, leaps into the very core of heat: *deus immortalis haberi / dum cupit Empedocles, ardentem frigidus Aetnam / insiluit, AP* 464–66). These lines, then, at the end of the second book look to the two opposite possibilities of mind in the *Eclogues* (intellectual understanding and imaginative re-creation), but also, by their position, would seem to offer a balance to the conclusion of the fourth book.

The *Georgics* is a poem of science, and Orpheus is its exemplary poet. Virgil's conception of the pastoral imagination is a large part of the third book, as we saw, but for the most part the scientific intellect dominates the poem, naturally enough. Orpheus' counterpart is not Linus but Aristaeus, who, as the discoverer of all human knowledge, is ultimately equivalent to Orpheus. We should remember, though, that Aristaeus appeared first (in the proem, 1.14–15, and at 4.317) as a *pastor*: by this touch, I suspect, Virgil recalled Orpheus' earlier counterpart, Linus. Aristaeus, though, will not again appear as a shepherd, and in fact Virgil immediately removed him from the pastoral landscape, *pastor Aristaeus fugiens Peneia Tempe* (4.317). Orpheus and Aristaeus are parallel figures, just as Orpheus and Linus had been opposites: both are figures of knowledge acquired through the understanding of science.

In Virgil's creation, pastoral imagination finds its place in the shade, a cool retreat from the heat of midday, which is why the pastoral alternative is summarized (at the end of the second book, 2.488–89), *o qui me gelidis convallibus Haemi / sistat, et ingenti ramorum protegat umbra.* (The whole concept of the heat of the pastoral world, as it evolves throughout the third book, ought to be recalled here of course, and particularly its *reductio ad extremum,* and inversion, in the Libyan/Scythian passage: the pastoral imagination, acting in cool shade, transforms the heat of the real world. Both halves of the third book end with the failure of the pastoral, overcome by the realities of the fire of passion and the *sacer ignis* of disease, just as Orpheus' failure of intellect is represented by the supremacy of northern cold.) We have just seen, conversely, Aristaeus wrestling Proteus in a struggle for knowledge in the fierce midday heat of midsummer, when even the rivers themselves are parched. Orpheus' ultimate failure is followed by a description similar to the lines on the drying heat of Aristaeus' struggle (401–2, 425–58), but a description of the very opposite:

> solus Hyperboreas glacies Tanaimque nivalem
> arvaque Riphaeis numquam viduata pruinis
> lustrabat.   (517–19)

(Alone he wandered through the Hyperborean ice and the snowy Tanais and fields never without Riphaean frost.)

The failure of intellect at the end of the second book was summed up in Empedoclean terms, *sin . . . frigidus obstiterit circum praecordia sanguis* (2.484): following Eurydice's return to the underworld (*illa quidem Stygia nabat iam frigida cumba*, 506), Orpheus inhabits this frozen landscape (so also 509, *gelidis . . . sub antris*) until his final dismemberment, still calling Eurydice with his last breath, *et frigida lingua* (525).

Such, in outline, are the terms that seem particularly Virgilian and therefore revealing: the elements and their qualities are yet again essential, unifying a number of ideas because of their very simplicity, making a unity of landscape and themes and ideas: from these simple elements, associating in any number of forms, complexity results, giving the poem its extraordinary web of associations. Orpheus' failure of intellect leads back to a number of significant earlier passages, each of which have further connections. As his failure is acted out, though, its cause is revealed simply and directly: *furor* again destroys all that his intellectual powers and his magic had achieved. By the power of his song he had visited the underworld and charmed its inhabitants and rulers, just as he could charm trees and wild beasts on earth; he had achieved victory, in fact, over death itself (*felix qui . . . inexorabile fatum / subiecit pedibus strepitumque Acherontis avari*, 2.490–92). His love for Eurydice, his human passion, overcame intellect (*immemor heu! victusque animi respexit*, 4.491) and his effort went in vain (*ibi omnis / effusus labor*, 491–92). Eurydice gives the reason: *illa 'quis et me' inquit 'miseram et te perdi-*

dit, Orpheu, / quis tantus furor?' (494–95). It is characteristic of Virgil to say no more than this.

★

We may now review Virgil's progression of ideas in this last half of the book. The outline is obvious:

The *bugonia* (281–314): how to (re-)gain a lost swarm.

Aristaeus (315–86): loss, the failure of knowledge; water.

Proteus (387–452): the winning of knowledge; drying heat.

Orpheus (453–527): the failure of knowledge, loss; cold.

The restoration of Aristaeus' swarm (528–58).

Proteus occupies the central panel, and central in it is the scene of wrestling in the blazing heat: violence, the victory over the delusions of change, the winning of knowledge, and because this is not a static, pictorial representation, but rather a progression, those scenes must dominate. First we have the simple fact of Aristaeus' loss of his swarm, which is (as he says) the loss of all agricultural science, which is (as Virgil has said) in effect the failure of intellect; he moves then to the *umida regna* of his mother, a setting obviously intended to contrast with the setting of his subsequent struggle with Proteus. The Orpheus panel moves from the possession of scientific understanding, which is power over nature and even over death, to its failure; it shows us how knowledge fails (the Aristaeus story shows only the *fait accompli*); and its final setting is the frozen north, the scene of the death of the singer himself. The elemental qualities have thus come finally to dominate the poem, just as they dominate lands and control every living thing taking its nature from the land and just as the world and the universe are shaped by the elements: in the center is the hot and the dry, balanced on the one side by the water that gives life and on the other by the cold of death.

These are the actors and the events in Virgil's final drama. They are playing, however, on a stage that was revealed before they entered and that remains after they depart, and we must consider again that basic question: is there a restoration of life, when Aristaeus finally regains his swarm? My answer would be no.

In the first place, as we saw, the *bugonia* is a *fama*, unreal in practical terms, a *thaumasion* and therefore intended to be seen as unreal even as an abstraction, but rationalized by Virgil specifically to suggest the annual generation of life from the Nile's spring flooding. Virgil's point, then, would seem to be not the regeneration or restoration demanded by the necessities of narrative, but rather simply generation, the fact of life itself, which indeed seems required by the necessity of the progression of ideas. The restoration of the swarm to Aristaeus complements the *bugonia*, but is strangely barren of the themes and motifs that have governed the action and meaning of the previous panels. Cyrene gives her instructions, and Aristaeus carries them out. Her first words ("Cheer up. This is the whole cause of the disease," 531–32) seem totally unreal, following upon Orpheus' loss and death, and her advice (*et facilis venerare Napaeas*, 535) sounds, in both content and in facility of manner, very much like that offered by Virgil previously, when, following the great storm of spring in the first book, he advised, *in primis venerare deos* (1.338)—again, it is too late to do much else. The *matris praecepta* (548) work, to be sure, and a swarm boils forth (*effervere*, 556) from the liquified (*liquefacta*, 555) viscera of the bulls, a *thaumasion* indeed (*subitum ac dictu mirabile monstrum,* 554). These details are enough to connect this restoration with the previous *bugonia* (the *thaumasion* of the creation of life from the *tepefactus umor* of the spring), but there is little else here of substance or reality.

These outer panels are thus the frame, or rather the stage, for the events acted within them. In the narrative they must present rebirth, regeneration, and restoration, but I think Virgil has made it clear that there is a level beyond the simple narrative, a level on which his ideas have a life of their own. At this level themes and motifs indicate that the outer panels are concerned with birth, the spontaneous generation of life as from the moist warmth of some primal spring: on this stage, then, the ideas presented by the scenes of Aristaeus, Proteus, and Orpheus play out their parts in turn, sequentially, but leaving as well the impression of a whole. The end, however, is Orpheus' death, for the final panel is simply an empty reminder of the beginning, of where it all started.

★

The two halves of the fourth book are complementary, and together stand as a dramatic synthesis of the first three books. The bee society began in a well-tempered spring, protected from enemies, and developed in a setting of unreality, much like the unreality of the world inhabited by the Corycian old man, himself an easterner like the bees. Jupiter's bees, however, have all the *artes* of civilization, which presuppose *pestes* (also Jupiter's gift) and disease and death as well. Knowledge, science, the *artes*: all are won by violence and lead inevitably to death, for there is something even more powerful than any manifestation of the mind.

CHAPTER SIX

AN OVERVIEW

Virgil does not offer conclusions: the final lines of the poem provide no grand answer. We have had, though, the final patterns, created from familiar pieces, revealing shapes similar to those seen before but different still in dimensions and outline. The pieces are again the elements, both the real matter of the actual world and the basis of our perceptions and understanding, our knowledge. Here, in fact, is Virgil's poem: it is concerned with nature (the real world) and our knowledge of it.

Our study of the *Georgics* is only half completed. We should now begin again and read the poem with the awareness of the pieces and patterns we achieved only at the end (as we were in fact so often tempted, or compelled, to do while reading the last book). The process could continue indefinitely, for every part is related in some way to every other. At the beginning we also noted that Virgil was a reflective poet, meaning just this quality: it is a matter of actual reflections cast from one object to another, as precise yet as illusive and transitory as a beam of light from a reflecting surface passing suddenly over and illuminating briefly different objects. But there is no dreaminess or romantic trance here, nor visions of Xanadu: the marvel of Virgil's reflective sensitivity is its clear reality.

We cannot, obviously, begin again, but it might be helpful simply to reconsider the broadest outlines of the poem, from book to book. The general movement of the first two books was clear enough. The first book shows us man in the universe and through time: cosmology offers a corresponding view of the earth's globe, which explains how man is the creature of that one zone "granted to wretched mortals by the gods' gift," between fire and ice; it shows too how man's present condition is the result of external forces in the past (how Jupiter changed man's condition). The first book is thus the most impersonal of the three, since the scale (of both space and time) is too great to allow much significance to the human figure. The second book, however, is concerned with man's present condition and his immediate environment: he appears now as the product of a particular land, sharing its local character, and acts in a present reality (not against an immense, almost timeless, past): but the environment and the present condition are Virgil's particular focus in the book.

In the last two books, however, man seems to be in the center of attention. The third book is concerned primarily with human passion and fallibility, and the fourth extends this view of man to an historical past. We can discern a controlling movement through the entire poem, I think, a narrowing of focus to its center, and a corresponding expansion from that point to the ends: to sum up, the first half moves from man in the universe and through time (I) to man's immediate environment and present condition (II), and the second from man's individual character (III) to the development of this character in the history of a people (IV).

This view of the poem is valid only to a certain extent (Virgil's poem is hardly so simple). What is missing is a clear realization of the poem's actual subjects. More specifically, we can say that the first half sees man in relation to nature, and the second is concerned with man's knowledge (his understanding and control of nature). From this vantage point, and returning to generalizations offered in the Introduction, we can make a final survey of the poem.

We are now able to appreciate far better what Virgil was doing in his reworking of Varro at the beginning of Book I. Varro's four divisions of his subject were (it is worth repeating):

1. knowledge of the farm's situation and its soil;
2. necessary equipment;
3. what needs to be done;
4. when it must be done.

In the very first section of the poem (43–70), Virgil inverted Varro's order (lines 43–53), then presented three sets of three *exempla* each (54–59), then resumed Varro's divisions in reverse order (60–70)—but with two significant changes: Varro's "necessary equipment" became "the farmer," and in the restatement of the divisions the farm became the world with its universal laws and the farmer became Deucalion's "hard race" of men. The next four sections continue from this:

3. the work, but in terms of wet and dry, water and fire (71–99);
4. when, but with the farmer as soldier, and the conflict of fire and water (100–117);
1. the nature of Jupiter's world (118–59);
2. equipment, *duris agrestibus arma*—the farmer again as soldier (160–75).

As we review these sequences, or patterns, we can see what was not so apparent the first time. We see how inevitably knowledge of the world (the farmer's science of agriculture) and its use involve conflict, and hence how the farmer acts with violence to distort and subdue (so especially in the final section, 160–75); and we see how the external world opposes, by Jupiter's design, the farmer's efforts. Our first view of the subject, then, presents unrelieved conflict at every level and in every aspect: knowledge and nature are thoroughly antagonistic, and are so by the force of absolute necessity, due to the conflict of the elements themselves.

As we consider these sections, we must make the effort of a readjustment of our instinctive attitudes: for Virgil's readers this opposition of knowledge and nature was somewhat paradoxical and certainly disturbing. To the Roman, the farm offered a comforting setting for man's control of nature, to the extent that the farmer and nature (*natura* as "begetting") are identified emotionally, and to the extent that nature (*natura* in the sense of the processes of life) *is* the farm; beyond the borders of the farm lie chaos and destructive disorder, which is not *natura* either by definition or by Roman instinct. The discussion of the first book of Varro's treatise is set in the temple of Tellus on the festival of the Sementivae, while the participants await the arrival of the sacristan: at the end of the book, suddenly and with extraordinary realism, the sacristan's freedman rushes in, in tears, to announce the murder of his master in Rome, and the group disperses—*descendimus de aede et de casu humano magis querentes quam admirantes id Romae factum, discedimus omnes* ("We left the temple and all went our separate ways, lamenting more at human misfortune than surprised that this had happened at Rome"). Sudden, unexpected, and unnatural violence happens not just at Rome (that is not surprising to them), but outside the agricultural setting; irrational violence (the knifing of the sacristan was a case of mistaken identity, or at least a mistake—*exaudisse vocem, perperam fecisse*) belongs to the world beyond the temple of Tellus, where the discussion of farming took place, where man orders and controls. There can be no other point to this extraordinary conclusion to Varro's first book, and no other reaction it could have elicited from a Roman reader.

Virgil can be observed starting with the instinctive assumption that the farm is order and growth introduced and fostered by the farmer, who achieves a balance of the elements, draining and irrigating, but inevitably and consistently this assumption, in each section, is revised by a change in the patterns created, so that the result is the farmer, through violence, opposing nature within the boundaries of his farm. When we first followed the development of lines 100–117, with Virgil's reworking of the simile from *Iliad* 21 and the suggestions of the Troad and of Achilles (as fire) fighting the Scamander, we were unclear how the farmer who irrigates in Virgil's context could be related to the destructive fire of the allusion or to the clear suggestion of the farmer as soldier, occurring in the poem for the first time. It has now become clear, but only from our understanding of the whole.

The rest of the first book proceeds from and with this paradox: that the very idea of Roman order—that is, the deepest exemplum of creation and fostering nurture, where man is in fact the creator (rather than the creature), the nurturer and, by his knowledge, the controller—is in fact the scene of an inevitable conflict in which violence is brought against the natural world and a natural order external to man. His knowledge (the *veterum praecepta* of 176–203) opposes the world, and water flows inevitably downstream. Knowledge of the universe, of storms and calm weather, occupy Virgil for the remainder of the book, but the result is always the same. The charioteer has lost control:

> sic omnia fatis
> in peius ruere ac retro sublapsa referri.   (1.199–200)

The beginning of the second book offers no relief: Virgil's conception of the farmer opposed to *natura* is given a scientific basis at the beginning of Book II, where the technical distinction, going back to Theophrastus, between wild (nature's) and cultivated (man's) plants is insisted upon by repetition (lines 9–34 and 47–72). Nature's growth is strong and productive, while man's cultivation inevitably degenerates and man's knowledge (as in grafting) inevitably and with violence produces the monstrous and unnatural. The book's focus is on the immediate environment, that each land has its own character and thus shapes and influences everything growing and living on it: the *ingenium* of a land is glossed by *rebus natura ferendis* (2.178). Everything, then, is subject to nature: through the rest of the book Virgil is creating patterns testing and exemplifying this domination of nature. Man's plant is the vine, requiring rich soil, demanding continual labor, and in return requiting violence with violence. The wild olive is nature's, growing in poor soil, requiring no attention, able to survive even fire. The first digression takes the cliché of Italy as both the tempered ideal of the ethnographers and as Saturn's golden age and reveals the truth behind the cliché: that a land of richness produces war just as it produces the vine. Again, Spring and the Rustic Life are false dreams, at best: there is no *ver aeternum* in the real world of spring storms, when winter opposes summer, and there is no peace on the land that bears the vine.

The progression of the first two books is clear. Virgil begins with the Roman assumption of the farmer who is the creator and nurturer (the *agri-cola*, again), who in fact has created and fostered *natura* within the *termini* that separate this world of order from the wild, un-natural, and unproductive chaos beyond. This assumption, however, immediately begins to change, even within the Varronian contexts of the first sections, and continues in various ways to change until the final inversion, which reveals man as the product of his land, and therefore subject to it, just as his efforts were subject to nature's *pestes* and degeneration. Through much of this, nature has likewise been stripped of its agricultural associations to become the laws and processes of the universe (*rerum natura*); the physical reality of science replaces, in a sense, the wilderness of mountain and thicket beyond the farm's borders. In this physical world of elemental oppositions, man is necessarily subject to fire and water, just as Spring is no dream but rather the season of conflict between winter's wet and cold and summer's drying heat.

The third book continues this focus, from the universe, to the immediate environment, and now to man himself. Its subject is the pastoral, which Virgil explores again by opposing ideals and realities. There is the real world of horses and sheep, and then there is the pastoral ideal of peace in a land of perpetual warmth. The real horse is created for war: he is fire itself. Transformations are gradually effected until, beginning with the suggestion of the ideal pastoral setting of Silarus and Sila, the gadfly begins the process that brings on the final *furor equarum*: the fire of war is itself consumed by a greater fire. A similar transformation leads to the destruction of the smaller animals by disease: the warmth necessary to the pastoral ideal becomes the *sacer ignis*. Likewise, the Libyan nomad becomes the Roman soldier, and the ice-bound Scythian enjoys *secura otia*.

The pastoral, too, is a way of understanding, not through scientific knowledge, but by re-creating the world, by altering its realities into acceptable images, escaping the heat of midday by singing in the cool shade. As Virgil had anticipated at the end of the second book, this pastoral understanding is never far from Virgil's reflections in the third. Virgil's concentration on man is a narrowing of focus on his mind. The pastoral warmth that becomes (by extension) the burning heat and finally the fire of passion and of disease, destroys pastoral understanding as a possible intellectual alternative: the cool shade again offers no retreat.

Virgil is left, then, with the knowledge of Aristaeus and Orpheus, to be won by struggle in the blazing heat, the fire of Empedocles' Aetna. Such knowledge, offered as the miraculous restoration of a people who have grown sick and died, is as great a failure as the pastoral understanding. Science, the struggle of unremitting labor and violent domination, wins no victory, though the domination of fire is complete.

The *Georgics* is a poem *about* science—about agriculture, about all the other sciences related to agriculture, about science as understanding of and control over nature. It is also a poem *of* science: if there is a reality for Virgil, it is the reality of the elements.

The central books are especially concerned with illusions, dreams, or what we called the great lies—the second book with certain conceptions of the world, and the third with a way of understanding. Even if Italy were in fact a land of tempered balance (which it is not), it must still contain the fire of war in its constitution and will thus still breed and nourish the warrior horse and a fierce race of heroes. The dream of Spring is a scientific impossibility: spring is rather a time of elemental conflict, in which any day of quiet (between hot and cold) can be assumed to be both accidental and transitory. The entire poem points to the futility of the dream of country peace: the farmer must (paradoxically) wage a war to create a balance of opposing elements, setting one against the other without cease. So, too, the pastoral warmth of the third book is a delusion: it is all too easily resolved into the realities of heat and cold. The cool shade of summer's midday is invaded by the gadfly—*furor*, the fire of passion, must come to dominate, which is the same element that transforms the landscape into the final scene of devastation, *desertaque regna / pastorum et longe saltus lateque vacantis* (3.476–77).

★

Behind appearances and in our own conceptions there are only the elements. Nature is not man's creation, because in reality the universe, our world, and any part of it are all the result of elemental oppositions. Knowledge likewise: true understanding is won by struggle in the blazing heat and is thus identical with the violence and destruction inherent in elemental fire. Balances can only be temporary or illusory. The first spring of the bee's creation, the peace of their first swarming, and the balance of their young and healthy society gave way finally and inevitably to elemental instability, sickness, and death. The different patterns are all made with the same few pieces.

Virgil's poem is profoundly pessimistic: conflict is the ultimate reality in that fire and water are the ultimate elements of all things; peace, conception and growth, a tempered climate or a fine spring day are only passing hopes and temporary illusions. The farmer must change the course of nature to create a balance, which is to say that he works with perversions, creating, with violence and unceasing labor, what is unnatural, and he cannot achieve even this for long because the ultimate nature, beyond the farm, is unresolved opposition. There are moments of extraordinary bleakness and passages of dark depression in the poem, certainly, and even revelations of quiet loveliness are most characteristically offered only when they have ceased to be, such as the land that Mantua lost, *pascentem niveos herboso flumine cycnos* (2.199), or the *nemora . . . multos ignava per annos, / antiquasque domos avium* destroyed by the *arator* (3.207–10). If the *Aeneid* can be summed up by the line beginning *sunt lacrimae rerum*, then the *Georgics* is characterized by the sudden intensity of *optima quaeque dies miseris mortalibus aevi / prima fugit* (3.66–67). Virgil's pessimism is thorough, deep, and inescapable: there is no relief. It is, however, the pessimism of the grand vision, which, like that inherent in the tragic struggle, offers (if not a catharsis) something clarifying and supportable. Orpheus is not ennobled but becomes deeply human, even through the end; his humanity is the result of the stark immensity against which he is projected. All things are phenomena of the elemental oppositions and conflicts—fire and water, the drying heat and the moist cold. It is the pessimism of one who sees not only the immensity of the starry night, but has looked into its history, back to the darkness of its beginning and ahead to its inevitable end.

BIBLIOGRAPHICAL NOTES

Bibliography on the *Georgics* is easily accessible (especially since Suerbaum) and will be familiar to most readers of this book. Therefore, in these Notes I cite only (a) a few standard works, *pro forma*, for those who may be unfamiliar with the poem, or (b) work I have relied on in areas that may not be known territory to readers of the poem, or (c) a few recent articles with good bibliography or of special interest.

A bibliography of work on the *Georgics* (by topic and by Book, with further divisions) from 1875 to 1975 has been compiled by W. Suerbaum in (H. Temporini and W. Haase, ed.) *Aufstieg und Niedergang der Römischen Welt* II.31.1 (Berlin and New York, 1980), 395–499—a supplement to his "Hundert Jahre Vergil-Forschung: . . . Aeneis" in the same volume, 3–358. He lists other bibliographies on pp. 399–400.

I have cited Virgil from the Oxford Classical Text of R.A.B. Mynors (1969); occasional departures have been noted.

The only modern commentary of scholarly merit is by W. Richter (Munich, 1957), to which I am of course much indebted. The standard vintage English commentary is J. Conington – H. Nettleship (London, 1001'), and the "school" commentary by T. E. Page (London, 1898) is still often useful. The forthcoming commentaries by R.A.B. Mynors and R. F. Thomas are eagerly awaited.

For Servius, I have used the text of G. Thilo and H. Hagen (Leipzig, 1887, repr. Hildesheim, 1961). An excellent introduction to the Servian tradition is provided by G. P. Goold, "Servius and the Helen Episode," *HSCP* 74 (1968), 101–68; see too R. A. Kaster in *CP* 75 (1980), 216–41, and *HSCP* 84 (1980), 219–62.

A good introduction to the *Georgics*, its literary background and historical context, and to modern scholarship, interpretation, and criticism can be had from the following five books:

Büchner, K., "P. Vergilius Maro," in Pauly-Wissowa-Kroll, *Realencyclopädie der classischen Altertumswissenschaft* VIII A 1–2 (1955–58), 1021–1486: repr. as *P. Vergilius Maro, der Dichter der Römer* (Stuttgart, 1961).

Klingner, F., *Virgils Georgica* (Zürich, 1963), repr. in *Virgil: Bucolica, Georgica, Aeneis* (Zürich and Stuttgart, 1967), 177–363.

Wilkinson, L. P., *The Georgics of Vergil* (Cambridge, 1969).

Putnam, M.C.J., *Virgil's Poem of the Earth* (Princeton, 1979).

Miles, G. B., *Virgil's Georgics: A New Interpretation* (Berkeley, 1980).

On Roman agriculture, two books may be singled out:

Billiard, R., *L'Agriculture dans l'Antiquité* (Paris, 1928).

White, K. D., *Roman Farming* (Ithaca, 1970).

Chapter One

The standard introduction to the history of the period is H. H. Scullard, *From the Gracchi to Nero* (London, 1975⁴). R. Syme, *The Roman Revolution* (Oxford, 1939), is essential. For a detailed but lucid account of these years, the *Cambridge Ancient History* should not be forgotten: F. E. Adcock, *CAH* IX (1932), and W. W. Tarn and C. P. Charlesworth, *CAH* X (1934). Appian (*BC* 4.2.5) gives what may be exaggerated figures of the number murdered in the proscriptions (300 senators and 2000 knights—Livy (*Per.* 120) reports 130 senators, for instance). Livy's account of Cicero's death is quoted by Seneca, *Suasoriae* 6.17.

For the redating of the publication of the *Eclogues* (from 37 to 35 B.C.), see G. W. Bowersock, "A Date in the *Eighth Eclogue*," *HSCP* 75 (1971), 73–80; W. V. Clausen, "On the Date of the *First Eclogue*," *HSCP* 76 (1972), 201–5; E. A. Schmidt, *Zur Chronologie der Eklogen Vergils*, Sitzungsber. Heidelberg, Phil.-hist. Kl. 1974, 6; D. O. Ross, "*Non sua poma*: Varro, Virgil, and Grafting," *ICS* 5 (1980), 63–71. (See also R. J. Tarrant, with a response by Bowersock, *HSCP* 82 [1978], 197–202.)

S. K. Langer is cited from *Philosophy in a New Key: A Study in the Symbolism of Reason, Rite, and Art* (Mentor edition, New York, 1948), 72 and 75: see esp. chap. 4, "Discursive and Presentational Forms."

On the agricultural stratum in Latin, see J. Marouzeau, "Le latin langue de paysans," in *Mélanges linguistiques offerts à J. Vendryes*, Collection linguistique, 17 (Paris, 1925), 251–65.

On primitive Roman religion and the country, see W. Warde Fowler, *The Religious Experience of the Roman People* (London, 1911), esp. pp. 209–18 (on *lustratio*) and 132–33, on Mars Silvanus of the forest (in Cato, *De Agr.* 83), speaking of "the time when Mars was really the wild spirit of the 'outland,' where wolves and human enemies might be met with. . . ." C. Bailey is quoted here from *Phases in the Religion of Ancient Rome*, Sather Classical Lectures, 10 (Berkeley, 1932, repr. 1972), 44–45: see esp. chap. 2 (pp. 35–108), "The Spirits." Some have downplayed Mars as in origin an agricultural *numen* (so, recently and emphatically, G. Dumézil, *Archaic Roman Religion* (Chicago, 1966: trans. P. Krapp), 1, 205–45. The only recent survey in English is R. M. Ogilvie, *The Romans and their Gods in the Age of Augustus* (London, 1969): see pp. 9–23 for the importance of the agricultural roots of Roman religion. In great detail on one particular figure, L. A. Holland, *Janus and the Bridge*, Monogr. of the Amer. Acad. in Rome, 21 (Rome, 1961).

There is surprisingly little on "nature" and the Romans. Older studies are of the "ach, wie schön ist die Natur" school: e.g., H. R. Fairclough, *Love of Nature among the Greeks and Romans* (New York, 1930, repr. 1963). Two recent studies (with extensive bibliography) are concerned especially with landscape in literature, painting, and architecture (mostly imperial, naturally), and with the ideas of artificiality and man's domination of nature: Z. Pavlovskis, *Man in an Artificial Landscape*, Mnem. Suppl., 25 (Leiden, 1973); and J. Römer, *Naturästhetik in der frühen römischen Kaiserzeit*, Europäische Hochschulschriften, Reihe xv, Band 22 (1981).

Chapter Two

On the ethnographical tradition in antiquity, two studies were seminal: K. Trüdinger, *Studien zur Geschichte der griechisch-römischen Ethnographie* (diss. Basel, 1918); and E. Norden, *Die germanische Urgeschichte in Tacitus Germania* (Leipzig and Berlin, 1922; Stuttgart, 1959⁴). We now have the exhaustive two-volume study of K. E. Müller, *Geschichte der Antike Ethnographie und Ethnologischen Theoriebildung . . .*, Studien zur Kulturkunde, 29 (1972) and 52 (1980).

For Virgil's use of the ethnographical tradition, the lucid study of I. Borzsák is exemplary and essential, "Von Hippokrates bis Vergil," in *Vergiliana*, ed. H. Bardon and R. Verdière (Leiden, 1971), 41–55: in what follows here I must presume that his collection of sources and his discussion is familiar to readers. How Virgil and Horace (among others) used this tradition has been perceptively studied by R. F. Thomas, *Lands and Peoples in Roman Poetry: the Ethnographical Tradition*, Cambridge Phil. Soc. Suppl., 7 (1982): it will be obvious that we share many basic assumptions about the *Georgics*.

General, readable, and recent introductions in English to ancient medicine are E. D. Phillips, *Greek Medicine* (London, 1973) and J. Scarborough, *Roman Medicine* (Ithaca, 1969). For the development of Greek humoral theory, see Phillips' Index of medical topics, s.v. "humours"; on p. 149 Phillips speaks of "the dominance of humoral theory" on Alexandrian medicine and of the fact that "In Galen, for instance, the humours are still canonical." Several essays by L. Edelstein provide excellent introductions (and of course much more) to important aspects of Greek medicine: *Ancient Medicine: Selected Papers of Ludwig Edelstein* (Baltimore, 1967).

The standard text of the Hippocratic corpus is still E. Littré, *Hippocrates: Oeuvres Complètes* (Paris, 1839–61, repr. Amsterdam, 1961), 10 vols. A convenient selection can be found in the four volumes of the Loeb Classical Library (London, 1923–31), edited by W.H.S. Jones and E. T. Withington, from which my citations are taken.

On the elements, qualities, and humors in philosophy and medicine, there are good observations in the general introduction by Jones in the Loeb, vol. I, pp. ix–lxix; see also Jones' *Philosophy and Medicine in Ancient Greece, with an Edition of περὶ ἀρχαίης ἰητρικῆς* , Suppl. to the Bull. of the Hist. of Medicine, 8 (Baltimore, 1946). For an excellent specific discussion, see I. M. Lonie, *The Hippocratic Treatises "On generation," "On the nature of the child," "Diseases IV,"* Ars Medica: Texte und Untersuchungen zur Quellenkunde der Alten Medizin, II. Abteilung, Band 7 (Berlin, 1981), esp. pp. 54–62 ("Introduction: 4. The theory of four constituent humors and the De natura hominis"—the passages quoted above are from pp. 56 and 61). On the humors from antiquity onwards, see R. Klibanski, E. Panofsky, F. Saxl, *Saturn and Melancholy* (London, 1964), esp. pp. 3–66 (Chapter I, "Melancholy in the Physiological Literature of the Ancients"); and H. Flashar, *Melancholie und Melancholiker in den medizinischen Theorien der Antike* (Berlin, 1966).

For an excellent discussion of the qualities in early Greek philosophy and medicine, see G.E.R. Lloyd, "The Hot and the Cold, the Dry and the Wet in Greek Philosophy," *JHS* 84 (1964), 92-106 (with his earlier study of other polarities, *JHS* 82 (1962), 56–66, and his subsequent book, *Polarity and Analogy: Two Types of Argumentation in Early Greek Thought* [Cambridge, 1966]): Lloyd concludes "that while the first extant physical theory based on the hot and the cold, the dry and the wet as the four primary elements of other things appears in *On the Nature of*

Man, the doctrine of the balanced interaction of opposed substances occurs in various forms in earlier theorists and goes right back to Anaximander himself" (p. 100); Lloyd then considers what values (positive or negative) these qualities may have had (100–106).

On the background of "balance" (*isomoiria* or *isonomia*) as a political metaphor, see G. Vlastos, "Isonomia," *AJP* 74 (1953), 337–66 (on Alcmaeon, esp. 344–47, 363–65), and "Equality and Justice in Early Greek Cosmologies," *CP* 42 (1947), 156–78 (esp. 156–58, on "Medical Theory").

Chapter Three

For a fuller discussion of grafting and its significance for Virgil (with the relevant bibliography), see my "*Non sua poma*: Varro, Virgil, and Grafting," *ICS* 5 (1980), 63–71.

On the *laudes Italiae*, see esp. Thomas, *Lands and People*, 36–49, with further bibliography in his notes. The essay of M.C.J. Putnam, "Italian Virgil and the Idea of Rome," in *Janus: Essays in Ancient and Modern Studies* (Ann Arbor, 1975), 171–99, ought to be mentioned as the first (to my knowledge) study to point out certain negative aspects in Virgil's praise of Italy.

On spring and the golden age, see esp. H. Reynen, "Ewiger Frühling und goldene Zeit: zum Mythos des Zeitalters bei Ovid und Vergil," *Gymnasium* 72 (1965), 415–33. On the Golden Age and primitivism, A. O. Lovejoy and G. Boas, *Primitivism and Related Ideas in Antiquity* (Baltimore, 1935), remains a gold mine. There is more recent bibliography in P. A. Johnston, *Vergil's Agricultural Golden Age*, Mnem. Suppl. 60 (Leiden, 1980).

On aetiologies in the *Georgics*, see S. Shechter, "The *Aition* and Virgil's *Georgics*," *TAPA* 105 (1975), 347–91.

The Virgilian significance of the epithet *ingens* (= "native, natural") was revealed by J. W. Mackaial, "Virgil's Use of the Word *Ingens*," *CR* 26 (1912), 251–55, and has been ignored since (even by the lexicographers of the *Oxford Latin Dictionary*).

Chapter Four

On gadflies, see R. F. Thomas, "Gadflies (Virg. *Geo.* 3.146–48)," *HSCP* 86 (1982), 81–85, with further references.

Mt. Sila has been exhaustively mapped by M. Geymonat, "Paesaggio drammatico ed esperienza biographica nella 'Sila' Virgiliana," *Storia e Cultura del Mezzogiorno: Studi in memoria di Umberto Caldora* (Rome, 1979), 9–20.

Chapter Five

The most recent, and very thorough, reviews of the problem of Servius and the *laudes Galli* are by H. D. Jocelyn, "Servius and the 'second edition' of the *Georgics*," *Atti del Convegno mondiale scientifico di studi su Vergilio* 1 (Rome, 1984), 431–48; and H. Jacobson, "Aristaeus, Orpheus, and the *Laudes Galli*," *AJP* 105 (1984), 271–300.

On the bees and the fourth book, see Thomas, *Lands and Peoples*, 70–92. By far the most stimulating and perceptive recent study (I have found) is J. Griffin, "The Fourth *Georgic*, Virgil, and Rome," *GR* 26 (1979), 61–80: otherwise, with a few exceptions (such as H. Dahlmann's standard *Der Bienenstaat*, Abh. Akad. Mainz, 10 (1954), modern work is extraordinarily impressionistic.

A recent review of the Old Man of Tarentum is that by C. G. Perkell, "On the Corycian Gardener of Vergil's Fourth *Georgic*," *TAPA* 111 (1981), 167–77.

INDEX LOCORUM

INDEX NOMINUM ET RERUM

Library of Congress Cataloging-in-Publication Data

ROSS, DAVID O.
VIRGIL'S ELEMENTS.

BIBLIOGRAPHY: P.
INCLUDES INDEXES.
I. VIRGIL. GEORGICA. I. TITLE.
PA6804.G4R6 1987   873'.01   86–22598
ISBN 0–691–06699–X
(ALK. PAPER)

David O. Ross, Jr.
is Professor of Classical Studies at the
University of Michigan